Global Complex Project Management

An Integrated Adaptive Agile and PRINCE2 LEAN Framework for Achieving Success

Robert K. Wysocki
Colin Bentley

J.ROSS
PUBLISHING

ISBN-13: 978-1-60427-126-3

Printed and bound in the U.S.A. Printed on acid-free paper.

10 9 8 7 6 5 4 3 2 1

Library of Congress Cataloging-in-Publication Data
Names: Wysocki, Robert K., author. | Bentley, Colin.
Title: Global complex project management : an integrated adaptive agile and PRINCE2 lean framework for achieving success / by Robert K. Wysocki and Colin Bentley.
Description: Plantation, FL : J. Ross Publishing, [2016] | Includes bibliographical references and index.
Identifiers: LCCN 2016028544 | ISBN 9781604271263 (hardcover : alk. paper)
Subjects: LCSH: Project management.
Classification: LCC HD69.P75 W9544 2016 | DDC 658.4/04--dc23 LC record available at https://lccn.loc.gov/2016028544

Phone: (954) 727-9333
Fax: (561) 892-0700
Web: www.jrosspub.com

TABLE OF CONTENTS

FOREWORD

Modern project management is a relatively new business process, having emerged in the last half of the 20th century. It grew out of a need for businesses' processes to integrate the emerging technologies, and it matured in parallel with information technologies. We think mostly in terms of computer technologies and see project management and information systems management as bedfellows that share a common history—they grew up together. That history is one of turmoil, high risk, lots of mistakes, failures, and disappointments. Learning and discovery through experience are the watchwords to any successes we might claim in project management and information systems management. It would be fair to say that each has benefited and learned from the experiences of the other.

Today, effective complex project management shows signs of morphing into a strategic tool, but the challenges to do so are significant. Critical business problems remain unsolved. Untapped business opportunities arise every day. Those who are creative, flexible, risk takers, agile, and lean will thrive and survive. Others will fail. There are no recipes for that survival. To respond to that complexity, we need *chefs*, not *cooks*, to create the recipes that will effectively execute complex and unique projects and deliver expected business value.

Without any known interactions, there are two frameworks that are prominent and have a structure that will survive this morphing process. PRINCE2 (P2) is one of the frameworks. It dates back to 1996. Colin Bentley was the designer of the original version of P2, which was called PROMPT II and eventually renamed PRINCE, and then PRINCE2. The other is the Effective Complex Project Management (ECPM) Framework, an adaptive and robust business-driven project management framework designed by Bob Wysocki, which has a history dating back to the 1990s and has evolved over the years to its current mature state. It originally grew out of some of Bob's practical and innovative concepts that were first shared in his bestselling book, now in its 7th edition, entitled *Effective Project Management: Traditional, Agile, Extreme*, which was most recently published in 2014. We have chosen to partner, and through our collaborative efforts from opposite sides of the pond, have produced this work and taken complex project management to the next level. What does this book offer?

> An Integrated Adaptive Agile and PRINCE2 LEAN Framework and a practical applications-oriented guide for managing complex projects in a manner that enable organizations to achieve maximum business value.

Does it have a pedigree? It is based on two methods with well-proven pedigrees:

- PRINCE2, a framework with a worldwide reputation for delivering products of good quality, while taking care of costs, timescale, risks, and changes.
- ECPM, a framework based on Agile principles, but with added lean features that are particularly suited to complex projects.

Our goal for the integration of several artifacts from the ECPM and P2 frameworks was to create a new and improved framework that is agile, lean, and adaptable, which would complement both the Project Management Institute's (PMI) Body of Knowledge as well as the Association for Project Management's (APM) Body of Knowledge. Why? To provide a framework that is useful to project or program managers most anywhere in the world for managing complex and mission-critical projects or programs.

We decided to name this version of our integration efforts the PRINCE2 LEAN (P2 LEAN) Framework. In no way should it be confused with the P2 Agile framework that was recently developed by AXELOS. P2 LEAN is our legacy and will prove to be a significant contribution to the success of the selected integration of the ECPM Framework with P2!

We want to make it very clear to the P2 community that it is not our intention to replace P2. Rather we offer the P2 LEAN Framework as an addition to the P2 and PMI community's toolbox. As stated previously, it is designed for those projects that are very complex and filled with uncertainties. Their fulfillment comes only with high risk.

Just as P2 and ECPM are frameworks, so also is P2 LEAN a framework. It is not a methodology. As a framework, we have designed it to be robust. In order to be used, it will have to be further tailored to comply with any complex project that will use it, while staying true to the lean principles on which it is based. In this book we offer the agile and lean processes and activities to do that. Be warned however, that chefs are needed to do this work—cooks need not apply!

Our collaboration has demonstrated the alignment of the purposes underlying two different frameworks. Hopefully our efforts have created value and an improved path to success for practitioners and professional communities on both sides of the pond! But we caution both of these communities, the P2 LEAN Framework is different—it is not P2 and it is not ECPM—it is its own framework. For clarity, it is described using an intuitive process flow diagram (PFD). As such, there will be processes and practices that are at odds with either P2 or ECPM, but those differences pay allegiance to a higher order—the P2 LEAN Framework. That higher order is the need for a lean and agile framework that meets the needs of the 21st century organization.

We believe we have designed a framework to meet that need and leave it to the practitioners and professionals on both sides of the pond to validate our claim. All we ask of them is that they approach our framework with an open mind. Recognize at the outset that the P2 LEAN Framework is different and that it is not based on convention. We designed it to be lean, agile, and applications-oriented and to be an integration of the best of both the P2 and the ECPM Frameworks.

Enjoy!

Robert K. Wysocki
Colin Bentley

ABOUT THE AUTHORS

Robert K. Wysocki, Ph.D. has long been considered one of the world's major thought leaders and a top expert within the field of project management. He has over 45 years of combined experience as a project manager, business analyst, business process consultant and trainer, information systems manager, systems and management consultant, author, and training developer and provider. He has written 25 books on project management and information systems management and seven monographs. One of his books, *Effective Project Management: Traditional, Adaptive, Extreme*, has been a best seller for many years and is currently in its seventh edition. His books have been repeatedly recommended by the Project Management Institute for the library of every project manager. He has also written over 30 articles and papers published in professional and trade journals and has made more than 100 presentations at professional and trade conferences and meetings. He has developed more than 20 project management courses and trained over 10,000 project managers worldwide. His most recent book entitled *Effective Complex Project Management: An Adaptive Agile Framework for Delivering Business Value* was published in 2014 by J. Ross Publishing.

In 1990 he founded Enterprise Information Insights, Inc. (EII), a project management consulting and training practice specializing in project management methodology design and integration; business process design; project support office establishment; the development of training curriculum; and the development of a portfolio of assessment tools focused on organizations, project teams, and individuals. In 2011 he revised the company focus and renamed it EII Publications.

His client list includes AT&T, Aetna, BMW, British Computer Society, Boston University Corporate Education Center, Computerworld, Czechoslovakian Government, Data General, Digital, Eli Lilly, IBM, J. Walter

Thompson, Novartis, Ohio State University, Sapient Corporation, Technical Learning Institute, The Limited, The State of Ohio, The State of Vermont, Travelers Insurance, TVA, U.S. Army 5th Signal Corp., U.S. Coast Guard Academy, Wal-Mart, Wells Fargo, ZTE and several others.

He is also a Senior Consultant at the Cutter Consortium where he is an active member of the Agile Project Management Practice. He is past editor of the Effective Project Management Series for Artech House, a publisher to the technical and engineering professions. He was a founding member of the Agile Project Leadership Network and served as its first Vice President and President Elect. He earned a BA in Mathematics from the University of Dallas, and an MS and Ph.D. in Mathematical Statistics from Southern Methodist University.

Robert Wysocki resides in Worcester, Massachusetts, U.S.A.

Colin Bentley, Original Author and Chief Examiner of PRINCE2. Colin Bentley has long been perceived as one of the world's major thought leaders and top experts within the field of project management. He has been a project manager since 1966 and has managed many projects, large and small, in several countries. Colin is particularly well-known in the United Kingdom and throughout the European Union for his work related to PRINCE2, the most widely used project management framework outside of the United States.

Colin wrote the original PRINCE2 manual and was the author of all revisions to the manual for the Central Computer and Telecommunications Agency (CCTA) until the 2009 version, where he acted as Lead Reviewer and Mentor. He was also the Chief Examiner for PRINCE2 from its beginning until 2008 and wrote all Foundation and Practitioner Exams. He still answers the "Ask an Expert" questions on PRINCE2 for the APMG, an international professional certification organization.

PRINCE2 derives from an earlier method called PROMPT II (Project Resource Organisation Management Planning Techniques). Mr. Bentley was one of the original creators of PROMPT II and one of the team members that brought PROMPT II to the marketplace. He has been working with PROMPT II, PRINCE, and PRINCE2 since 1975. In 1989, the CCTA adopted a version of PROMPT II as a UK Government standard for information technology (IT) systems project management and called it PRINCE. However, it soon became regularly applied outside the purely IT environment, both in the UK government and in the private sector around the world. PRINCE2 was released in 1996 as a generic project management method and became the most widely used project management framework in the world. PRINCE2 governs projects as a whole and complements the Project Management Institute's Body of Knowledge, as well as the Association for Project Management Body of Knowledge, making it useful to project managers anywhere in the world for various types of projects.

Colin has had over twenty books published, lectured widely on PRINCE2, and acted as a project management consultant to such firms as The London Stock Exchange, Microsoft Europe, Tesco Stores, Commercial Union, and the BBC.

In his retirement, Colin has been working on project management methods for complex projects, as well as for small projects.

Colin Bentley resides in Waterlooville, Hants, UK.

Web
Added
Value™

This book has free material available for download from the
Web Added Value™ resource center at *www.jrosspub.com*

At J. Ross Publishing we are committed to providing today's professional with practical, hands-on tools that enhance the learning experience and give readers an opportunity to apply what they have learned. That is why we offer free ancillary materials available for download on this book and all participating Web Added Value™ publications. These online resources may include interactive versions of material that appears in the book or supplemental templates, worksheets, models, plans, case studies, proposals, spreadsheets and assessment tools, among other things. Whenever you see the WAV™ symbol in any of our publications, it means bonus materials accompany the book and are available from the Web Added Value Download Resource Center at www.jrosspub.com.

Downloads for *Global Complex Project Management: An Integrated Adaptive Agile and PRINCE2 Lean Framework for Achieving Success* include slide presentations for use in training and academic instruction that visually depict and briefly explain the P2 Lean Framework and associated processes.

PART 1

OVERVIEW

We take a bold step forward with this book, but we take a necessary step forward at the same time. Modern project management has been trapped in less-than-acceptable performance, and this has been the case for several years now. There does not appear to be any signs of an escape from the self-imposed trap! We offer an escape and share it here, for the first time anywhere.

Our escape plan comes from having made an observation that there is a way out that has remained under everyone's radar screen for 15 years. We have discovered that by integrating a selected set of artifacts from the Effective Complex Project Management (ECPM) Framework (Wysocki, 2014) into the PRINCE2 (P2) Framework (AXELOS, 2009), we will define a P2 LEAN Framework that holds the promise of increasing project performance and delivered business value. P2 is well-established, and we don't need to defend its value to the project management community. The ECPM Framework is relatively new in print, but has been successfully practiced for nearly 20 years now and has earned its reputation from those successes.

Both the P2 and the ECPM Frameworks are closely aligned from a process and practice perspective, and this is explored in Chapter 1. Since the ECPM Framework will be relatively new to the P2 practitioner and professional, we offer a brief summary of it in Chapter 2: *Overview of the Effective Complex Project Management Framework.*

P2 will be familiar to our readers and is not summarized here, but P2 LEAN is new to the entire project management community on both sides of the pond, so we introduce it in Chapter 3: *PRINCE2 LEAN: Are you a Cook or a Chef?* The backbone of any agile and lean project management process is its planning process. In Chapter 4: *PRINCE2 LEAN: Project Planning,* we introduce a robust 11-step planning process template and the five types of plans that use it.

1

INTRODUCTION

---

*I never did anything worth doing by accident, nor did any
of my inventions come by accident; they came by work.*
—Thomas Alva Edison, American inventor and entrepreneur

There is no data on the future.
—Laurel Cutler, Vice Chairman, FCB/Leber Katz Partners

New ideas... are not born in a conforming environment.
—Roger von Oech, President, Creative Thinking

CHAPTER LEARNING OBJECTIVES

This chapter will provide readers the knowledge or ability to:

- Understand the similarities and differences between PRINCE2 (P2) and the Effective Complex Project Management (ECPM) Frameworks
- Know that P2 principles, themes, processes, and activities apply to the ECPM Framework
- Gain some insight into enhancing P2 using artifacts from the ECPM Framework

In addition to several project management models (Scrum, Dynamic Systems Development Method [DSDM], etc.), the complex project landscape is supported by two unique and adaptive frameworks that are designed to provide the best-fit management approaches based on the characteristics of the project and its internal/external environments. These approaches are launched during initiation activities that eventually lead to an approval from Project Executive Management to execute the project. Despite the fact that they share similar goals, the way they execute projects has some marked differences. It is those differences that can be leveraged for the benefit of the other. In this book we explore how P2 can be enhanced using selected artifacts from the ECPM Framework.

P2 is the first of those adaptive frameworks to be introduced to the project management community. Its history dates from 1975 with the development of PROMPT II by a team whose members included Colin Bentley. He wrote the first P2 manual in 1996. He was also a major contributor to P2 in the 2003, 2005, and 2009 editions of the P2 Manual. Up to his retirement, he was the Chief Examiner of P2 examination papers. Colin is still active in the profession.

P2 has been an unqualified success since its introduction in 1975. It was adopted by the UK Government in 1989 as the standard for all information technology (IT) project management. It quickly expanded outside the IT domain and is now used in most industries. The name PRINCE2 was adopted in 1996 when the specific IT content was dropped and the method became generic. Today P2 is used in over 150 countries. Its application in the U.S. is recent and growing, especially among companies with significant operations or headquarters in the EU.

P2 was designed and deployed before the agile, adaptive, and lean movements were on anyone's mind. Actually, P2 was designed to be an adaptive framework. It was positioned to accommodate lean and agile variations with minimal disruption. In fact, that can and does happen. However, P2 doesn't give them any guidance on how to make that happen. There is a choice though. Leave it to the project managers to figure out how to adapt P2 to be lean or agile, or to help them with some tools, templates, and processes to create a version of P2 that is both lean and agile. We choose the latter, and that is the purpose of this book.

The ECPM Framework is the other adaptive framework. Its history dates from 1985 with the development of *Effective Project Management: Traditional, Agile, Extreme* by Robert K. Wysocki, now in its 7th edition. It was followed by *Adaptive Project Framework: Managing Complexity in the Face of Uncertainty* (Wysocki, Robert K., 2010, Addison Wesley) and most recently by *Effective Complex Project Management: An Adaptive Agile Framework for Delivering Business Value* (Wysocki, Robert K., 2014, J. Ross Publishing). Together these three books document the entire development history of the ECPM Framework. That history has evolved out of actual client engagements, but it does align with the accepted research tradition.

The P2 and ECPM Frameworks are similar in intent. Both are PMBOK® (Project Management Body of Knowledge) compliant. They have many similarities and also many differences. Those differences are what prompted our writing this book. They can be exploited to the benefit of each framework. We integrate several artifacts from the ECPM Framework into the P2 Framework for the improved performance of P2. The reverse integration is out of scope for this book.

INTRODUCTION

Our framework is a hybrid of P2 and the ECPM Frameworks. This book contains the first published description of what we have named P2 LEAN. The book will be a definitive work on not only *what* processes and activities are contained in the P2 LEAN Framework but *how* these processes and activities can be executed. In the spirit of lean, the *how* will come in several flavors (i.e., versions). These versions are driven by three critical components of every complex project situation:

- The defining characteristics of the project itself
- The environment and culture of the organization of both the consumer of the project deliverables and the producer of the deliverables for the market
- The market situation viewed as a dynamic entity

Definition: P2 LEAN Framework

The P2 LEAN Framework is an integration of selected artifacts from the ECPM Framework and the P2 Framework in order to create not just an agile and lean version of P2, but a better framework for handling complexity in projects:

P2 Framework + ECPM Framework = P2 LEAN Framework

These components define a project landscape that is a continuum that ranges from the small and simple projects to projects of increasing complexity and uncertainty. As you move across this landscape, the depth and sophistication of the tools, templates, and business processes used in P2 LEAN increases. There will be business rules for choosing the *what* and *how* for a variety of project management situations. For example, consider risk management. In the smallest and simplest of projects, that might be a simple risk/reward (low, medium, high) matrix. As project size, complexity, and uncertainty increase, that might be replaced with probabilistic models, multi-criteria scoring models, or sophisticated weighted criteria models. The other themes would have similar choices ordered by project *size, complexity,* and *uncertainty.*

P2 AND THE ECPM FRAMEWORKS: DIFFERENCES AND SIMILARITIES

Since its 1989 adoption by the UK Government, P2 has expanded into more than 150 countries. It has established itself as the de facto project management standard in the EU and perhaps elsewhere. It is now gaining a footprint in the U.S. as validated by the growing number of P2 training opportunities available. As the P2 community grows in the U.S., there is an unmet need to share how some of the agile artifacts that have worked so well in the U.S. can improve P2 performance. There is a clear synergy to be gained from that integration.

P2 and the ECPM Framework are conceptually similar. They are both adaptive and designed to produce best-fit project management models tailored to the project characteristics. Quoting from each of their descriptor documents:

- *P2 is not a "one-size-fits-all" solution. Rather, it is a flexible framework that can readily be tailored to any type or size of project.*

  One could argue that P2, because of its flexibility, already contains P2 LEAN and P2 Agile. And it does, but only potentially, because it is not only hidden from view, but also undefined. We take the position that if you leave it to the Project Team to take the covers off, they might, but the result will be to create an unmanageable situation for program managers, portfolio managers, executives, resource managers, and other senior-level managers. Whether you consciously align with the Capability Maturity Model Integration (CMMI) or not, you will have put your project organization back into Level 1 Maturity—a *Do It Your Own Way* organization, and that is unmanageable!

- *ECPM is not a methodology. Rather, it is an adaptive agile framework that utilizes robust decision processes to build best-fit management models driven by project characteristics and the internal/external environments in which it is executed.*

  You can think of the ECPM Framework as an umbrella that covers all Project Management Life Cycle (PMLC) Models, including P2, as well as a decision model for choosing and adapting from among them the best-fit PMLC Model. P2 LEAN takes selected artifacts from the ECPM Framework and integrates them into P2 to produce P2 LEAN. This defines the *what*, but P2 LEAN goes one step further and documents the *how*. This book is a guide to using P2 LEAN. Part of P2 LEAN is a P2 LEAN/kit. This is a comprehensive vetted portfolio of tools, templates, and business processes for managing any project. It is customized to the process and practice needs of the organization. The guide goes further by documenting w*hen to use* and *how to use* this guide as a desk reference to the Project Team.

The P2 and the ECPM Frameworks have a number of features in common, as well as several differences too. Those differences are what prompted us to combine our efforts. This book is the result of those efforts to *reach across the pond* and take selected artifacts from the ECPM Framework to show how they can be integrated into the P2 Framework for improved performance and delivery of expected business value. The label we have chosen for that integrated framework is the P2 LEAN Framework. We choose to include *Framework* in its name to remind the project management community that it is not a methodology. It is a framework that includes all project management methodologies and the decision processes to choose and adapt the best-fit methodology to manage a specific complex project.

Our hope is that the book will help you improve your P2 project management performance, regardless of where you call home.

Rationale

There are high-level similarities (Figure 1.1) between the ECPM and P2 Frameworks. The 3 ECPM Framework Stages overlap the 7 P2 Processes, but there are differences as well. For example, the ECPM Framework is designed around *Lean Principles*; P2 is not. That difference is significant in today's competitive marketplace and opens a number of opportunities to improve P2 performance and business value through integrating selected ECPM Framework artifacts. In fact, many of the ECPM Framework artifacts can be integrated into P2 with minimal disruption. This derives from the fact that P2 is adaptive. That is an awesome feature because it allows the P2 community to pick and choose from among the recommended artifacts for maximum business value and performance improvement. There is a great deal of synergy that can result from such integrations. The ECPM Framework has a long and successful history based on over 20 years of U.S. client

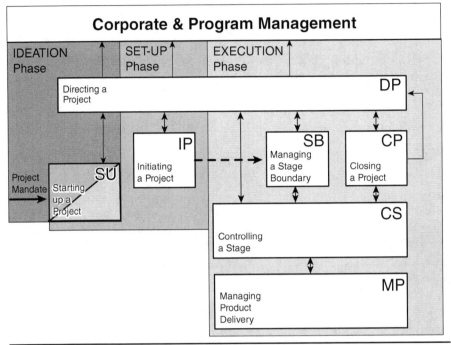

Figure 1.1   The relationship between PRINCE2 processes and the ECPM Framework phases

experiences. The ECPM Framework was designed around these successful client experiences. So we know that the ECPM Framework works because Bob was there to see that it worked. Furthermore, the selected ECPM Framework artifacts, when integrated into P2, deliver measurable benefits because Colin participated in that integration.

ECPM Framework Foundations

The ECPM Framework follows from a few observations:

- Projects are unique
- Because projects are unique, expect their management approach to also be unique
- The best-fit approach to managing a project is driven by:
  - ✦ The project characteristics

+ The organizational environment in which the project will be executed
+ The market conditions in which the project deliverables will apply
• The best-fit project management approach is dynamic because the world is dynamic

P2 Framework Foundations

P2 is defined by 7 principles, 7 themes, 7 processes, and 40 activities. We discuss these briefly here for the purposes of showing the degree to which P2 is aligned with the ECPM Framework.

P2 Principles Align with the ECPM Framework

P2 is based on 7 principles (see Figure 1.2). This set of principles is unique to the P2 method. Unless all these principles are applied, it is not a P2 project.

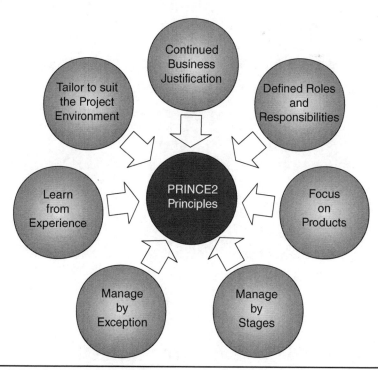

Figure 1.2   The 7 PRINCE2 principles

➤ **Continued business justification:** P2 believes that a project must be driven by a viable Business Case. The existence of a valid Business Case should be proved before the project is authorized, and it should be confirmed at all major decision points during the project. It should also be documented and approved by the Project Board:

- Don't start a project unless there is a sound Business Case for it
- Make sure that the Business Case is stated in measurable terms
- Check at regular intervals during the project to see that the project is still viable
- Stop the project if the justification disappears
- The Business Case:
    - ✦ Should inform and drive the decision-making processes
    - ✦ Allows for intermittent checks as to whether or not the project can still achieve the stated business objectives and benefits

Even projects that are compulsory require justification—this permits a check that the most cost-effective solution has been selected. Internal and external events may change the business justification, but it must remain valid.

The Business Case drives all three phases of the ECPM Framework:

IDEATION uses a customized brainstorming session to define a number of possible projects to address the Project Mandate and chooses the project that will be proposed.

SET-UP designs the best-fit project management approach using a vetted portfolio of tools, templates, and processes.

EXECUTION conducts the project using the designed management approach, subject to changes due to the dynamics of the situation.

The Business Case is the underlying control tool.

➤ **Learn from experience:** Lessons should be sought at the beginning of a project (in the process *Starting up a Project*), learned as the project progresses, and passed on to other projects—optionally at each stage end, and always at the close. There is no reason for any project manager to enter into a project with no experience or help from a base of lessons. Those involved in the project may have previous experience, there may have been prior projects in the company from which lessons were learned, and there are other sources (e.g., the web, suppliers, sister companies) of valuable lessons that can be used by the project.

ECPM Framework cycles (equivalent to P2 Stages) include Probative Swim Lanes which are experiments to learn *and* discover solution components using lean practices.

➤ **Defined roles and responsibilities:** Project management is different from line management. Projects require a temporary organization for a finite timescale and for a specific business purpose. Managing the project staff can be a headache for a project manager. A project may include staff who report to different line managers or even work for other organizations. The project resources may change for different parts of the project and be a combination of full-time and part-time members. So how does everyone know who is responsible for what?

An explicit project management team structure is required. People must know what their own responsibilities are, along with the responsibilities of other people. This depends on good communication.

The ECPM Framework is built upon a shared management model. Each ECPM project has two project managers. One is from the developer side (the P2 Supplier); the other is from the client side (the business and or user side). These co-managers have equal responsibility and authority as decision makers over the project.

➤ **Manage by stages:** This comes from two different thoughts:

- If the Project Board is, in P2 terms, ultimately accountable for the project and P2 doesn't like the idea of regular progress meetings, there must be some key points during a project when the Project Board needs to review progress and decide if it wants to continue with the project
- Very often a project will last longer and contain more detail than can be planned with any accuracy at the outset

Based on these thoughts, P2 divides a project into stages. P2 has a Project Plan—an overview of the whole project—which is often a *best guess* at the outset. The project manager plans only the next stage in detail—only as much as can be accurately judged—and the Project Board approves only one stage at a time, reviewing the status at stage end and deciding whether to continue or not.

A P2 project will have a minimum of two stages. The first is an initiation stage, where we confirm the organization structure, create the Project Plan and the Business Case, consider the risks, and decide if it is okay to continue. The second stage is where the product is created. This second stage may be broken down into a number of stages, depending on the size, complexity, and risk content of the project.

At the end of each stage, a plan is presented together with an updated view of the Business Case, the Project Plan, the risks, and suggested tolerances for the next stage. Thus, senior management can review progress so far and decide from the information presented to them whether to authorize the next stage or not.

> ECPM projects require an adaptive approach built upon learning and discovery that occurs through repeated Cycles (P2 Stages). At the completion of each Cycle, a Client Checkpoint is conducted to decide how the project should go forward, if at all. The client checkpoint is similar in many respects to the end stage assessments in P2. The decision criterion aligns with the requirements and success criteria as specified in the Business Case and Project Overview Statement (POS). The POS is similar to the Project Brief.

> **Manage by exceptions:** P2 recognizes four levels of authority in a project. Authority is delegated from one management level to the next. Each management level is allocated tolerances within which they can continue without the need to refer to the next higher level of management. This is called *management by exception*. There are six tolerance limits:

1. Time: +/– an amount of time boundary on each side of the target completion date within which it is okay to vary
2. Cost: +/– amounts of money on either side of the planned budget within which it is okay to vary
3. Quality: +/– degrees off a quality target, (e.g., a product that weighs a target 10k, with an allowed –50g to +10g tolerance)
4. Scope: permissible variation in delivery of the plan's products (e.g., mandatory requirements +/– desirable requirements)
5. Risk: limits on the plan's exposure to threats (e.g., the risk of not meeting the target date against the risk of overspending)

6. Benefit: +/– allowable degrees off an improvement goal (e.g., 30 to 40% staff saving offers a 10% tolerance)

To cut down on unnecessary meetings or problem referrals, P2 has the principle of allowing a management level to continue its work as long as there is no forecast that a tolerance will be exceeded. Only when there is a forecast of a tolerance being exceeded does the next higher level of authority need to be consulted.

> The Client Checkpoint takes all previous project results into account and adapts Cycle Plans and the overall Project Plan as appropriate. As such, there is no separation of management by exception. It is absorbed into the normal conduct of the project's business, which is similar to the P2 End Stage Reports.

➢ **Focus on products:** P2 focuses on the *products* to be produced by the project, which later leads to the activities to produce them. This affects the method of planning, many of the controls, and the approach to ensure quality.

> The high-level requirements include performance criteria that define product quality. These are documented in the Business Case and are in the Client Checkpoint (similar to the end-stage assessment). Process quality is monitored and assessed through a continuous process improvement program that is built into the ECPM Framework.

➢ **Tailor to suit the project environment:** Ensure that the level of project management is relative to the project's environment; the project's scale, importance, and risk; and the formality required. The whole method may be suitable for larger projects, but it may need to be tailored for smaller projects, such as making some reports orally, combining roles, or merging some registers.

> The ECPM Framework SET-UP Phase is a critical process. It establishes a customized version of the PMLC tailored to the project characteristics, the internal organizational environment, and the external market conditions. That is unique with the ECPM Framework.

From a principles perspective, the ECPM Framework is equivalent to P2.

P2 Themes Align with the ECPM Framework

The P2 method has a number of *themes* (Figure 1.3) to explain its philosophy about various project aspects, why they are needed, and how they can be used. This philosophy is implemented through the processes.

Themes are the specific aspects of the project that must be continually addressed throughout the life span of the project. They are part of the design of every effective project management approach. This is true for P2 and it is true for the ECPM Framework. Seven themes characterize P2, and the ECPM Framework aligns with those themes. The P2 themes are briefly discussed below:

> ➤ **Business case:** P2 emphasizes that a viable Business Case should drive a project. Its existence should be proved before the project is given the go-ahead, and it should be confirmed at all major decision points during

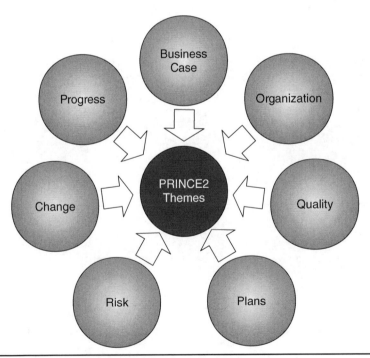

Figure 1.3   The 7 PRINCE2 themes

the project. Claimed benefits should be defined in measurable terms so that they can be checked after delivery of the product.

> A thorough Business Case is written during the IDEATION Phase. It is the thread that runs through the project life span and is used to decide on the future course of the project and how the business value delivered aligns with the expected business value.

➤ **Organization:** A structure of the project management team, the organization is based on a definition of the roles, responsibilities, and relationships of all staff involved in the project. P2 describes these roles. According to the size and complexity of a project, these roles may be combined, shared, or allocated to an individual.

> The ECPM Framework uses a Project Review Board. The Project Review Board members are the senior managers who have a functional connection with the project and a few senior project managers who have no vested interest in the project. On a periodic basis, the Project Co-Managers appear before the Project Review Board to report on the progress of their project since the last review.

➤ **Quality:** The P2 method recognizes the importance of quality and incorporates a quality approach to the management and technical processes. It begins by establishing the customer's quality expectations and follows these up by laying down standards and quality inspection methods to be used and verifying that these are being used.

> In any ECPM project, there are two types of quality: product quality and process quality. The developer team is responsible for performing up to the level of the processes available and delivering the product quality as specified in the high-level requirements. The client team is responsible for assuring that the product quality measures up to expectations.

➤ **Plans:** The P2 method offers a series of plan levels that can be tailored to the size and needs of a project, and an approach to planning that is based on products rather than activities.

> In the ECPM Framework, the journey to the learning and discovery of the solution proceeds through a series of Cycle Plans (in P2 these are Stage Plans). These Cycle Plans are dependent upon each other in the sense that the output from a Cycle Plan is input to the next Cycle Plan. An overall Project Plan exists only at a high level and describes generally how the Project Team expects the project to proceed. As learning and discovery takes place, the overall Project Plan is often revised due to revisions in the scope of the project. At this level both P2 and the ECPM are equivalent and P2 LEAN simply accommodates both.

> **Risk:** Risk is a major factor to be considered during the life of a project. The P2 method defines the key moments when risks should be reviewed, outlines an approach to the analysis and management of risk, and tracks these through all the processes.

> Complex projects are high-risk projects. A sound Risk Management Plan is included in P2 and P2 LEAN, except P2 LEAN assigns a team member to be responsible for keeping the Risk Plan updated and keeping the team members informed of all project risks, their status, and any other updates. P2 would normally assign maintenance of the Risk Register to Project Support, but as this is a role, the role may be allocated to a team member.

> **Change:** The P2 method emphasizes the need for change control, and this is enforced with a change control technique plus identification of the processes that apply to change.

Tracking the key components of a final product and their versions for release is called configuration management. There are many methods of configuration management available. The P2 method does not attempt to invent a new one, but defines the essential facilities and information requirements for a configuration management method and how it should link with other P2 key themes and techniques.

> The ECPM Framework uses its own bundled Change Management Process. Change requests are held in the Scope Bank until the Cycle ends. As part of planning for the next Cycle, those change requests are each decided upon as part of a group rather than individually.

➤ **Progress:** The organization should have a set of controls which facilitate the provision of key decision-making information, allowing it to pre-empt problems and make decisions on problem resolution. For senior management, controls are based on the concept of *management by exception*, i.e., if we agree on a plan, let the manager get on with it, unless something is forecast to go wrong.

A project is split into stages as an approach to defining the review and commitment points of a project, in order to promote sound management control of risk and investment.

> In the ECPM Framework, progress is measured as actual performance against planned performance and this is tracked over time. This primitive earned value analysis can be used to track trends that are indicative of convergence towards or divergence from an acceptable solution.

P2 LEAN FRAMEWORK

The P2 LEAN Framework is a hybrid. It has a P2 foundation upon which seven ECPM Framework artifacts are embedded.

The Recommended ECPM Framework Artifacts

There is a clear synergy to be realized by integrating certain artifacts from the ECPM Framework into P2. Such is the rationale for this book. The ECPM Framework grew out of over 25 years of client experiences and provided the concept and design of the ECPM Framework. This book brings those experiences to the forefront. The strength of these experiences is that they not only identify *what* must be done (as does P2), but also *how* to do it. This takes P2 to the practitioner and even professional levels and much closer to defining how to accomplish performance improvements. To that end, this book discusses the seven artifacts summarized below. They are introduced in Chapter 2 and discussed in detail in Chapter 3:

- Co-Manager Model
- High-level Requirements Definition
- Scope Triangle
- Bundled Change Request Process
- Scope Bank

- Probative and Integrative Swim Lanes
- Vetted portfolio of tools, templates, and processes

These artifacts are to be treated just like the activities in P2. They are to be used in every project to some extent.

The P2 LEAN Framework Has No Equals

The P2 LEAN Framework is new. Its name says that it is different from P2—and it is, but through that difference it opens the door to agile and adaptive instantiations of P2. The P2 LEAN Framework is an agile and lean framework, but it is not just another version of P2 Agile. It is that and much more, too!

The terms *agile* and *lean* have a close relationship and dependence on each other. An agile model is almost always a lean model, but a lean model is usually not an agile model. The P2 LEAN Framework is obviously lean, but it also happens to be agile. That positions the P2 LEAN Framework as an adaptive framework that aligns with the management needs of the complex project landscape. It also aligns with the complex project management models that support the learning and discovery efforts that are so important to successful complex project planning and execution.

MANAGING A P2 LEAN PROJECT

The P2 LEAN framework is new, but it is perhaps the most powerful approach to date to manage the complex and uncertain projects that populate the contemporary landscape. How can we make such a bold statement? The Co-Manager Model is at the center of this claim. The Project Team includes all of the subject matter expert expertise needed to manage the project and deliver the best business value possible. For this project the client-side members are the experts at product definition and the developer-side members are the experts at product discovery and development—and they are the only team that contains that expertise. The only input needed from outside the Project Team is up or down approval of resource requirements for a specific cycle or Project Plan. That is the responsibility of Project Executive Management (see Chapters 5 and 8). In some cases program/portfolio managers may ask the co-managers to submit prioritized alternatives with the resource requirements of each alternative included. This is an aid in the resource allocation decisions the program/portfolio managers must make.

The P2 LEAN Framework May Not Need a Project Board

The Co-Manager Model is self-contained. All of the subject matter expertise is represented by one or more team members. They are vested with the authority to change the project within the tolerances set by the Executive. Once a plan or cycle plan is created, Project Executive Management approves the resources needed and gives an up/down/delay decision on the project. For reference purposes we call them the P2 LEAN Project Review Board. In effect, part of the authority of the P2 Project Board is vested in the P2 LEAN Project Team. That part is content-based.

The P2 LEAN Framework Allows for Model Changes During Execution

As the solution comes into clearer focus, occasions will arise where the earlier chosen PMLC Model may no longer be appropriate and a change of models may be needed. This is a complex decision because there are several conflicting factors. However, the team has all of the expertise needed for that decision. In most cases those revisions will be to the P2 LEAN Model already in use for the project. In extreme cases the revision might be to a PMLC Model other than a P2 Model. For example, if the complete solution is discovered at the end of the current cycle, should the model be changed to a simple traditional linear model (i.e., Waterfall, Rapid Development Waterfall, or Staged Delivery Waterfall). This is a complex decision, involving several factors. A discussion of this decision model is out of scope for this book.

SETTING UP A P2 LEAN PROJECT

P2 LEAN incorporates the three-phased ECPM Framework: IDEATION, SET-UP and EXECUTION (see Figure 1.1). The ECPM Framework IDEATION Phase is closely aligned with P2: Starting up a Project Process. It includes a Business Case, high-level requirements, and a one-page Project Brief. The approval to plan the management approach to the project is a four-step SET-UP Phase:

- Determine Project Quadrant (Traditional, Agile, Extreme, Emertxe)
- Choose the Best-fit PMLC Model Type (Linear, Incremental, Iterative, Adaptive, Extreme)
- Assess Project Characteristics and its Internal/External Environment

- Choose and adapt a specific PMLC Model Template (Waterfall, Rapid Development Waterfall, FDD, DSDM, P2, etc.)

The SET-UP Phase is unique to the P2 LEAN Framework and has its roots in the ECPM Framework. You won't find it in any other PMLC Model. It is a robust template that incorporates all known PMLC Models and a decision rule to design the best-fit project management approach for a specific project. In our case, we are going to limit these four steps to a P2 environment but recognize that it applies to all PMLC Models.

Once the project characteristics and the internal/external environment have been determined, P2 LEAN comes into play. There are two major directions that can be taken:

- **There is a specific PMLC Model that can be a good starting point to design the model that will be used.** In our case that model is P2. It may or may not fit the project situation and some minor adjustments will be needed. The key here is *minor adjustments*. These are subjective and made by the co-managers in compliance with any required activities imposed by executive management.
- **There is no specific PMLC Model that can be used as a starting point and the model that will be used must be built from the bottom up.** In that case, we start with a minimal version of P2. Chapter 3 identifies and prioritizes the 44 activities that are part of the P2 LEAN Framework. That minimal version is defined by 27 of the 44 activities that align with the 7 processes. These 27 activities are a minimalist set that are needed to execute the smallest and simplest of projects for which the P2 LEAN Framework is an appropriate choice. With that minimalist set as the starting point, we add other activities until the resulting model is the best-fit model for this specific project. This exercise must be seen as subjective. The Project Team, under the guidance of the co-managers, decides on the activities to be included in their bottom-up model. These are subjective and taken by the co-managers in compliance with any required activities imposed by Project Executive Management.

So either we start with P2 and adapt it, or we start with the P2/kit and choose the activities and the vetted tools, templates, and business processes that will be our *recipe* for managing the project. This is a lean management solution development phase not found in any contemporary PMLC Model. It puts the P2 LEAN Framework in a class by itself.

THE FUTURE OF P2 LEAN

We are just scratching the surface here. So far we have learned that P2 LEAN is more powerful than we originally envisioned. It is far more than just an integration of lean tools, templates, and processes from the ECPM Framework into P2. Without realizing it, we have created a synergy. P2 LEAN is more powerful than either P2 or the ECPM Framework could be when used on their own. Its value is being discovered as we move forward with application and further development of P2 LEAN.

P2 defines a flexible framework that specifies *what* with little reference or guidance on *how*. P2 LEAN does that and more. *How* is an important addition. The flexible and adaptive opportunities that are presented to the Co-Managed Project Team are strange territory for most Project Co-Managers. These are not to be interpreted as a license to *do it your own way*. Rather, the Project Team is constrained to a vetted portfolio of tools, templates, and business processes from which they will create the *recipes* they will use to manage their project. The burden is on the Executive to make sure that the vetted portfolio does not constrain the Project Team to the point that their performance is limited and their ability to deliver business value reduced. Completing the vetted portfolio and providing the support to use it effectively is a major undertaking. So it is best to think of that vetted portfolio as a *work in progress* and it will never be completed. Experience with complex project management will give rise to changes or additions to that vetted portfolio. In the spirit of continuous process improvement, those suggestions must be considered.

WHY WE WROTE THIS BOOK

Project failure rates have been unacceptably high for several years running at 65% or higher. Efforts to improve this number have not been too successful. This book is a bold attempt to combine the best of two project management worlds. The purpose of that collaboration is to improve the performance and delivered business value of those projects that align with the P2 Framework. Both authors have come to the same conclusion—that several artifacts from the ECPM Framework (from the U.S. side of the pond) can be integrated into the P2 Framework (from the EU side of the pond). What those artifacts are and how they can enhance P2 is what has motivated us to partner and bring these benefits to the forefront.

It is that alignment and the resulting compatibility of the two frameworks that have been our inspiration. We have recognized that the net benefit from that integration follows from recognizing that P2 was developed during a time when the more traditional approaches to project management were popular. More recently, the P2 gurus are adapting P2 to the agile world. That version is called P2 Agile. The evolution from P2 to P2 Agile is more complex than those gurus have envisioned.

> The evolution from P2 to P2 LEAN requires a systemic evolution.

That includes adding, revising, and deleting processes and practices inherent in P2 to deliver effective P2 LEAN. That is the driving motivation for our book.

This is the first book that demonstrates the strong linkage between the ECPM Framework and the P2 Framework. Of the many artifacts in the ECPM Framework, seven are unique to the ECPM Framework. We discuss how they can be fully integrated into the P2 Framework for significant performance enhancement and increased delivery of business value.

This book offers enhancements to the processes and practices of project management in those organizations that use P2. That number includes most organizations in the EU that depend on effective project management processes and practices for competitive advantage. The number of adoptions of P2 in the U.S. is growing. Some of that growth is due to the fact that the U.S. companies are rooted in EU companies. Some of that growth is also due to the fact that U.S. companies have come to realize the benefits of using P2 in place of the processes and practices they are currently using. Our book reaches out to both of those communities.

HOW THIS BOOK IS ORGANIZED

Foreword
Part 1: Overview
    Chapter 1: Introduction
    Chapter 2: Overview of the Effective Complex Project Management
        Framework
    Chapter 3: PRINCE2 LEAN: Are You a Cook or a Chef?
    Chapter 4: PRINCE2 LEAN: Project Planning
Part 2: PRINCE2 LEAN and the IDEATION Phase
    Part 2 Introduction
    Chapter 5: Preparing the Business Case

HOW TO USE THIS BOOK

The real meat in this book can be found in Parts 2, 3, and 4. After reading Chapter 2, P2 practitioners and professionals can proceed directly to Part 2. There they can further direct their reading to the specific artifacts that address P2 practitioners' issues and challenges. After reading Chapter 3, complex project managers with an interest in P2 can proceed directly to Part 2. There they can further direct their readings to see how their processes and practices can be applied to the P2 Framework.

Those for whom both the ECPM and P2 Frameworks are new to their project management processes and practices should read Chapters 2 and 3. As they investigate the commonalities between the two frameworks in Part 2, our expectation is that we will open a whole new world populated with a greater success of project execution.

WHO SHOULD USE THIS BOOK

Any organization that uses or anticipates using P2 is an end-user target. So the focus is on application. To that group, any P2 professional services consulting or training organization would be included. That market includes virtually every organization in the EU and, by association, any of their partners worldwide including in the U.S.

A NOTE ON CAPITALIZATION OF TERMS

Terms that are reserved are capitalized. So for example, *plan* is not a reserved term and is not capitalized. *Stage Plan* refers to a specific type of plan which is reserved and hence, is capitalized. As another example, *swim lanes* is not a reserved term and is not capitalized. *Probative Swim Lanes* refers to a particular type of swim lane which is reserved and hence, is capitalized. The context in which a term is used will dictate the use of capitalization.

This book has free material available for download from the
Web Added Value™ resource center at *www.jrosspub.com*

2

OVERVIEW OF THE EFFECTIVE COMPLEX PROJECT MANAGEMENT FRAMEWORK

It would be difficult, if not impossible, to provide a highly structured environment that enhances a knowledge worker's method of functioning.
—Ira B. Gregerman, President, Productivity Associates

"We" rather than "I."
—Charles Garfield, President, Performance Sciences Corp.

Few ideas are in themselves practical. It is for want of imagination in applying them, rather than in acquiring them that they fail. The creative process does not end with an idea—it only starts with an idea.
—John Arnold, Massachusetts Institute of Technology

CHAPTER LEARNING OBJECTIVES

This chapter will provide readers the knowledge or ability to:

- Understand the IDEATION, SET-UP, and EXECUTION phases of the Effective Complex Project Management (ECPM) Framework
- Understand the robustness and adaptability of the ECPM Framework

- Understand the role of the ECPM/kit and its contents
- Explain the 12 steps of the ECPM Framework process flow
- Gain a working knowledge of the Linear, Incremental, Iterative, Adaptive, and Extreme Project Management Life Cycle (PMLC) Model types that populate the complex project landscape
- Understand the PMLC Model Templates as they relate to the five types of PMLC Models
- Gain familiarity with the decision process for changing PMLC Model Templates during complex project execution
- Know how to use the ECPM Framework for the Proof of Concept, revision of the version plan, and embed the ECPM in traditional project management

The ECPM Framework is a robust project management environment that thrives on business challenges and the creativity of the team, with the change process as the driver to solution discovery and the courage of conviction. The ECPM Framework is the only project management approach that is driven totally by the characteristics of the project, its internal culture, and changing external market dynamics. It embraces all project management methodologies, from the simplest linear models (such as Waterfall) to the most complex agile models (such as Scrum and PRINCE2). Included in the ECPM Framework are the following:

- A customized brainstorming process that begins with an idea and concludes with a project to be proposed
- A decision model and process for choosing and continuously adapting the best-fit project management approach, tailored to the specific characteristics of the project and the changing environment in which the project is executed
- A portfolio of specific PMLC Model Templates to be chosen and customized for the project situation
- A portfolio of vetted tools, templates, and processes for building and continuously adapting to the chosen PMLC Model Template to fit the changing project situation

In that sense, the ECPM Framework is the closest we can get to a *silver bullet*. So, in addition to providing a model for managing complex projects using Rational Unified Process (RUP), Scrum, or several others, the ECPM Framework is a structure that includes all project management methodologies as special cases. For that reason, the ECPM Framework stands alone among complex project management processes and practices.

The full realization of the ECPM Framework is itself an ongoing agile project. The instantiation documented here is a significant step forward in that journey. The immediate goal is to have the ECPM Framework become a major addition to your portfolio of tools, templates, and processes and to be implemented. Feedback from practice is essential as the ECPM Framework's process improvement will be a continuous effort. Thus, you should always view the ECPM Framework as a work in process. It will get better as those who use it provide feedback on their experiences.

In this chapter, we take a high-level tour through the three phases of the ECPM Framework. It sets the complex project management solution space. We expect this book will be a significant step forward in improving the success rate of projects.

ECPM PROCESS FLOW DIAGRAM

If you think of the ECPM Framework as a decision model whose purpose is to design a project management model in addition to executing that project management model, you will have a good start on understanding the ECPM Framework and how it can revolutionize all your approaches to complex project management. My beginning assumption is that projects are unique, thus, the best way to manage them must be unique also. There are no recipes, but only project management experts who can design recipes for these unique and constantly changing projects. These Project Managers are the *chefs* of the ECPM Framework. Effective complex project management is not accomplished by following a predefined recipe. Effective complex project management can only come from first having designed the project management approach for a specific project, and then following it with the assumption that it will probably change before the project is complete. But that is the nature of an ECPM Framework-guided project! So, an ECPM Framework Project Manager must be a creative and courageous leader, and certainly not a follower. Chefs are needed. Cooks need not apply.

The ECPM Framework consists of three dependent phases: Project IDEATION Phase (Steps 1–3), Project SET-UP Phase (Steps 4–7), and Project EXECUTION Phase (Steps 8–12). Figure 2.1 illustrates these three phases and their 12 Steps, and the feedback relationship that links Step 11 in the Project EXECUTION Phase to Step 5 in the Project SET-UP Phase:

- **The Project IDEATION Phase** begins the ECPM Framework with an untested idea to solve a recognized problem or take advantage of an untapped business opportunity, and ends with a brief explanation of

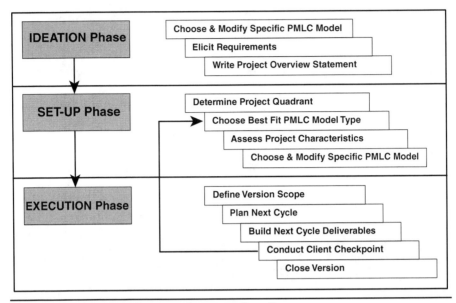

Figure 2.1   The ECPM Framework process flow diagram

a project to be proposed. StageGate #1 is received at the approval of the Project Overview Statement (POS), which is very similar to the Project Brief, and the granting of the authority to begin the Project SET-UP Phase.

- **The Project SET-UP Phase** is where the decision is made as to what is the best-fit project management methodology and how it needs to be adapted to be the best-fit approach for the specific project at hand. StageGate #2 takes place for the approval of the Modified PMLC Model and the granting of the authority to begin the Project EXECU-TION Phase.

- **The Project EXECUTION Phase** is where the project is executed using the best-fit approach that was defined during the Project SET-UP Phase, and contains a feedback loop to maintain that alignment over the project life span. StageGate #3 occurs when the High-level Project Plan is approved and the budget authorized to launch the project.

The ECPM consists, therefore, of three dependent StageGates:

- **StageGate #1:** The deliverable from the Project IDEATION Phase is the POS. One purpose of the POS is to gain sponsor approval to continue to the Project SET-UP Phase. Minimal resources will be required to complete the Project SET-UP Phase. That means that the Business Case has demonstrated the validity of the project from the perspective of the likely business value that will be delivered from a successful project.

- **StageGate #2:** The approval granted in StageGate #2 is for the feasibility of the PMLC and the granting of resources to complete the project plan. It is not approval to do the project—that comes later.
- **StageGate #3:** StageGate #3 approval is the last approval prior to executing the project plan for traditional projects or the next cycle plan for a complex project.

Each StageGate is a milestone event in the project life span and presents an opportunity for review by senior management, sponsor, and clients.

Project IDEATION Phase

A simple and intuitive process must be in place so that anyone in the enterprise with an idea for generating business value will be encouraged to come forward with their idea without any prejudging and with minimal documentation.

Step 1: Develop a Business Case

Driven by the sponsor, with the participation of the client and perhaps the project manager, a Business Case is developed and documented. The process to develop a Business Case consists of the following:

- Define the problem or untapped opportunity
- Identify alternative solutions
- Gather data relevant to each alternative solution
- Analyze, prioritize, and choose an alternative
- Document the chosen alternative

There is nothing new here. Every ECPM project is initiated by a Business Case. It establishes the *what, why,* and business value of a project. To do that, it will contain at least the above actions and may be further customized to align with specific enterprise processes and practices. A simple model for developing the Business Case is discussed in Chapter 4.

Step 2: Elicit Requirements

In an ECPM project, elicitation of requirements is a two-part effort. The first part gathers a high-level list of the necessary and sufficient requirements that an acceptable solution must meet. This list is often documented in the POS in IDEATION Phase, Step 3: Write the POS. For simpler situations, a conditions of satisfaction discussion can be used for the first part. For more complex situations, one of the many approaches to requirements elicitation can be used.

The second part of the Elicit Requirements step is found in the ECPM EXECUTE Phase, Step 8: Define Version Scope. In Step 8, the high-level requirements are decomposed to provide a better understanding of the functions and features that define them. This is the requirements breakdown structure (RBS), which describes *what* must be done, but not *how*. The RBS is then further decomposed into the work breakdown structure (WBS). The WBS defines how the deliverables will be built. The RBS and WBS are developed iteratively over the cycles of an ECPM project.

Step 3: Write a Project Overview Statement

This is a five-part, *one-page* document that includes:

- Statement of business problem or opportunity
- Project goal
- Project objectives or high-level solution requirements
- Quantitative business value and success criteria metrics
- Risks, assumptions, and obstacles

The POS is written in the language of the business so that anyone in the organization who has the occasion to read it will understand it.

Project SET-UP Phase

The POS is an input to the process that decides whether the project justifies further investigation. If it does, the authorization and resources are allocated by the sponsor for project planning. With the POS as input, the remaining steps for the Project SET-UP Phase consist of classifying the project and choosing the best-fit project type from among the linear, incremental, iterative, adaptive, and extreme projects. Within the chosen type, a specific PMLC Model Template is chosen and adapted to fit the project characteristics and the internal/external environments.

The Project SET-UP Phase consists of four steps. This is radically different to the approach used in many organizations. In fact, it may happen without any conscious effort. Their portfolio of project management methodologies is limited to just a few choices, and SET-UP happens with little analysis and ceremony.

Warning

Standard Waterfall and Scrum are the only two project management methodologies in many organization's PMLC Model Template portfolios. For the ECPM to be effective, this is too constraining.

Step 4: Classify the Project

Based on the initial understanding of the goal and solution, the project is classified into the appropriate quadrant of the four-quadrant Project Landscape shown in Figure 2.2. Further explanation of these four project quadrants is given in Chapter 5.

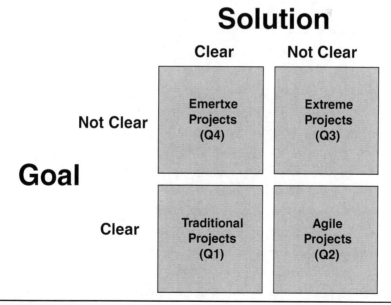

Figure 2.2   The Project Landscape

Step 5: Choose the Best-fit PMLC Model Template

There are several choices of specific PMLC Model Templates chosen from among Linear, Incremental, Iterative, Adaptive, or Extreme types (see Figure 2.3). These five project management types are further defined in Chapter 5. Each enterprise will have its own PMLC Model portfolio for each of these five project management types. That will include specific PMLC Model Templates such as Waterfall, Scrum, and others. The larger and more complex the organization, the richer their PMLC Model Template Portfolio will be.

With the exception of home-grown models, some subset of the 12 specific PMLC Model Templates shown in the right-most panel of Figure 2.4 will be the portfolio of models in use in most organizations. The contents of this portfolio should be carefully chosen and built. The specific PMLC Model Templates will have to cover a potentially wide range of project types.

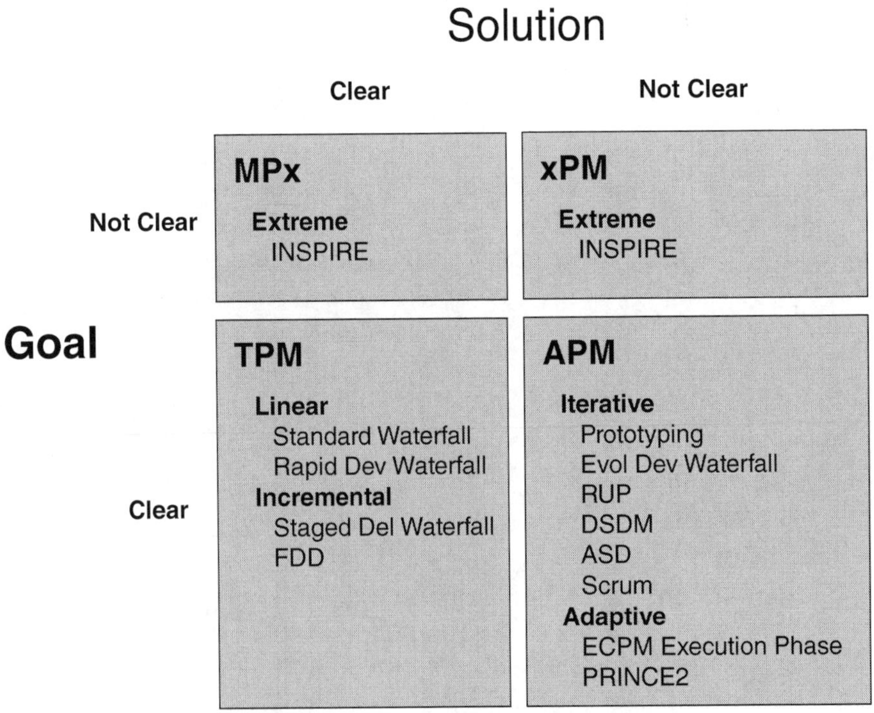

Figure 2.3 Five project management categories mapped into the Four-Quadrant Project Landscape

Once the portfolio of PMLC Model Templates is chosen, the next task for the organization is to build the skilled cadre of project managers and developers that will be able to utilize their portfolio of PMLC Model Templates. This is not only a matter of delivering training, but also the scheduling of that training and the participants to be trained. This has to be aligned with the need for complex project managers and their development team members: how many will be needed, and when will they be needed? That puts the human resources managers in the position of having to forecast needs by skills and competencies. Do not underestimate the challenges they will face. That is a major effort and requires a career and professional development program that aligns with the forecasted portfolio of project types that will be encountered by the organization. See Chapter 8 for a discussion of how this program might be defined. We will return to Figure 2.4 later with a detailed discussion of Steps 4 and 5.

Step 6: Assess Project Characteristics

There are several variables that can impact how the chosen PMLC Model Template is adapted for use. In addition to the specific characteristics of the project, the internal business environment and the external marketing environment are included, and their impact on the chosen PMLC Model Template determined.

Step 7: Modify PMLC Model Template

Projects are dynamic. They can change for a variety of reasons, including changes in business conditions and priorities, as well as other internal and external environmental factors listed in the details of Step 6. That translates into a need to continuously review the chosen PMLC Model Template for adaptations, and even for reconsideration. For example, at some point in an iteration during a Scrum project, the client says: "Aha, now I see what the complete solution will look like!" and the project manager replies, "And I know how we can build that solution." Does that mean that Scrum should be abandoned in favor of a Staged Delivery Waterfall model, for example? That question is difficult to answer because there are so many moving parts to consider. For example, some of the more obvious implications are:

- Changes to resource requirements and development team membership
- Schedule changes due to resource availabilities
- Cost of abandonment of one PMLC Model in place of another
- Budget implications

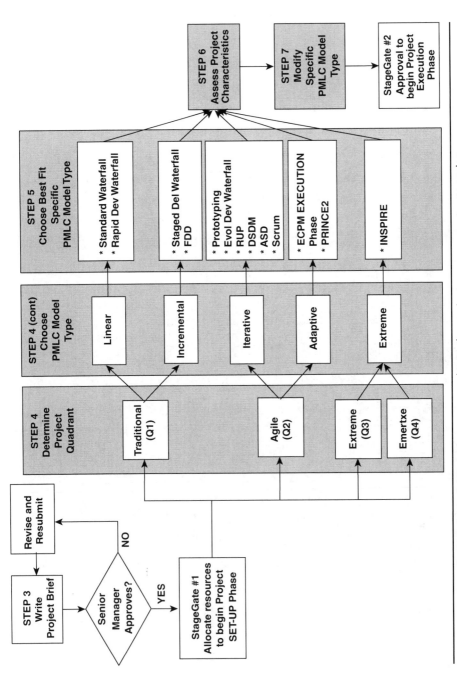

Figure 2.4 Specific PMLC Model Templates mapped into the project management categories

These added costs need to be balanced against the benefits of such a change, which could include:

- Pricing changes to products/services
- Sales and marketing implications to product/service rollout dates
- Cost avoidance implications

Revise the management model(s) accordingly and prepare a business proposal that will increase revenues, avoid costs, or improve service, and evaluate the business proposal based specific quantitative metrics.

Project EXECUTION Phase

At this point, reflect on your current comfort level with project execution using the ECPM. For example:

- Do you know how your project aligns with the strategic plan, especially its priority?
- Do you know how well your adapted PMLC Model Template fits the project, and where potential problems and obstacles might arise?
- Is your approach a lean approach, based on just-in-time planning?
- Have you made a good start on the risk mitigation plan and appointed a team member to manage it?

Once a specific PMLC Model Template has been chosen and modified, it is time to start project work. At this point in the ECPM process flow, the initial recipe is complete and it is time to deliver.

The Project EXECUTION Phase consists of five steps that will be familiar to most project managers. The only new feature that you will encounter in project execution, compared to traditional models, is the feedback loop from Step 11: Client Checkpoint, to Step 5: Choose the Best-fit PMLC Model Template. This feedback loop is unique to the ECPM. Plus, it contributes to the lean principles that the ECPM protects. Taken together, these two steps and their history track the status of the goal and solution convergence to clarity and completeness. Armed with that information, the project team is prepared for Step 10.

Step 8: Define Version Scope

The POS, including the project objectives, is a high-level description of what this ECPM version is all about. In anticipation of possible future projects that might extend the delivered business value, I call this a *Version*. The Version Scope includes some preliminary planning activities like cycle lengths, number of cycles, and cycle objective statements to help the sponsor and the client, whom are related to the project.

Step 9: Plan the Next Cycle

The Version Scope statement is the basis for identifying cycles of learning, discovery, and deployment. In the simple case where the project is a traditional project, there will only be one cycle. In more complex projects, there will be any number of cycles including an unspecified number of cycles. Across all project types, cycle length can vary from a few hours (prototyping) to several months (Staged Delivery Waterfall). Goal and solution clarity are the major factors in determining cycle length.

Step 10: Build the Next Cycle Deliverables

The deliverables from a Cycle Plan are fixed and are not affected by any scope change requests. Any suggestions for scope change are stored in the Scope Bank and considered in Step 11. Once the deliverables are produced or the cycle duration is reached, the cycle ends. Any incomplete deliverables are returned to the project Scope Bank for reprioritization and possible consideration in some later cycle. There are a few situations that would cause a deviation from the Cycle Plan.

Step 11: Conduct Client Checkpoint

This is a critical milestone in the life of the project. The Client Checkpoint includes an analysis of:

- The cumulative planned versus actual requirements delivered from all completed cycles
- The Scope Bank, which contains the prioritized list of requirements not yet met
- Separate prioritized lists of future Probative and Integrative Swim Lanes (see Chapter 11: Preparing for the Next Stage)
- A review of the adapted PMLC Model Template for any needed changes
- The decision about the next cycle and its requirement content

The feedback loop from the Project EXECUTION Phase: Conduct Client Checkpoint to the Project SET-UP Phase: Choose the Best-fit PMLC Model

Type (shown later in Figure 3.1) is a unique feature of the ECPM. This feature will be new to most readers. No other known PMLC Model includes this option.

The sole purpose of the feedback loop is to keep project execution aligned with the unique and changing nature of the project. The uniqueness of the project makes such a feedback loop essential to successful complex project execution. It arises from the fact that the less we know about the solution, the less we know about the best way to manage the project. As knowledge about the solution changes, so might the way the project is managed. Our initial choice of a PMLC Model Template might turn out at some later cycle to be the wrong choice for future cycles. While the initial choice was based on what was known about the solution at that time, learning and discovery of the goal and solution might render that decision no longer valid.

What it communicates is that changes that emerge during project execution can result in a reconsideration of the PMLC Model Template choice. Those changes can be simple or significant. Complex project management presents its own unique set of challenges and risks, but we don't want the management methodology to be a barrier to success.

Changing the PMLC Model Template mid-project is not a decision to be taken lightly. There are several competing factors to weigh. Here are some of the possible reasons for revisiting the choice of a PMLC Model Template:

- **A radical change in the priority of the project:** This happens more frequently than one would expect. We might be great starters, but we are often lousy finishers. Projects are re-prioritized, interrupted, postponed, re-scoped, and even canceled, and the resources re-assigned to other projects. These changes are often the result of politics, reorganizations, change of sponsors, and peer pressure rather than the result of sound business decisions. The best protection against the risk of investment loss is to use a PMLC Model Template that produces production-ready deliverables as early as possible. That means adopting models that have a cycle length as short as possible, and that create production-level deliverables as often as possible.
- **A significant proposed scope change:** Market forces and changes are not always predictable, or, we know that they will occur, but not when. These can often cause significant changes in scope, either by reducing scope or greatly expanding the scope in order to react to the market changes. This will warrant the revisiting of the model choice with the prospect of a better fit, given the new conditions. Understand that scope change is not the enemy in a complex project, as it is in a

traditional project. The solution is not known and must be learned and discovered through iteration. That means there will be several false starts and redirections. The more "aha's!" the team gets, the better the progress toward an elusive solution. So, change is not only encouraged, it is essential. Special design features are built into the Plan Next Cycle Step to minimize the false starts and misunderstood directions. See the discussion of *Integrative Swim Lanes* and *Probative Swim Lanes* in Chapter 11.

- **The loss of a scarce resource:** This loss can have devastating effects on an in-process ECPM project. If the Risk Management Plan did not identify this as a risk, the impact can be even bigger and can stop a project. The short-term solution is to go to the market and hire a consultant with the same skills that were lost. Every project that utilized the same scarce resource will have the same problem. The impact might be a scope reduction to remove the need for that lost resource, and perhaps a switch of the PMLC Model Template choice to fit that reduced scope. A good Risk Management Plan should identify this risk and have a mitigation plan in place. Popular mitigation plans include shadowing and use of outside contractors.
- **Actions of a competitor:** Increased functionality, price reductions, and other actions of a competitor can stop your ECPM project dead in its tracks. Sometimes an incremental release strategy may be the best strategy as a hedge against the competitor's actions. Getting to market faster can establish a foothold that the competitor will find hard to counter.
- **The entry of a new competitor:** The new competitor might be a company that operates from the dining room table in a small apartment in Mumbai, India. They will be offering a product or service that looks exactly like the one you are offering, but at a much lower price. As you design your ECPM environment, think in terms of creating barriers to entry.
- **The release of a new technology:** The entire market will be impacted and speed to market will be affected. There is also a strategy that gets you to market without incorporating the latest technology: only implementing it in the next release, once the technology has matured.

Changing the PMLC Model Template during the Project EXECUTION Phase is not a decision to be taken lightly for the following reasons:

- **The cost of abandonment:** Here you will abandon one PMLC Model Template and switch the remaining project execution to a different

PMLC Model Template. In this case, cost is not just measured in dollars. In complex project situations, knowledge gained during project execution is not necessarily documented. It may exist only in the experiences of the client and development teams. It is intrinsic to the ECPM project experience and used whenever appropriate. Changing PMLC Model Templates during project execution risks losing that knowledge and any future benefits that may derive from it. Yes, you might put a practice in place to document that knowledge. That's okay, but now it adds:

- ✦ The actual dollar cost of creating that documentation, which is okay if the PMLC Model Template is changed.
- ✦ Non-value-added work if the PMLC Model Template is not changed, which is counter to the lean principles of ECPM.

- **The impact on resource requirements and committed schedules:** This has all sorts of implications to the continuation of project execution. These include:

  - ✦ The new PMLC Model Template may require fewer or less experienced development team members.
  - ✦ The client team and/or the development team may not have any experience with the new PMLC Model Template and be taken outside of their comfort zone. To relieve their anxiety, it may require holding some type of workshop. A workshop takes time and money.

- **The impact on the schedules of other projects:** Changing the PMLC Model Template during the Project EXECUTION Phase can have a simple or devastating impact not only on your project schedule, but also on the project schedule of any other project that utilizes the same resources. The concern is more focused on the immediate plan, which should not be detailed beyond the next cycle (if there is one):

  - ✦ If the current PMLC Model Template being used is a Linear or Incremental Model, the remaining schedule and complete plan will be seriously impacted, as can the schedules of any projects utilizing the same resources.
  - ✦ If the current PMLC Model Template is an Iterative or Adaptive Model, the impact will be somewhat greater because of the increased complexities and uncertainties.

Not every change of the PMLC Model Template results in added costs, added non-value work, or delays in the schedule. There are a few benefits:

- **The use of a simpler PMLC Model Template:** Usually the change in PMLC Model Templates will be to simpler models (i.e., from an agile PMLC to a traditional PMLC Model Template). This allows the new model to take advantage of some of the planning and scheduling benefits of the now-known, complete solution. The time between increments or cycles can be reduced, and that contributes to being lean.
- **The use of less experienced and skilled team members:** This can have a big impact on resource cost reduction. The use of distributed development team members may now be an option, where it was an inconvenience for agile projects.
- **Risk reduction:** The simpler model will have a lower risk, and hence a higher probability of project success.

Step 12: Close the Version

Closing a Version is no different than closing a traditional project. There will have been acceptance criteria that the client and sponsor deem to have been met, followed by a list of closing activities. If it is an ECPM project, the closing activities will also include an evaluation of the Scope Bank contents at the time the work was completed on the current version. The final Scope Bank contents will be input to the decision to proceed with a Version 2 solution.

Note about the ECPM Framework

You will probably find many other reasons to adapt ECPM. Feel free to do that. ECPM is not a rigid structure to be followed without question. The bottom line has always been to do what is right for the client. If that flies in the face of some established process or procedure, you need to take a serious look at your process or procedure. It may not be serving your needs, at least for this project. You may need to build a case for your sponsors and managers.

At the end of every ECPM cycle, you can deliver a production version of the known solution. It may have enough business value to be released, but that is not even necessary. Organizational velocity with respect to change and the support capabilities of the project team are major determinants of the release plan. The process can stop at any time and the solution deployed.

Organizations will probably have a release plan in place (quarterly, semi-annual, or annual), and your ECPM release strategy should be aligned with it.

Advice

At this early point in the project, results may not be forthcoming as planned. Do not be afraid to kill the plan. In almost every case, you will be making the correct decision. Abandonment is costly, but not as costly as wasting resources and time on a project that is going nowhere.

THE RECOMMENDED ECPM FRAMEWORK ARTIFACTS

There is a clear synergy to be realized by integrating certain artifacts from the ECPM Framework into P2. Such is the rationale for this book. The ECPM Framework grew out of over 25 years of client experiences and provided the concept and design of the ECPM Framework. This book brings those experiences to the forefront. The strength of these experiences is that they not only identify *what* must be done (as does P2) but also *how* to do it. This takes P2 to the practitioner and even professional levels and much closer to defining how to accomplish performance improvements. To that end, the book discusses the seven artifacts summarized below. They are introduced in Chapter 3 and discussed in detail in Parts 2, 3, and 4.

The ECPM Co-Manager Model

Meaningful client involvement has been cited (Standish Group, 2013) as a critical success factor to project success. The best way to accomplish this is to give the client a leadership role in project planning and execution. Having them as co-managers of their projects is the most effective way of achieving that involvement.

The ECPM High-level Requirements Definition

Project management thought leaders are in unanimous agreement that defining and clearly documenting complete requirements at the initiation stage of a project is not possible. The world is dynamic and so are the deliverables from a successful project. But what is possible is the definition of high-level requirements that identify *what* a successful solution must include, without any conditions placed on *how* that solution will be achieved. Stage Planning is based on high-level requirements.

The ECPM Scope Triangle

The iron triangle (cost, time, scope) does not work in the complex project landscape. Rather the ECPM Scope Triangle (cost, time, scope, quality, resource availability, and risk), shown in Figure 2.5, defines a project as a system in balance. When changes occur that put the system out of balance, problem solving and decision-making processes are invoked that restore that balance.

The ECPM Framework Scope Triangle is the conceptual foundation for problem solving, decision making, and change management processes in the project. Resource availability deserves special attention because it is the link to program and portfolio staffing and scheduling. Enterprise resources are often fixed in the short run, thus all approved and scheduled projects are constrained by that resource. Human Resource Management Systems (HRMS) have not sufficiently addressed the decision process for allocating resources across the project portfolio. The nature of the complex project landscape further complicates those decision processes. Much remains to be developed.

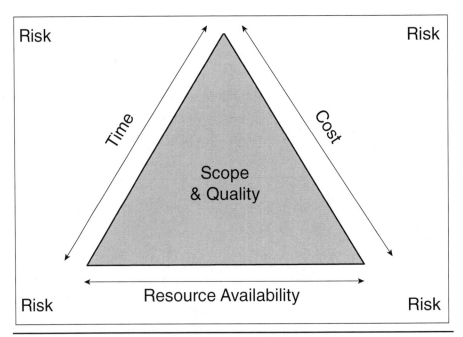

Figure 2.5   The ECPM Framework Scope Triangle

The ECPM Bundled Change Request Process

Change management processes are notoriously *not lean*. In the ECPM Framework project space this is unacceptable. P2 is not a lean process. The ECPM Framework utilizes a Bundled Change Request Process designed specifically to preserve its lean principles and assure better decision making with respect to analyzing, approving, and prioritizing change.

The ECPM Scope Bank

In the complex project landscape, a project is a dynamic environment looking for a previously unknown solution in the face of complexity and uncertainty. To effectively manage such a high-risk situation, a clearinghouse is a requirement. In the ECPM Framework, that clearinghouse is the ECPM Scope Bank. Think of it as the documented history of how the solution has evolved. As such it contains all of the information needed to make good business decisions regarding the future course of the project's journey.

The ECPM Probative and Integrative Swim Lanes

A complex project is a journey in search of an unknown solution to a critical business problem or untapped business opportunity. As such, it is high-risk. An acceptable solution may not even exist, given current knowledge and technologies. Such projects must be founded on lean principles and nowhere is that more critical than in how resources are spent looking for that solution. Those *looks* are based on a sequence of *investigating feasible ideas*. But the project team must be frugal in how and where it spends its limited resources. Such is the nature of the Probative and Integrative Swim Lanes that are the components of a single ECPM cycle.

The ECPM Vetted Portfolio of Tools, Templates, and Processes

Every organization is unique with respect to the portfolio of tools, templates, and processes that it uses to manage project and other business processes. The portfolio contents are usually vetted by the Project Management Office. Once vetted, the ECPM Framework gives the co-managers the authority and responsibility to choose how to use the portfolio to best manage its projects.

PUTTING IT ALL TOGETHER

The intention, from the beginning, of developing the ECPM Framework was to provide the project manager and client with a tool that would guide their thinking toward constructing a best-fit project management approach that is unique to each project, and adapting that decision as the project work commences. This has been done, and will continue to develop ECPM so that it can easily align with the changing project environment in your organization.

ECPM is not limited to any specific PMLC, software development life cycle, business process, or domain, and in that sense, is a robust and timeless project management approach. It might help by viewing ECPM as a decision model and thought process that provides a guide as to how a specific project is best managed, and following that decision by assembling the tools, templates, and processes to execute that management approach. The portfolio of applicable management models is dynamic. In most cases, that portfolio is limited to the vetted tools, templates, and processes within the needs, competencies, and capabilities of the organization. Finding an outside provider to assist in meeting some of those needs is part of the equation, too.

3

PRINCE2 LEAN: ARE YOU A COOK OR A CHEF?

We like to test things... No matter how good an idea sounds, test it first.
—Henry Block, CEO, H&R Block

If a man can write a better book, preach a better sermon, or make a better mouse-trap than his neighbor, though he builds his house in the woods, the world will make a beaten path to his door.
—Ralph Waldo Emerson, American essayist and poet

We weren't forced to follow the old ideas.
—J. Georg Bednorz, IBM researcher and Nobel laureate

CHAPTER LEARNING OBJECTIVES

This chapter will provide readers the knowledge or ability to:

- Understand the IDEATION, SET-UP, and EXECUTION Phases of the Effective Complex Project Management (ECPM) Framework and their overlap with the PRINCE2 (P2) processes
- Know the differences between the cook and the chef as a metaphor for the complex project manager and complex project management.
- See the value added by using the P2 LEAN Framework
- Have a high-level understanding of the P2 LEAN Framework and its impact on complex project success

Chefs can creatively adapt a recipe. Cooks can only use recipes developed by others—and such is the case with complex project management. The complex project landscape is populated with projects that are uncertain and high-risk. They are executed in a dynamic and changing environment, both from an internal and external perspective. It would be foolhardy to assume that an off-the-shelf project management model would fit the situation. A chef could do better.

When you enter the world of complex project management, you are in a world filled with risk and uncertainty. Your challenge as a project manager is to trade in your rule book because you will have to depend on your flexibility, creativity, and problem-solving skills to manage a complex project. The P2 LEAN Framework is the name of our integrated template. It is the framework that provides that starting point for managing a complex project using P2 as the starting template that is modified with artifacts adapted from the ECPM Framework.

The ECPM Framework is a robust project management framework with the change process as the driver of solution discovery. The ECPM Framework is the only project management approach that is driven totally by the characteristics of the project, its internal culture, and changing external market dynamics. It embraces all project management methodologies, from the simplest linear models (such as Waterfall), to the most complex agile models (such as Scrum and P2).

The cook/chef metaphor is a powerful tool for understanding the management environment of the complex project. Project managers are of two types. The cook is a manager who manages their project by following a recipe developed by others. They cannot succeed in the complex project world. The chef is a manager who creates the recipe for managing their project. They are the only type of project manager that can succeed in the complex project world. The P2 LEAN Framework is designed for the chef, not for the cook.

THE COMPLEX PROJECT LANDSCAPE

The complex project landscape was introduced in Chapter 2 and is illustrated in Figure 3.1.

Think of the complex project landscape as the land of the unknown unknowns and you won't be too far off. Testimonial data gathered from the U.S., EU, and Asia suggests that over 80% of all projects are complex projects. That is a staggering number and suggests that we have a job to do, to figure out how to best manage these projects that are high-risk and have

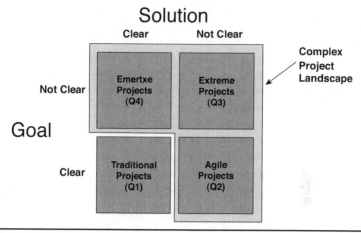

Figure 3.1 The complex project landscape

high failure rates. First of all, these projects will not be approved unless they are critical to the success of the enterprise or have been mandated by an external agency. Second, these are high-value projects and acceptable solutions have yet to be found. In some cases, business survival depends on finding acceptable solutions. The difficulty with complex projects is that either the goal or the solution is not clearly defined (or both). In some cases the goal may be nothing more than a desired end state without any knowledge of whether that end state is achievable. In other cases, the solution may be totally unknown and no one can even guess whether a solution exists and whether they have the ability to find it. And finally, there is not yet an effective project management approach that can find an acceptable solution for the most complex and uncertain projects. So risk is high and the rewards had better match the risk. Using the P2 and ECPM Frameworks, we have designed a framework that can find an acceptable solution, if one exists. That template is called the P2 LEAN Framework. We offer it as an add-on to P2, not as a replacement. P2 is an awesome framework and belongs in the organization's portfolio—but so does the P2 LEAN Framework. If it fits, use it!

A HIGH-LEVEL LOOK AT P2 AND THE ECPM FRAMEWORK ARTIFACTS

There are a few points worth mentioning regarding similarities and differences between P2 and the ECPM Framework. These are briefly noted in the following paragraphs.

ECPM Framework versus P2 Project Life Spans

P2 belongs to a family of products. Sitting above P2 is Managing Successful Programmes (MSP). Above that we have the Portfolio, Programs and Project Offices (P3O). It is this higher level that deals with subjects such as resource management and strategic decisions on which projects should be undertaken. Thus, P2 doesn't have to concern itself with such matters. The ECPM Framework doesn't have this all-embracing family, so resource management and project selection are included as appropriate. As not all readers of this book will use MSP and P3O, this book will start with the selection of a project from a prioritized list of contending potential projects.

Evolutionary Development

P2 has evolved from a method based on the traditional Waterfall method, where goal and solution are known at the outset. Complete project plans are routinely developed and approved. In more complex projects today, the solution is often not clear at the outset. The agile approach was developed for such situations and, therefore, has a lot to offer. The ECPM Framework is an agile and lean design and is perfectly suited to managing projects in the complex project landscape. The ECPM Framework uses Project Co-Managers with a sound knowledge of P2, and they can use the P2 LEAN Framework in situations where the solution must be learned and discovered in stages.

Time Boxing

The agile concept of time boxing can be fitted fairly seamlessly into the P2 Processes of Managing a Stage, Managing Product Delivery, and Managing a Stage Boundary. It is a very powerful addition to the P2 processes and many of its features will be brought into the combined method. P2 and P2 LEAN Frameworks are equivalent with respect to time boxing. The only difference may be that a P2 LEAN Framework time box is shorter than a typical P2 time box. But the concepts are the same.

Project Plan

There is a slight difference here in that the ECPM Framework approach is that the Project Plan is very high-level. It is more conceptual than functional. The ECPM Framework Business Case is the primary tool for maintaining the alignment of the project to the High-level Project Plan. This is a lean approach and saves a lot of work. In P2, the Project Plan is a key control for the Project Board, being part of the information it receives to check at end-stage assessments if the project's Business Case is still valid. Therefore, it needs updating to show the actual time and costs so far, as well as a new forecast for the total project.

Early in its history, P2 included Planning as the 8th Process. Discussions finally led to removing it as a process and adding it to the themes where it is currently parked. The P2 LEAN Framework is driven by a rather unique project planning approach and while planning runs continuously across the project life span, it has reinstated Planning as a process. The Plan Theme from P2 has been carried forward into the P2 LEAN Framework with some modifications. Chapter 4 discusses the particulars.

Tolerances

Tolerances can cover time, cost, quality, risk, scope, and benefits. This is a major control feature of P2. In the ECPM Framework, time and cost are generally fixed, while the scope varies to fit within those constraints. This links to the agile concept of time boxing. In our combined method the tolerance philosophy will shift toward the ECPM Framework attitude with zero tolerance for cost and time. Those tolerances apply at the stage level and control how a stage ends.

Start Point

P2 only deals with a single project. Subjects like programs, the company portfolio, and resource planning are dealt with at higher levels in the family, particularly in the P3O—Portfolio, Program, and Project Office. It seems sensible that subjects such as resource planning should be done at the same level as strategic planning—where are we going in the next 5–10 years; what products and systems will we need to get there and after we get there; and what should we be planning our workforce to look like when that time comes?

The ECPM Framework maintains a view at the portfolio level, because resources are finite and must support the portfolio. The ECPM Scope Triangle (Figure 2.5) includes Resource Availability as a constraining variable for a P2 LEAN Framework project. So approval, staffing, and scheduling of a project are constrained by resource commitments to other projects, programs, and portfolios. Our combined method will therefore start with the ECPM Project IDEATION Phase. So the P2 LEAN Framework IDEATION Phase is a result of integrating the ECPM Framework SET-UP Phase into activities from both the P2 Starting Up a Project (SU) and Initiating a Project (IP) Processes.

P2 is designed around stages. Stage Plans can change as a result of exceeding tolerances and are managed using Exception Plans. The ECPM Framework is designed around cycles. Cycle Plans do not change. Cycles may be terminated early and incomplete Work Packages are simply returned to the Scope Bank for later replanning and reprioritization. See these sections in Chapter 11: Update the Scope Bank, Create the Next Stage Plan, and Update the Project Initiation Document, for how the P2 LEAN Framework accomplishes stage planning.

People Autonomy and Empowerment

Agile is very strong on giving teams and individuals empowerment to get on with the job. P2 uses a Project Board for outside management control and project decision making. The ECPM Framework uses Project Executive Management for up or down decisions on Project and Stage Plans and Project Reviews but otherwise allows the Project Co-Managers to get on with the project with minimal interference or the need to refer to higher management levels. The two frameworks are quite similar. The differences come in the form of centralized authority. The ECPM Framework Project Team is more self-contained than the P2 Project Team. That translates into more centralized decision-making authority in the ECPM Framework than in the P2 Framework. The P2 LEAN Framework leverages the strengths of both frameworks. Understand that the P2 LEAN Framework is not the P2 Framework—and it is not the ECPM Framework, either. It is new. It is unique. It is agile and lean. It is the best of both frameworks.

THE ECPM FRAMEWORK ARTIFACTS

The P2 LEAN Framework is the product of the P2 Framework and the integration of these agile and lean artifacts from the ECPM Framework:

- Complex Project Co-Manager Model
- Requirements Elicitation
- Scope Triangle
- Bundled Change Management Process
- Scope Bank
- Probative and Integrative Swim Lanes
- Vetted portfolio of tools, templates, and processes

Each of these artifacts is unique to the ECPM Framework and sets it apart from all commercial PMLC Models. These artifacts were briefly discussed in Chapter 2 and will not be repeated here. Later, in Parts 2, 3, and 4, we discuss *when* these are used and *how* they are used.

P2 LEAN FRAMEWORK

The P2 and the ECPM Frameworks have a number of features in common, as well as several differences. Those differences are what prompted us to eventually develop the P2 LEAN Framework. We have introduced the seven artifacts from the ECPM Framework that when integrated into P2, result in the P2 LEAN Framework. This book discusses the tools, templates, and processes of the P2 LEAN Framework.

Definition: PRINCE2 LEAN Framework

The PRINCE2 LEAN Framework is an integration of selected artifacts from the ECPM Framework into PRINCE2 to create an agile and lean template for the management of any PRINCE2 complex project.

PRINCE2 + ECPM Framework = P2 LEAN Framework

The P2 LEAN Framework is not a fixed recipe for managing complex projects. It is a robust framework that draws on a vetted portfolio of tools, templates, and processes (the P2 LEAN/kit) that the P2 LEAN Project Co-Managers use to create a dynamic recipe for the management of their complex project. Understand that the P2 LEAN Framework is not a *Reader's Digest* version of P2, nor is it a subset of P2. The P2 LEAN Framework is a totally new approach to lean and agile project management based on a P2 infrastructure.

This book is the first published description of the P2 LEAN Framework. In this chapter we have presented the *what* and *why* of these seven artifacts. In Parts 2, 3, and 4 we will discuss *when* and *how* the P2 LEAN processes and activities can be executed. In the spirit of lean, for a few activities the *how* will come in several flavors (i.e., versions). For example, consider the Risk Management Model. In the smallest and simplest of projects, that might be a simple risk/reward (low, medium, high) matrix. As project size, complexity, and uncertainty increase, that Risk Management Model might be replaced with probabilistic models, multicriteria scoring models, or sophisticated weighted criteria models. These versions are driven by three critical components of every project situation:

- The defining characteristics of the project itself
- The environment and culture of the organization as both the consumer of the project deliverables and the producer of the deliverables for the market
- The market situation viewed as a dynamic entity embracing both the buyer and seller communities

These components define a project landscape that is a continuum that ranges from the small and simple projects to projects of increasing complexity and uncertainty. As you move across this landscape, the frequency, depth, and sophistication of the tools, templates, and business processes used in the P2 LEAN Framework increases. There will be business rules for choosing the *what* and *how* for a variety of project management situations. The other tools, templates, and business processes would have similar choices ordered by project *size*, *complexity*, and *uncertainty*. In the spirit of lean principles, we don't want to put the project manager in the position of *killing mosquitoes with sledge hammers*! Rather, they should have the flexibility of choosing the appropriate weapons for the situation.

We leave open the question about using or not using a particular activity. The answer is provided by the co-managers, based on the value added from using the activity, to the total cost of using it. So in the P2 LEAN Framework, a P2 activity can be used, modified, replaced with an equivalent tool, template, or process, or not used at all. We recognize that this is not the P2 way and will be viewed by some as heretical. But our reply is that the P2 LEAN Framework co-managers are responsible for delivering a successful project, not for following a prescribed process. We live and work in a project environment that requires flexibility and creativity. However the co-managers decide to manage the project, they do so within a portfolio of vetted tools, templates, and processes. The P2 LEAN Framework is not a free-for-all effort. To do otherwise would border on chaos. Clearly, no one can possibly anticipate all conditions that can occur in the execution of a project and hence, how these conditions must be managed. A fixed set of activities does not fit all projects.

The P2 LEAN Framework offers a new approach to managing complex projects, but it is conceptually aligned with contemporary thought. For example, it aligns with the 7 Lean Principles (Poppendieck & Poppendieck, 2003):

- Eliminate waste
- Amplify learning

- Decide as late as possible
- Deliver as fast as possible
- Empower the team
- Build integrity in
- See the whole

It also aligns with the 7 Principles of Continuous Innovation (Denning, 2011):

- Principle #1: Focus Work on Delighting the Client
- Principle #2: Do Work through Self-organized Teams
- Principle #3: Do Work in Client-driven Iterations
- Principle #4: Deliver Value to Clients Each Iteration
- Principle #5: Be Totally Open about Impediments to Improvement
- Principle #6: Create a Context for Continuous Self-improvement
- Principle #7: Communicate through Interactive Conversations

So the P2 LEAN Framework is well-suited for the management challenges of the complex project landscape. Its name says that in some way it is a *more efficient* version of P2, and it is; but through that difference it opens the door to agile and adaptive instantiations of P2. The P2 LEAN Framework is an agile and adaptive framework. It is not just another version of P2 Agile. It is that and much more.

The Aligned Frameworks

Figure 3.2 shows the extent to which the ECPM and P2 Frameworks align with one another. Because of that strong alignment, each framework can leverage certain features of the other for its benefit with minimal difficulty. Taking advantage of that, we have built the P2 LEAN Framework. It is a more effective framework than either the existing ECPM or P2 Framework acting alone. Be forewarned, however, that the P2 LEAN Framework is new. It is not the next version of P2 or the next version of the ECPM Framework. To that extent, certain processes and activities of P2 will be different or absent from P2 LEAN. The same is true of the ECPM Framework. The P2 LEAN Framework is not a replacement for either framework; rather it is another arrow to be added to the organization's quiver. The P2 LEAN Framework can co-exist with either of the other frameworks.

The P2 LEAN Framework has moved the Plan Theme from P2 to the Process Level (PL). P2 LEAN Planning has a number of similarities to the P2 Plan Theme, but it also has a number of marked differences. Those

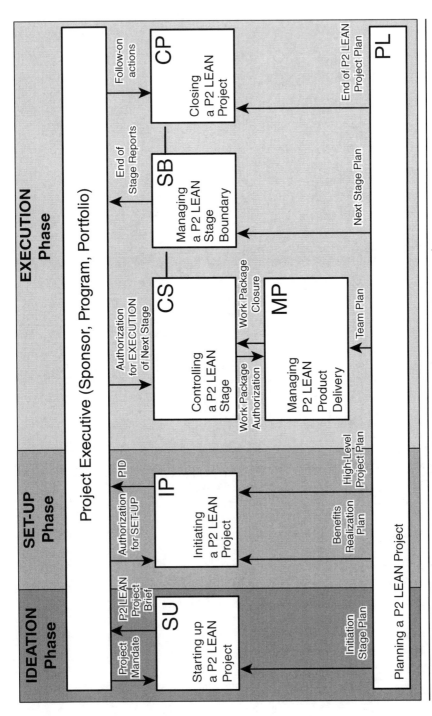

Figure 3.2 P2 LEAN Framework: An overlay of the ECPM and PRINCE2 Frameworks

marked differences are what led us to label the P2 LEAN Project Planning as a process, not a theme.

Setting Up a P2 LEAN Project

The P2 LEAN Process Model incorporates the three-phased ECPM Framework as an overlay, as shown in Figure 3.2. Those phases are: IDEATION, SET-UP, and EXECUTION. The Process Model is a good conceptual representation of P2 and perhaps a good study for certification examination preparation, but it is not a good representation for how to use P2. For that we have developed the P2 LEAN Framework Process Flow Diagram (PFD). Figure 3.3 is that PFD. It also provides an outline of Chapters 5 through 14, which are written to be the companion guide for applying the P2 LEAN Framework.

The three phases are clearly shown and the activities that make up each of these phases are shown in the order in which they are executed. The

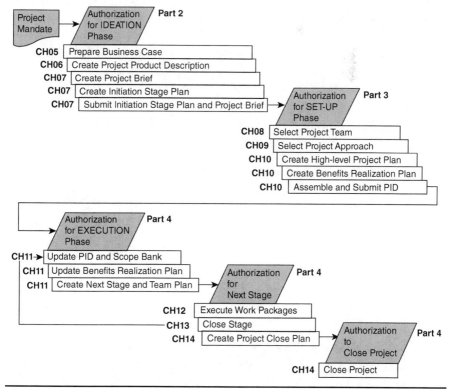

Figure 3.3   P2 LEAN Process Flow Diagram

details are discussed in Parts 2, 3, and 4 of this book along with how they are integrated into the P2 LEAN Framework. The PFD is intuitive and easy to follow, whereas the P2 Process Model is not. The Process Model does a good job of showing how the processes are related to one another, but it offers no help with understanding the chronological flow of processes and activities through the project phases.

Bottom-up Construction of a P2 LEAN Model

P2 LEAN makes two changes to the 7 P2 Processes. The Directing a Project Process has been embedded in the other processes as appropriate and does not appear as an identified process in Figure 3.2. Planning, which is a *theme*, has been moved to *process* status. In P2 LEAN, the planning process is different to that in the P2 Framework Planning 7-Step Process.

Across the 7 P2 LEAN Processes, there are 44 separate activities. Most can be found in P2, but there are some processes that are unique to P2 LEAN. The 44 activities are listed in the following sections. The labels A through D are ordered from most significant to least significant, so that the "A" activities are required of even the smallest and simplest of projects. As the project becomes larger, more complex, or uncertain, "B" activities are added, then "C," and finally "D." This classification scheme is based on the MoSCoW method of *must do, should do, could do, won't do*. This classification of activities is, of course, subjective, and using an activity is really a decision that the Project Co-Managers will make on a project-by-project basis. The co-managers are concerned about how they add value to the project by using an activity. Value can be measured in several ways. If that value exceeds the effort required to use the activity, the activity should be used. Even at that, it is still up to the co-managers to decide on its use. The decision to use an activity might be nothing more than a decision based on their comfort zone or usual practice. So *value add* will always remain a subjective call by the co-managers. The bottom line is still that there is no room in P2 LEAN for any non-value-added work. Using this approach, P2 LEAN remains lean. Obviously senior management is part of this business rule too. Except for the "A" Activities, these labels are our suggestions. Our goal is to preserve the lean principles, but we leave the final decisions to the co-managers.

Starting Up a P2 LEAN Project

A request has come to the Project Office from someone in the organization (perhaps through the management chain of command) proposing an idea for solving a previously unsolved but significant problem or for taking advantage of an untapped business opportunity. In the P2 LEAN Framework this is also called a Project Mandate, as it is in P2. It can be a well-thought-out request or scribbled on the back of an envelope. Some type of document is required; a verbal request at the water cooler is not sufficient. The Project Mandate is converted into a Business Case and a specific project proposed in the form of a one-page Project Brief. The Project Brief and an Initiation Stage Plan is submitted to Project Executive Management for authorization to enter the SET-UP Phase and Initiate the P2 LEAN Project. The question for Project Executive Management is whether or not the submitted documents describe a business opportunity that warrants further investment to produce a detailed project proposal that should be approved.

Here are the six prioritized activities for the process called Starting Up a Project (SU):

- A   Appoint Project Executive and Project Co-Managers
- D   Capture previous lessons
- A   Prepare the Business Case
- A   Identify High-level requirements (same as P2 Epics)
- A   Write the Project Brief
- A   Plan the Initiation Stage

Initiating a P2 LEAN Project

The Project Executive Management sees business value in the proposed project and authorizes IP. The Project enters the SET-UP Phase. This is a technical phase and may require recruiting Core Team members to provide the technical expertise beyond that of the co-managers to set-up the project. The primary purpose of the SET-UP Phase is to create the project management approach that will be used in the EXECUTION Phase. All of this results in a High-level Project Plan and the Project Initiation Documentation (PID), which are forwarded to the Project Executive Management for authorization to enter the EXECUTION Phase of the project.

Here are the 12 prioritized activities for the IP Process:

- A   Authorize the Initiation Stage
- A   Appoint the Core Team
- C   Select the project approach
- A   Choose and adapt the best-fit PMLC Model
- B   Prepare the Risk Management strategy
- B   Prepare the Quality Management strategy
- C   Prepare the Communication Management strategy

- C   Set up project controls
- A   Create High-level Project Plan
- A   Create Benefits Realization Plan
- D   Refine Business Case (if needed)
- A   Assemble Project Initiation Documentation

Controlling a P2 LEAN Stage

The Controlling a Stage Process (CS) is the day-to-day monitoring and management of the execution of the Stage Plan. In the P2 LEAN Framework, the Stage Plan is not changed. Any change requests are accepted and added to the Scope Bank for consideration during the Next Stage Plan. If for some reason some of the Work Packages cannot be completed during the Stage, they are simply returned to the Scope Bank for consideration in the Next Stage Plan.

Here are the seven prioritized activities for the CS:

- B   Capture, examine, and escalate issues and risks
- D   Review Stage status
- A   Take corrective action
- A   Conduct Bundled Change Management
- A   Authorize Work Packages
- C   Review Work Package status
- A   Receive completed Work Packages

Managing Product Delivery

Managing Product Delivery (MP) is the processing of the authorized Work Packages for the Stage. MP requires a Stage Plan and a Team Plan, if there is one. The Work Packages are developed as part of the Team Plans and cover both Probative and Integrative Swim Lanes.

Here are the three prioritized activities for the MP Process:

- B   Accept Work Package
- B   Execute Work Package
- A   Deliver Work Package

Managing a P2 LEAN Stage Boundary

The Managing a P2 LEAN Stage Boundary Process (SB) is essentially the management of the activities that connect one Stage to its successor Stage.

Here are the six prioritized activities for the Managing a Stage Boundary Process:

- A   Update Project Scope Bank
- A   Plan Next Stage
- C   Update Project Plan
- C   Update Business Case
- C   Update Benefits Realization Plan
- A   Report Stage end

Closing a P2 LEAN Project

The expectation is that an acceptable solution has been found that delivers the planned business value. Complex projects are high-risk and the results are not always as expected. In any case the product deliverables are installed and certain close-out activities are conducted.

Here are the five prioritized activities for the Closing a Project Process (CP):

- A   Recommend project closure
- A   Create End of Project Plan
- A   Hand over products
- D   Evaluate the project
- A   Prepare End of Project Report

Planning a P2 LEAN Project

It is commonly accepted that one of the most common causes of projects failing to deliver benefits is a neglect of the planning process. All too often a plan is created, approved, and then put on the shelf, never to be referenced again. Such behavior in a P2 LEAN project dooms the project to certain failure. The Planning a P2 LEAN Project Process (PL) is the real heart of the P2 LEAN Framework. There are five types of plans that describe the IDEATION, SET-UP, and EXECUTION Phases of the project life span.

Here are the five prioritized activities for the Planning Process:

- A   Initiation Stage Plan
- A   High-level Project Plan
- B   Team Plans
- A   Next Stage Plan
- A   End of Project Plan

PUTTING IT ALL TOGETHER

We have just scratched the surface here. So far, we have learned that P2 LEAN is more powerful than we originally envisioned. It is far more than just an integration of lean tools, templates, and processes from the ECPM Framework into P2. Without realizing it, we have created a synergy. P2 LEAN is more powerful than either P2 or the ECPM Framework could be when used on their own. Its value is being discovered as we move forward with application and further development of P2 LEAN.

P2 defines a flexible framework that specifies *what* with little reference or guidance on *how*. P2 LEAN does that and more. *How* is an important addition. The P2 LEAN/kit is a comprehensive collection of the *how*, *when*, and *why* for each of the 50+ activities. The flexible and adaptive opportunities that are presented to the Co-Managed Project Team are strange territory for most project managers. These are not to be interpreted as a license to *do it your own way*. Rather, the Project Team is constrained to a vetted portfolio of tools, templates, and business processes from which they will create the *recipes* they will use to manage their project. The burden is on the executives to make sure that that vetted portfolio does not constrain the Project Team to the point that their performance is limited and their ability to deliver business value is reduced. That is a major undertaking to provide a complete vetted portfolio and the support to use it effectively. So it is best to think of that vetted portfolio as a work in process and it will never be completed. Experience with complex project management will give rise to changes or additions to that vetted portfolio. In the spirit of continuous process improvement, those suggestions must be considered.

The stage is now set for us to develop the details of how each ECPM Framework Phase contributes to the formation of P2 LEAN. We do that using the three ECPM Framework Phases, but from the perspective of the 7 PRINCE2 Processes.

4

PRINCE2 LEAN:
PROJECT PLANNING

---

*It is a mistake to look too far ahead. Only one link of
the chain of destiny can be handled at a time.*
—Winston Churchill, English Prime Minister

Achieving good performance is a journey, not a destination.
—Kenneth H. Blanchard, Chairman,
Blanchard Training & Development

CHAPTER LEARNING OBJECTIVES

This chapter will provide readers the knowledge or ability to:

- Understand the relationship between Planning and the IDEATION, SET-UP, and EXECUTION Phases of the PRINCE2 (P2) LEAN Framework
- Understand the Product-based Planning Process Template
- Be able to adapt the Product-based Planning Process Template to the five types of plans used in the P2 LEAN Framework.

The P2 LEAN Framework is supported by a planning process defined by five types of interdependent plans. All five types are product-based and special cases of a single template, which defines 11 robust steps. In this chapter, we define each of those types of plans and how the template is applied to each type of plan.

WHAT IS PRODUCT-BASED PLANNING?

The P2 LEAN Framework provides a product-based planning template that can be applied to any project to give a logical sequence to the project's work. A *product* may be a tangible one, such as a machine, a document, or a piece of software; or it may be intangible, such as a culture change or a different organizational structure. Within the P2 LEAN Framework these are all called *products*.

There are two general product planning approaches that can be used to plan projects:

- **Plan-driven approaches:** These are for projects whose goal and solution are clearly stated at the outset. Usually they are projects that have been done several times (i.e., installing a computer network in a field sales office or conducting an annual conference). Over time and several repetitions, templates have been honed and are used. Everything that can be known about these projects is known and a complete plan can be developed as a precondition for executing the project. Little change is expected and risk is very low.
- **Just-in-time approaches:** At the other extreme are planning approaches for projects whose goal and or solution are not very well defined at the outset (i.e., finding a cure for cancer or integrating RFID (Radio Frequency IDentification) technology into current inventory management processes). A complete plan is not possible at the outset without considerable guessing. So from a lean standpoint, a just-in-time approach is the only approach that makes any sense. Planning can only occur for parts of the project that are known. Guessing is not a lean practice. So planning such projects to arrive at an acceptable solution can only occur incrementally. As the goal and solution come into focus, the plan can be extended a bit further. Learning and discovery are the lifeblood of such projects.

The P2 Framework and the Effective Complex Project Management (ECPM) Framework both use just-in-time planning. Both practice communities should find comfort in that because the P2 LEAN Framework is designed primarily as a just-in-time framework. The P2 LEAN Framework also uses product-based planning like the one used in P2. Consistent with P2, the P2 LEAN Framework follows a process that begins with a P2 LEAN Planning Template and provides a comprehensive platform for effective planning. It is the technique that enables the co-managers to:

- Define what the project has to deliver from a requirements and performance perspective
- Provide measurable statements of quality expectations and how they will be measured
- Manage the risks associated with the learning and discovery effort in complex projects
- Monitor and control progress and the supporting change process
- Manage convergence toward an acceptable solution

The Benefits of Product-based Planning

Product-based planning is designed into the P2 Framework and is also an integral part of the P2 LEAN Framework. Its primary focuses are on the quality and business value of the delivered products. By taking a product-based approach to planning, the project remains in the client's comfort zone as long as possible. That promotes their meaningful involvement and ownership of the deliverables.

There are three fundamental parts that drive product-based planning for each type of project plan.

- **Producing a Product Breakdown Structure:** The product breakdown structure (PBS) is a dynamic document. It may start out with not much more than a high-level set of requirements (see Chapter 6). Whatever is known at the time this document is written is included and as each stage is completed, the PBS detail is expanded until the complete solution emerges.

  The PBS is a functional decomposition version of the work breakdown structure (WBS). The P2 LEAN Framework is designed to keep the client meaningfully involved throughout the entire project life span. To support that intent, the PBS is a tool that keeps the project close to the comfort zone of the client. The PBS promotes client ownership of the products of the project just as the Co-Manager Model supports client ownership of the project and its deliverables.

- **Writing Product Descriptions:** A clear, complete, and unambiguous description of products is a tremendous aid to their successful creation. That begins with a Project Product Description and continues with the descriptions of the products produced in the stages. A Product Description carries important information about the product. It is a key element in the quality work of a project. It is also given to the quality checkers to establish if the required quality has been built into the product.

A documented and agreed upon Product Description of the known goal and solution ensures that all personnel affected by that product have the same understanding. A Product Description written for each known product helps to ensure that it is understood, to provide a pointer to the way in which the product is to be further developed.

Product Descriptions are written using the most recent PBS as input. The purpose of these descriptions is to document the characteristics of the product, including quality aspects and the activities needed to produce the product. The Product Descriptions are needed to identify and describe the Stage Plan at the swim lane level and the Work Packages that further describe the swim lanes.

- **Producing a Product Flow Diagram:** Every planner needs to know the answer to the question "What comes next?" The Product Flow Diagram (PFD) shows the sequence of development of the products of the plan and any dependencies between them. It also identifies dependencies on any products outside the scope of the plan. It leads naturally into consideration of the activities required and into network planning.

  This is the approach taken by P2 and is carried over into the P2 LEAN Framework. It is equivalent to the precedence diagrams used in the ECPM Framework. The PBS and Product Descriptions are input that is used to create the PFD. Later on in the planning process, the PFD is used to create the Work Packages that comprise the Team Plan.

The use of the product-based planning approach is recommended for all levels of any plan required in a project. In the agile and lean environment of the P2 LEAN Framework, these parts are done at the stage level and each stage continues the journey that concludes with convergence on the final version of the project product.

THE P2 LEAN PROJECT PLANNING HIERARCHY

The P2 LEAN Framework includes a Planning Hierarchy defined by six types of plans that are interrelated, as shown in Figure 4.1.

While the corporate strategic plan is outside the scope of this book, the P2 LEAN Planning hierarchy aligns with, or is the derivative of, the corporate strategic plan. So every P2 LEAN Project will, in some way, contribute to the corporate strategic objectives and align with that plan. P2 LEAN Project prioritizations will often follow from the contribution the project makes toward

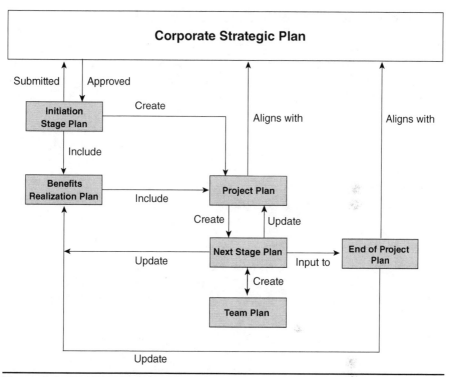

Figure 4.1 P2 LEAN Planning Hierarchy

corporate strategic goals. The Project Executive is very sensitive to maintaining that alignment and will be using it for any project prioritization decisions in the programs and portfolios. That same criteria will apply to the Project Executive decisions regarding the Project Plan and all Stage Plans.

The six types of plans in the P2 LEAN Planning Hierarchy are described in the following paragraphs.

Initiation Stage Plan

This is basically the plan for conducting the P2 LEAN SET-UP Phase and the activities in the Initiating a Project (IP) Phase. It is done only once, as it is a plan for the SET-UP Phase, which is also done only once per project. The Initiation Stage Plan is a product of the IDEATION Phase, which is an exercise to decide *if* and *how* a project can be justified to address the Project Mandate. The purpose of the Initiation Stage is to decide if the project should be approved and funded.

The contents of the Initiation Stage Plan are:

- Project product description
- Prerequisites
- External dependencies
- Planning assumptions
- Lessons incorporated
- Monitoring and controls
- Budgets
- Tolerances
- Benefits Realization Strategy and Plan
- Initiation Stage product descriptions

Benefits Realization Plan

The Benefits Realization Plan (BRP) is a term that appeared in P2 2009 but was never defined. P2 2009 includes the BRP and states that it will be part of the program's BRP. No discussion of a BRP was included by The Stationery Office (2008). The term fits very well with our treatment of benefits strategy and planning and so we have adopted it and have provided definitions and details appropriate to the P2 LEAN Framework. It will also add two activities to the P2 LEAN Framework Planning Process. The BRP is derived from the Benefits Realization Strategy (BRS) and updated at the completion of every stage. It is a fundamental tool for maintaining the project's focus on the delivery of business value. That business value derives from benefits realization. The BRS is discussed in Chapter 5, and the BRP at the project and stage levels is defined in this chapter and then discussed in detail in Chapter 10. The BRP is updated in Chapter 11 and finalized in Chapter 14.

The project was approved based on the business value that it will deliver to the organization. That won't happen by accident. It must be designed into the project, i.e., it requires planning. That will happen first through establishing a BRS, which we do in Chapter 5. It will become the guide to a continuous product improvement program and second, it will be supported by a plan at the stage level to maintain that improvement.

Definition: Benefit

A measurable positive impact on the business from having implemented one or more of the project products that have been accepted by the client.

Project products have to meet the acceptance criteria for the solution to be acceptable to the client. Once the client accepts and deploys the project products, the products should result in benefits accruing to the business. These benefits will be observable over a period of time, often long after the project has been closed and all but its Project Executive moving on to other assignments. Some benefits will be measured by existing business processes, but if measuring accrued benefits will be required, that must be spelled out with a plan.

Rather than simply walk away when the end product has been handed over, there is a requirement to create a BRP, describing when and how measurement should be made of the achievement of the expected benefits. This plan is outlined during initiation, refined at each stage end, and finalized as part of closing the project. The co-managers are responsible for its creation, but as the project team will be disbanded at the close of the project, responsibility for implementing the BRP belongs to the Project Executive.

Figure 4.2 is a graphical depiction of the BRS that we have designed into the P2 LEAN Framework. Implied in the BRS is a cause and effect relationship. The cause is meeting the acceptance criteria and implementing the

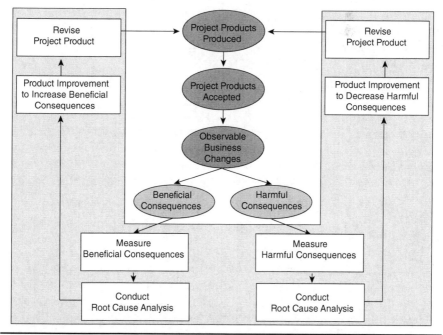

Figure 4.2   Benefits Realization Strategy

project products. The effect is to change the business in some way. Now, some of these benefits will have been identified in the Business Case and may be the basis for approving the project for further planning. There will also be benefits that accrue from effects that were not visualized. Let's delve more deeply into the consequences of deploying the project products.

The deployment of the approved project products will have consequences with respect to the benefits accrued. Most of those consequences will have been expected, others not. The intended consequences are those that will have been described in the Business Case and will generate business value, i.e., benefits. There will also be consequences that were not expected, i.e., unintended consequences. These could be positive or negative with respect to the business value generated. A continuous product improvement program is designed into the P2 LEAN Framework so the BRP will include programs to increase the beneficial consequences and decrease the harmful consequences. These will all involve adjustments to the project products. Some programs will be significant enough to initiate new project mandates.

There is one caveat that applies. For those in the P2 community who are new to the complex project world and agile projects, the P2 LEAN Framework will require an adjustment. An agile project can be a major cultural shock to many senior managers because it can take them outside of their comfort zone. They want to know exactly what they are going to get, when they will get it, and how much it will cost. That is old school. In an agile project, that specificity is not possible. All the developer could do is say something like, "If you give me $50,000 and six months, your representative and I (ah—the co-managers) will do our best to deliver an acceptable solution." There is no guarantee and in the most complex of situations there may not be one.

If the project involves an unsolved problem or an untapped business opportunity, how could anyone ever state the actual benefits that will be achieved? You can't. No one can. All a sponsor can do is make a statement like, "If you can deliver $1,000,000 in net profits or increase sales revenues by 10% within three years, I will approve your project." So now you know what the acceptance criteria are, and you set out to achieve it. However, there are unknown unknowns!

So you put a plan together that you and your co-manager hope will deliver that expected business value. You both have done the best you can with the plan. (You have fully implemented the P2 LEAN Framework by the way.) But you don't really know what you will achieve. No one does. All you and your co-manager can do is give your best effort. Hopefully it will be good enough, but it might not. So what do you do? Shoot the co-managers for failure to deliver?

But nobody can really tell you that, or even if, the project will find a solution, let alone one that achieves the expected business value. Maybe there is no solution. That could be one reason why it is an unsolved problem or an untapped business opportunity. So how do you approach a P2 client given this reality?

High-level Project Plan

Since either the goal or solution is not clearly described at the outset, this plan can only be specific with what is known. As stages are completed, the goal and solution become clearer, and this plan is updated with that learned and discovered knowledge. At the completion of the last stage, the goal and solution will have been clearly stated.

This plan is created at the start of the project and updated at the end of each stage. The initial High-level Project Plan is a part of the Project Initiation Documentation. It is mandatory for every P2 LEAN Project.

Project Executive Management does not want to know about every detailed activity in the project at this point. Depending on the complexity and uncertainty associated with the project, many of those details are not and cannot be known until the project work has commenced and the learning and discovery events occur. They only require a high-level view of:

- How long the project will take
- What the major deliverables or products will be
- Roughly when the major deliverables or products will be delivered
- Which people and other resources will have to be committed in order to meet the plan
- How control will be exerted
- How quality will be maintained
- What risks there are in the approach taken
- The estimated cost of the project

Next Stage Plan

The Next Stage Plan learns from the just completed stage and puts forward the plan for the next stage, which includes both Probative and Integrative Swim Lanes as described in the upcoming sections. The Scope Bank will have been updated with the products delivered from the last stage. This includes the High-level Project Plan too. This is the primary input to identifying the objectives of the next stage. The High-level Project Plan will have originally included the objectives of each stage. For this next stage those objectives will be reviewed and finalized as a result of all the intermediate stages that have been completed. The objectives of the next stage will be further detailed to the swim lane levels.

Stage plans are mandatory, and unless a project is very small, it will be easier to plan, in detail, one stage at a time. Another part of the philosophy that makes stage planning easier is that a stage is planned shortly before it is due to start, so you have the latest information available on actual progress to date.

When planning a stage, the major products in the High-level Project Plan that were initially assigned to that stage are taken and decomposed into two or three levels of additional detail (i.e., the PBS for the products in the stage being planned). Stage Plans have the same format as the High-level Project Plan except for the greater detail and specificity.

The tools that you are already familiar with and use are directly applicable to stage planning, but on a much smaller scale. A P2 LEAN stage is typically two to six weeks in duration and composed of one or more swim lanes. The swim lane with the longest duration defines the stage's critical path. Unlike P2, in a P2 LEAN project, any products planned for this stage and not delivered are simply returned to the Scope Bank for later prioritization and consideration. Stage length was fixed during stage planning and not extended for any reason; and Stage Plans are not changed once they have been authorized.

- **Swim Lanes**

  Swim lanes are the building blocks of a stage. Swim lane is a common term that is familiar to project managers in the context of process flow diagrams, but in a P2 LEAN Project, they take on additional significance. A stage is a collection of streams of work activities called *swim lanes*. They are planned sequentially and concurrently. This is not new. However, a P2 LEAN swim lane can extend from a few hours to a few weeks. This *is* new—and not characteristic of P2. Ideally, swim lanes are scheduled independently of one another, but due to resource constraints, that is often not possible. Each swim lane or sequence of swim lanes must have a total duration less than or equal to the stage duration.

In a P2 LEAN Project there are two distinct types of swim lanes: Probative Swim Lanes and Integrative Swim Lanes. They are very different from one another; may have a unique dependency relationship, and have very different planning requirements. That dependency results from the outcome of a Probative Swim Lane providing planning input to Integrative Swim Lanes.

- **Probative Swim Lanes**

  Probative is the label we use for swim lanes whose purpose is to investigate new ideas or whether a particular variation of a product's functions or features could be part of the final solution, and what that might look like. New ideas are tested for feasibility using Probative Swim Lanes. Probative Swim Lanes are speculative. These are not unlike simple designs of experiments. Planning is minimal. If the results from a Probative Swim Lane show encouraging signs of solution discovery, then either more Probative Swim Lanes would be planned to further analyze the discovery or an Integrative Swim Lane would be planned and prioritized for a future stage. Probative Swim Lanes are unique to the P2 LEAN Framework and are entirely consistent with the lean and agile principles espoused.

- **Integrative Swim Lanes**

  Integrative is the label for those swim lanes that will be used to fully develop and integrate new functions and features into the current solution. There is nothing here that is new. Many will have been the direct result of successful Probative Swim Lane investigations. That *is* new. The Integrative Swim Lanes are approved and prioritized, but not yet integrated. They are in the Scope Bank awaiting integration into the solution in a future stage.

Both types of swim lanes draw upon the members of the project team and their scheduling is constrained by the project team capacity. So there is a delicate balance between the two. In Chapter 11, in the sections discussing updating the Project Initiation Documentation (PID), the Scope Bank, and Creating the Next Stage Plan, we will get into the specific details of protecting that balance with the appropriate stage planning. This is a challenging planning activity that does not arise in any other Project Management Life Cycle Model.

Team Plan

The Team Plan starts with the approved Next Stage Plan which includes the products that are planned for each Probative and Integrative Swim Lane for that Next Stage. Each swim lane will be described in a Work Package, and a Team Plan will cover one or more Work Packages.

Team Plans are optional. They deliver the Work Packages that support the Stage Plan. Their need is dictated by the size, complexity, and risks associated with the Stage Plan. The co-managers will request Team Plans for some swim lanes. For the most part, Probative Swim Lanes do not require a Team Plan while Integrative Swim Lanes will require one because these swim lanes will include many more tasks to build the product.

Stage Plans discuss *what* products will be delivered for that Stage. Work Packages discuss *how* those products will be built, i.e., the work of the stage. A Work Package describes the *how*, and may contain any or all of the following elements as listed in the P2 Process and modified for the P2 LEAN Process:

- The start and end date for the Work Package
- The Work Package description
- The person responsible for delivering the product of the Work Package
- The Work Package PBS and the Work Package Dependency Diagram
- The Work Package Performance Metrics
- Reference to the predecessor and successor Work Packages
- The Work Package Team members and work schedule
- Constraints, risks, and assumptions

Not all products in Stage Plans require a Team Plan. The need for a Team Plan is driven by what makes sense. For example, many of the Probative Swim Lanes will not require a Team Plan because the content may include a few simple activities that can easily be accomplished within the swim lane time frame.

End of Project Plan

Once the client has accepted the delivered products as having met the acceptance criteria and delivered the requirements and expected business value, the project can enter the closing steps.

The end of the project is triggered when the client accepts the products of the project. The acceptance criteria were summarized in the Project Brief success criteria and detailed in the High-level Project Plan. The success criteria reflects the fact that the delivered products produced the performance requirements, quality standards, and expected business value that justified doing the project in the first place.

The End of Project Plan includes work to produce:

- Project product implementation plan and schedule
- Post-project Lessons Learned audit
- End-user training deployment
- Administrative and contractual close-out
- Preparing and archiving:
  - ✦ Project Note Book (drawn from the Daily Logs)
  - ✦ Scope Bank Contents (products not incorporated into this version)
  - ✦ End of Project Report

These six plans are very different in purpose, but they are all based on the 11-Step Planning Process Template and are adapted to the characteristics of the project being planned and the type of plan for that project.

WHAT IS THE PRODUCT-BASED PLANNING TEMPLATE?

This template is a robust template that applies across all planning activities of a P2 LEAN Project. We have taken the Plan Theme, redesigned it to meet the unique characteristics of the P2 LEAN Framework, and reintroduced it as a process. It defines the standards to be used for developing all future plans. The result is a consistent set of plans—a common parlance among them that avoids any confusion and misunderstandings among the entire project team. The P2 LEAN Planning Template integrates the planning approaches of both the ECPM and P2 Frameworks resulting in these 11 Planning (PL) steps:

- PL1   Designing a plan
- PL2   Creating the PBS
- PL3   Writing Product Descriptions
- PL4   Creating the PFD
- PL5   Identifying the activities and dependencies
- PL6   Defining Work Packages
- PL7   Estimating
- PL8   Identifying resource requirements
- PL9   Scheduling
- PL10   Analyzing risks
- PL11   Completing a plan

This is a robust template. Figure 4.3 is the PFD for these 11 planning steps.

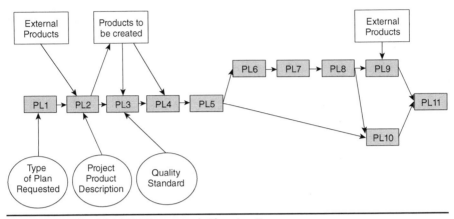

Figure 4.3 The P2 LEAN Framework Planning Process

This template can be adapted to meet the plan specifications of each type of plan. As discussed in the following sections, there are five types of plans. Each plan will adapt these 11 steps. For some types of plans, not all 11 steps are appropriate; they might even be considered overkill for the needs of a particular plan. A particular planning step may be different depending on the type of plan being prepared.

The products identified when using this template to develop the Project Plan will also appear in the relevant Stage and Team Plans, where they will normally be broken down into their component parts to suit the level of detail required for the lower-level plan.

PL1—Designing a Plan

The first step begins with specifying the *type* of plan being generated, and knowing that the plan is what crafts the details of how each step will be done for that kind of project. A plan is the backbone of every project and is essential for a successful outcome. Good plans cover all aspects of the project, giving everyone involved a common understanding of the work ahead. Designing a plan will ensure that all aspects are adequately covered. It is important that all team members involved can easily understand the plan.

The activity PL1 includes decisions on the approach to planning for the project and therefore, needs to be used early in the project. These decisions must be made before any of the other PL processes can be used. PL1 is normally only done once, at the start of the project, and applies to all the project plans.

Choices need to be made for presentation and layout of the plan, planning tools, estimating methods, levels of plan, and monitoring methods to be used for the project. Any recipients of plans and their updates should be identified. There may be a central function that consolidates all plans for senior management, particularly if the project is part of a program or portfolio.

One of the first decisions will be to identify any planning and control aids to be used by the project. There may be a company standard or the client may stipulate the use of a particular set of tools. The choice of planning tool may depend on the complexity of the project. If so, the choice may need to be deferred until after some of the other planning processes. Planning tools may also include giving consideration to the approach toward risk analysis and management.

The method(s) of estimation must be chosen. Each facet of the project may need its own estimation method. Estimating may be supported by:

- Computer tools
- Experienced planners
- Templates or tables of estimates based on previous work
- Top-down or bottom-up methods
- Discussion with those who will do the work
- Any combination of these

There are several methods from which one or more might be chosen. These are discussed later under the heading of PL7—Estimating. They should be evaluated, and comments about their effectiveness made in the End of Project and Lessons Learned Reports, when the project ends.

The estimating methods to be used in the plan may affect the plan design so decisions on the methods to be used should be made as part of plan design.

There are two possible allowances that may have to be considered for inclusion within the project's plan structure—a change budget and a contingency budget. These are not mandatory and their use depends on each project's circumstances.

PL2—Creating the Product Breakdown Structure

The PBS begins with the specification of the high-level project requirements (see Chapter 6). The PBS is a hierarchical decomposition of the project product into its constituent products; and those are further decomposed into products of less scope. This decomposition process continues until the completeness criteria discussed below are satisfied. At that point we will have built the PBS. Chapter 6 begins with the specification of the high-level requirements of an acceptable solution. This is done during the IDEATION Phase. These are not guesses or speculation; they are established fact and are complete in that they are the necessary and sufficient set of requirements. Delivering and meeting those requirements in the solution is assurance that the solution has done its job as requested by the client and Project Executive Management.

The Project Co-Manager meaningfully participated in the specification of those requirements as defined by the required products. This occurred during the Brainstorming Process that identified the project that will be proposed, and finally the Business Case (Chapter 4) and Project Product Description (Chapter 6). The results of those activities will be included in the various plans.

The objectives of this planning step are to:

- Identify the products to be created or obtained by the planned work
- Identify any additional products needed to build and support the end products
- Build a consensus on the best product groupings that should be used to generate ideas on what products have to be created or obtained

A difficult question to answer is, "Have I decomposed the PBS to the right level for this plan?" *The Project Management Body of Knowledge (PMBOK® Guide)* recognizes the PBS as the physical WBS and, in fact, that is what it is, with one notable exception mentioned later. At the top of this hierarchical decomposition is the project product. The first-level breakdown is the high-level requirements of the project product (see Chapter 6 for more details). Each of these requirements is then decomposed into its major products or product groups to form the next level of the structure. Each of these is then further decomposed until an appropriate level of detail for the plan in question is reached. Decomposition of a product is complete if it meets the following criteria:

- Status and completion are measurable
- Product development is bounded
- Time and cost to develop the product is easily estimated
- Product development duration is less than stage duration
- Product development assignments are independent

A High-level Project Plan should only show the major products to be developed. A Stage Plan will consist of a small number of the products shown in the High-level Project Plan, i.e., those that are to be developed in the next stage. These products will be broken down into their subproducts until a level is reached where each subproduct will take five days or less to complete—easy to estimate and easy to control. When the decomposition has reached its lowest level, those lowest level subproducts are called *tasks*, for the purpose of our discussions.

A product in a Stage Plan may be left at too high of a level for the purposes of estimation and control in the PBS, if the intention is to create a Team Plan for it that will show the product broken down into its subproducts, activities, and tasks. This level of decomposition assures that the *what* has been clearly defined. The WBS defines all of the work but this PBS does not include work. That is the notable exception mentioned before. The task level decomposition (the *how*) is the Work Package Plan that defines the Team Plan. So the Team Plan defines the work to be done to develop the products defined in the Next Stage Plan.

PL3—Writing Product Descriptions

A Product Description must be written for each lowest-level product of the plan. Those products are identified in the PBS and carried forward into P2 LEAN. It should include:

- Product name
- Purpose
- Content
- Derivation
- Format
- Development skills
- Quality:
    + Performance metrics
    + Acceptable tolerance
    + Assessment method
    + Assessor skills required

Product Descriptions should be written as soon as possible after their identification. To begin with, this may only be a *skeleton* with little more information than the title, identifier, and purpose; but the more knowledge you have about a product, the better your planning to create it will be. It will be refined and amended as the product becomes better understood and future planning steps are done.

Although responsibility for writing Product Descriptions rests officially with the Core Team, it is wise to involve representatives from the area with expertise in the product and those who will use the product in question. The latter should certainly be asked to define the quality they expect.

PL4—Creating the Product Flow Diagram

The PFD is created from the PBS and the Product Descriptions (discussed in PL3) and precedes the identification of activities in Identifying Activities and Dependencies (discussed in PL5).

A PFD uses very few symbols and is an intuitive presentation of the sequence in which a product's component parts are developed. Each product to be developed within the plan is enclosed in a box. Arrows denote development sequences and connect the boxes. Any products that already exist or exist in their own right outside the project, or are developed in a previous stage, should be clearly identified by using a different type of enclosure; an ellipse works well here. Bentley (2015) is a good reference for further discussion and details.

The diagram begins with those products that are available at the start of the plan (perhaps many of these are documents, such as statements of requirements or designs) and ends with the final product(s) of the plan.

Creation of a PFD may reveal new products that are required. These should also be added to the PBS; and Product Descriptions should be written for them when the need for them is recognized.

Although a Project Co-Manager or Team Leaders are responsible for creation of the PFD, it is sensible to utilize the help of those who are to develop or contribute the products contained in the stage plan.

Depending on the type of plan being produced, whoever is responsible for preparing the plan should verify that the lowest level of product in the PFD meets the completion criteria defined in PL3.

PL5—Identifying the Activities and Dependencies

The inputs to this step are the PBS and Product Descriptions, and the output is the PFD. But keep in mind that the PBS is incomplete and so is the PFD that is developed from it. This PFD has great value in that it helps identify the Next Stage objectives and swim lane contents.

The planner who is responsible will be either the Project Co-Managers or a Team Manager. Depending on the type of plan being produced, the planner should:

- Break each product in the PFD down into the activities needed to produce it. Where a product has been broken down into several activities, put the activities into their correct sequence.
- Review the dependencies between products and refine them to give dependencies between the new activities. For example, where PFD dependencies went from the end of one product to the start of the next, is there now an opportunity to overlap or start some activities on a product before all the activities on its preceding product have been done?

The diagram begins with those products that are available at the start of the plan (perhaps many of these are documents, such as statements of requirements or designs) and ends with the final product(s) of the plan. Some of the products may already exist in other products.

PL6—Defining Work Packages

The input to this step is the Next Stage Plan. Defining Work Packages is a challenging step because the results of the previous Stages, which are posted in the Scope Bank, must be taken into account as the fixed human resources must be allocated across both the Probative and Integrative Swim Lanes identified in the Next Stage Plan. That will require some number of iterations between the Next Stage Plan and the Work Packages that are needed to fulfill that Next Stage Plan; i.e., the Next Stage Plan may have to be revised to meet the time and resource constraints.

Some Work Packages will be simple, others will be technically complex and require special skills to plan. Work Packages are defined by the Development Co-Manager and usually planned by the person who will manage the Work Package or do the *work* of the Work Package. To the extent that this is possible, it should be done. There will be cases where the skills required to do the work can be defined, but the actual person cannot be named until a schedule has been developed. Recall that Resource Availability is one side of the P2 LEAN Scope Triangle. This project is contending for those same resources and many of them will have already been committed to other projects.

The Stage Plan has been approved. It identifies the products to be delivered from this stage. With the products defined, the Integrative Swim Lanes can be identified, and from that the Work Packages created and planned for the Team Plan. The Probative Swim Lanes will be defined based on any parts of the PBS that lack the *how*.

PL7—Estimating

The Work Packages define the work that is needed to deliver the products in the Next Stage Plan. Within each swim lane there will be one or more Work Packages whose duration estimates will be used to calculate the duration of the swim lane. The longest duration swim lane will provide an estimate of the Next Stage duration. As swim lanes have resource contention problems, the Next Stage duration may be extended.

The objective is to identify the resources and effort required to complete each activity or product. The approval of the estimates is the responsibility of the Project Co-Managers, but there may possibly be expert help available on the project team to create those estimates.

Estimation has been a continual problem for many teams. Often there is little consistency, and that is not good. P2 LEAN operates under the following assumptions:

- Estimates are best done by those who will do the work
- Estimates are based on the typically skilled person doing the work
- Estimates are based on the typical resource loading to do the work
- Estimates are either the labor hours required or the duration needed to complete the work or both
- Duration estimates are for scheduling purposes
- Labor hour estimates are for budgeting purposes
- Duration times are always longer than labor time

P2 LEAN recommends using the following five methods to estimate either duration or labor. They are listed in the order of preferred use:

- Similarity
- Historical data
- Expert advice
- Delphi technique
- Three-point technique

Similarity

Those who have experience doing the task will be the best person for estimating this task.

Historical Data

Past recorded experience with similar tasks can be used to estimate this task.

Expert Advice

Those with expertise in this task can also provide the estimates.

Delphi Technique

The Delphi technique extracts and summarizes the knowledge of a small group to arrive at an estimate. After the group understands the task, each member of the group is asked to make his or her best guess of the task duration. The results are tabulated and presented to the group in a histogram labeled First Pass, as shown in Figure 4.4. Participants whose estimates fall in the outer quartiles are asked to share the reason for their guess. After listening to the arguments, each group member is asked to guess again. The results are presented as a histogram labeled Second Pass, and again the outer quartile estimates are defended. A third guess is made, and the histogram plotted is labeled Third Pass. Final adjustments are allowed. The average of the third guess is used as the group's estimate. Even though the technique seems rather simplistic, it has been shown to be effective in the absence of expert advice.

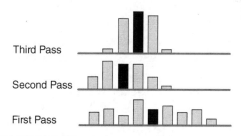

Figure 4.4 The Delphi technique

Three-point Technique

Task duration is a random variable. If it were possible to repeat the task several times under identical circumstances, duration times would vary. That variation may be tightly grouped around a central value, or it might be widely dispersed. Figure 4.5 illustrates the point.

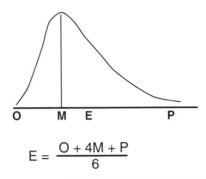

$$E = \frac{O + 4M + P}{6}$$

Figure 4.5   The three-point technique

- **Optimistic (O)**—The shortest duration ever experienced
- **Pessimistic (P)**—The longest duration ever experienced
- **Most likely (M)**—The typical duration you would expect
- **Expected (E)**—The estimated time

PL8—Identifying Resource Requirements

Identifying and scheduling resources across project, programs, and portfolios has always been a challenge. Current P2 LEAN does not escape that challenge. Most organizations are not equipped to handle those challenges, thus, resource contention problems abound. Human Resource Management Systems (HRMS) are not sufficient. The problem is somewhat mitigated by P2 LEAN in that its plans do not include naming specific resources. Instead, any P2 LEAN plan identifies resources by position title and additional skills, along with the window of time within which those resources are needed. The resource managers negotiate with the co-managers and commit to providing those resources in the window of time needed. (See Chapter 15 for more details on these negotiations.) This exercise becomes complex as resources are used across swim lanes. To the extent possible, these cross swim lane dependencies should be minimized.

Types of resources are specified in the following paragraphs.

Facilities

Project work takes place in locations. Planning rooms, conference rooms, presentation rooms, and auditoriums are but a few examples of facilities that projects require. The exact specifications of the required facilities as well as the precise time at which each facility is needed are some of the variables that you must take into account. The Project Plan can provide the required details. The availability of the facilities will also drive the project and stage schedules.

Equipment

Equipment is treated exactly the same as facilities. The availability of equipment will also drive the stage and work package schedules.

Money

Accountants will tell you that everything is eventually reduced to dollars, which is true. Project expenses typically include travel, accommodations, meals, and supplies.

Materials

The timely availability of parts to be used in the fabrication of products and other physical deliverables will be part of the project work schedule. For example, the materials needed to build a bicycle might include nuts, bolts, washers, and spacers. The delivery of these in a timely manner also needs to be carefully planned.

People

Resource Availability is part of the P2 LEAN Scope Triangle and has been the most complex resource from a scheduling perspective. In most cases, the most challenging resource you will have to schedule are human resources.

People are the most difficult type of resource to schedule because you plan the project by specifying the types of skills you need, when you need them, and in what amounts. Generally you do not specify the resource by name (that is, the individual you need), which is where problems arise. So the staffing plan for the Stage Plan and the Team Plan cannot be completed without the participation of the managers of the people resources. This is a complex process, especially since the schedules of the people resources have to accommodate the business unit and the project, programs, and portfolios. The best approach is to request people resources by position title and skill requirements and to stipulate when those resources will be needed. The managers of these people resources have to commit to meeting those staffing plans.

PL9—Scheduling

Scheduling is part of the Team Plan and spans all of the swim lanes in the Next Stage Plan. Because of resource availability constraints, both the Next

Stage Plan and/or Team Plans may have to be revised to reach an acceptable scheduling solution.

A plan can only show whether it can meet its targets when the activities are put together in a schedule against a time frame, showing when activities will be done and by what resources. Therefore, the following activities should be undertaken:

- Draw a planning network
- Assess resource availability—this should include dates of availability as well as the percent available; any known information on holidays and training courses, etc., should be gathered
- Allocate activities to resources and produce a draft schedule
- Revise the draft to remove as many peaks and troughs in resource usage as possible
- Negotiate a solution with the resource managers to resolve scheduling problems, such as too few or too many resources, or the inability to meet fixed target dates
- Add in management and quality activities or products (Stage and Team Plans only)
- Calculate resource utilization and costs

The PFD and the duration estimates for each of the lowest-level products in the PBS are the input to the scheduling activity. The Early Starts, Early Finishes, Late Starts, and Late Finishes can be calculated. While there are four different types of dependency, P2 LEAN uses the Finish-to-Start dependency to construct the schedule. If the schedule does not meet the project deadline requirement, other dependencies can be introduced to reduce the total project duration.

PL10—Analyzing Risks

A strong Risk Management Plan is a requirement of every P2 LEAN Project. That starts with a Core Team member being assigned the responsibility for developing, monitoring, and managing risk over the entire project life span. That assignment begins during the Starting Up Process with the Project Brief.

You should not commit to a plan without considering what risks are involved in it, and what impact the plan might have on risks already known.

- Look for any external dependencies. These always represent one or more risks; for example they may not arrive on time, they may be of poor quality, or they may be wrong in some other way.

- Look for any assumptions you have made in the plan, such as the resources available to you. Each assumption is a risk.
- Look at each resource in the plan. Is there a risk involved? For example, a new resource may not perform at the expected level, or a resource's availability may not be achieved.
- Are the tools or technology unproven?
- Take the appropriate risk actions. Where appropriate, revise the plan. Make sure that any new or modified risks are shown in the Risk Register.

Risk management consists of:

- Risk identification
- Risk assessment
- Risk mitigation
- Risk monitoring

P2 2009 discusses the Risk Theme in great detail and should be referenced while the Risk Management Plan is being prepared. In the P2 LEAN Framework, risk management is a critical component of every effective P2 LEAN project approach. It aligns with the P2 2009 Risk Theme with one exception. In the P2 LEAN Framework, a Manager of Risk Management is appointed from among the Core Team to monitor and report the status of every identified risk over the entire project life span. That begins with a Risk Management Plan. Do not commit to a project plan without considering what risks are involved in it and what impact the plan might have on risks already known.

PL11—Completing a Plan

The PID includes an updated Project Plan and a detailed Next Stage Plan. A plan in diagrammatic form is not self-explanatory. *A decision needs to be made on the format of the presentation of the plan to the authorizing body. A plan needs supporting and explanatory text to*:

- Set agreeable tolerance levels for the plan.
- Document what the plan covers, the approach to the work, and the checking of its quality.
- Document any assumptions you have made.
- Explain the context:

Who is the audience? Write the plan to fit the audience. The broader the audience, the less technical and more business oriented it should be. Having completed the schedule and assessment of the risks satisfactorily, the plan, its costs, the required controls, and its supporting text need to be consolidated into an Executive Summary.

- Document the process description:

  Narrative needs to be added to explain the plan, any constraints on it, external dependencies, assumptions made, the risks identified and their required countermeasures. Oftentimes these descriptions can be plan technical and allocated to an appendix.

- Plan controls:

  Some risk monitoring events may have been added to the plan, but at this point there is also a need to add the creation of any required management products to the plan because these take time and effort. The P2 LEAN Framework uses a primitive earned value analysis for all periodic reports to Project Executive Management. For problem and issue resolution, specific reporting requests are handled.

- The products of the planning cycle are easily checked for completeness and reasonableness by people experienced in planning and who know the product of the project.

PUTTING IT ALL TOGETHER

There are those who would say that planning is a waste of time. They would argue that no sooner is the plan approved, then it is changed due to unexpected circumstances. The P2 LEAN Framework will not work in the absence of the five planning types discussed previously. The 11-Step Template drives all of these plan preparations. It functions much like a checklist to assure all relevant components have been taken into account. Detailed planning is reserved for the Stage Plans and Team Plans. These are short-term plans (two- to six-week planning horizons) and are quite accurate. That is consistent with a just-in-time planning approach and protects the lean principles upon which the P2 LEAN Framework is based.

PART 2: PRINCE2 LEAN AND THE IDEATION PHASE

The objective of Part 2 is to take the Project Mandate, formulate it, and get the approval to plan a project using its given definition and business justification. That involves three steps plus StageGate #1:

- Developing the Business Case
- Creating the Project Product Description
- Preparing for the Initiation Stage
- StageGate #1

Part 2 will integrate the Brainstorming Process and the Requirements Elicitation Process from the Effective Complex Project Management (ECPM) Framework into the PRINCE2 (P2) Business Case and Project Brief from P2. This defines the P2 LEAN IDEATION Phase.

Chapter 5: *Preparing the Business Case* begins with the Project Mandate, then through a brainstorming session designed specifically for the P2 LEAN Framework, identifies and prioritizes a few potential projects and selects the best one for addressing the Project Mandate. A Project Brief is then prepared.

Chapter 6: *Creating the Project Product Description* uses a new definition of requirements taken from the ECPM Framework and integrated into the P2 LEAN Framework Starting Up Process. That definition mitigates the problems of incomplete requirements and the guessing that usually accompanies requirements elicitation. These newly defined requirements start the process of creating the product breakdown structure.

Chapter 7: *Preparing for the Initiation Stage* discusses the processes for creating the documentation that will eventually lead to the authorization to enter the SET-UP Phase and further define the project approach.

5

PREPARING THE BUSINESS CASE

---

*Nothing creates more self-respect among employees than
being included in the process of making decisions.*
—Judith M. Bardwick, University of California at San Diego

*Which of you, intending to build a tower sitteth not down first
and counteth the cost, whether he have sufficient to finish it?*
—New Testament, Luke 14: 28

CHAPTER LEARNING OBJECTIVES

This chapter will provide readers the knowledge or ability to:

- Capture the real needs of the client and separate them from the wants
- Think openly and creatively without fear of retribution
- Share responsibility and authority with your client
- Understand the Ideation Phase of a project
- Take a problem or opportunity from a desired end state (Project Mandate) through an analysis of alternative projects and the choice of an executable project

In this chapter, we begin with a Project Mandate—a request for help in solving a problem or taking advantage of an untapped business opportunity. The request can come from anywhere in the organization and the process for receiving them must be open. In most organizations, those requests will be received from an executive rather than directly from the originator.

We end the chapter with a detailed Business Case that justifies doing a specific project to address the problem or business opportunity. The chosen project meets all business criteria for a successful delivery and approval to enter the PRINCE2 (P2) LEAN SET-UP Phase. That approval follows from having prepared a Project Product Description (Chapter 6) and the Project Brief (Chapter 7). This is quite similar to P2 except we will introduce some *technique* details that are appropriate for a P2 LEAN project.

The Business Case and its updates provide the infrastructure and decision advice for the P2 LEAN Project throughout the entire project life span.

OVERVIEW

The P2 LEAN IDEATION Phase spans the P2 Starting Up (SU) and Initiating a Project (IP) Processes. P2 LEAN approaches IDEATION in three steps. In this chapter, the project leadership is appointed using the Effective Complex Project Management (ECPM) Co-Manager Model (Artifact #1). A Business Case is developed and a specific project is chosen from among alternatives.

In Chapter 6, we build the high-level requirements using the ECPM Requirements Elicitation Process (Artifact #2). And finally, in Chapter 7, the Project Brief is prepared. The approval of the Project Brief and Initiation Stage Plan signals the completion of the IDEATION Phase and is the approval to enter the SET-UP Phase of the P2 LEAN Framework.

STARTING UP A P2 LEAN PROJECT: THE BUSINESS CASE

The Input/Process/Output Model for generating the Business Case is shown in Figure 5.1.

The purpose of this model is to gather basic information about:

- What the project's scope is
- What level of quality is required from the final product
- What the approach to providing a solution will be
- What measurements the customer will apply to check that the final product is acceptable

At least one decision maker (the Project Executive) must be appointed in order to look at the information gathered and decide if it justifies proceeding

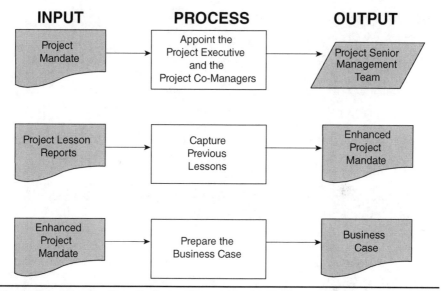

Figure 5.1   Starting Up a Project—Generating the Business Case

to the IP Process. In most cases, that Project Executive will be the originator of the Project Mandate, but the Project Executive could also include the Program Manager and Portfolio Manager depending on how the project is attached to the Corporate Strategic Plan. All of this work must be managed, so we need Project Co-Managers (ECPM Artifact #1) to be appointed. The Co-Manager Model is fully explained later in this chapter.

This beginning part of the SU Process includes the following activities:

- Appoint the Executive and the Project Co-Managers and, if needed, a few subject matter experts (SMEs) with specialized knowledge
- Factor in previous lessons learned to enhance the Project Mandate
- Prepare the Business Case including:
  1. What is to be done
  2. Who will make the decisions
  3. What alternatives have been identified
  4. What quality is required
  5. Solution acceptance criteria
  6. Who will provide the resources to do the work
  7. How the proposed project was chosen

Capture Previous Lessons

Lessons can be learned from every project. Every completed project should be followed by a Lessons Learned Report to answer questions such as:

- What worked?
- What didn't work?
- What can be done to improve the next P2 LEAN project?
- Did the Development Team perform as expected? Why or why not?
- Did the Client Team perform as expected? Why or why not?

One of the first tasks of a new project is to look at the Lessons Learned Reports from previous projects and glean from them any lessons that will be useful in the new project.

Enhanced Project Mandate

History is the best teacher and that is certainly true of a P2 LEAN Project. That history will temper the Project Mandate with reality and clarify its scope, giving the Senior Management Team a better perspective and understanding of what lies ahead. That tempering will identify risks, obstacles, and challenges gleaned from previous experiences. That clarification will set the bounds of what could be included in the products delivered and what probably is outside the scope of an acceptable response to the Project Mandate. All of this collective wisdom is a guide to the preparing of the Business Case.

P2 LEAN is designed so that an idea can originate anywhere and be submitted by anyone in the organization. The person proposing the idea must get the endorsement and support of a manager, who will often become the Project Executive. This is the first *step* in the process of developing a Business Case. A sponsor (usually a senior manager from the client organization who will fund the project) makes a request (the Project Mandate) of senior management to undertake a project to solve a mission critical problem, or take advantage of a significant yet untapped business opportunity. Whether it is a problem or an opportunity, the organization is presented with a major challenge. The challenge arises from the fact that the problem has remained unsolved, despite any prior attempts at resolution and it is unclear how to take advantage of the untapped business opportunity. That uncertainty is a fundamental characteristic of complex projects.

A representative from the development organization is assigned to work with the client sponsor. In keeping with the principles underlying the P2 LEAN Framework, this individual from the development organization will become one of the Project Co-Managers, and someone from the sponsor's business unit (the client) will become the other Project Co-Manager (Wysocki, 2014b). That could be a responsible business analyst, but it usually is a line manager from the affected business unit(s). Whoever is chosen, they must represent the sponsor's interests and have decision-making authority for the business unit(s) they represent.

PREPARING THE P2 LEAN BUSINESS CASE

There are several models and processes that could be used to develop the Business Case. The P2 LEAN Framework has adapted the model developed by Maul (2011) to accommodate the range of projects in the P2 LEAN Framework.

The Project Mandate provided by the IDEATION Phase should contain the basic justification for the project—at least enough to justify the expenditure needed to initiate the project. At this point, it may only be a set of reasons why the project is needed. The outline will be expanded into a full Business Case in the IP Process.

It is very easy to rush forward in a project conception to get to the design and creation of products. This is the interesting work, but there is often a lot of senior management pressure to *just do it*. With this attitude, it is easy to overlook why the project is being done and whether the long-term business value of the project will outweigh the total cost of the project.

What Is a P2 LEAN Business Case?

A Business Case is a document that identifies an unmet need, and provides evidence and justification for initiating or continuing a project investment to address that need. Combining the thinking of ECPM with P2, the P2 LEAN Business Case typically includes:

- A statement of a critical need and the overall justification for a project to address that need
- A description of the product, process, or service that the project will deliver
- The scope of the project and its deliverables
- How the project aligns with the business strategy
- A financial analysis comparing alternative project ideas
- A prioritization of the alternatives and the preferred option
- The incremental business value that will result

The P2 LEAN Framework Brainstorming Process

Figure 5.2 includes the brainstorming process that drives the development of the Business Case, beginning with a Project Mandate. The typical brainstorming process is mapped across the IDEATION Phase. (Figure 5.2 is the P2 LEAN Framework adaptation of a model originally developed by Gray et. al., 2010.)

The P2 LEAN Brainstorming Model consists of four parts:

- Project Mandate
- Divergent Phase
- Emergent Phase
- Convergent Phase

Divergent Phase

The purpose of the Divergent Phase is to elicit as many ideas as the brainstorming group can produce. No evaluation is done at the time, except for clarification. The more ideas that can be generated, the better the final results will be. No idea is too extreme to be rejected. One idea might not be used, but it may be the catalyst for other ideas. The best way to start the Divergent Phase is with a brainstorming session. What is presented here is a

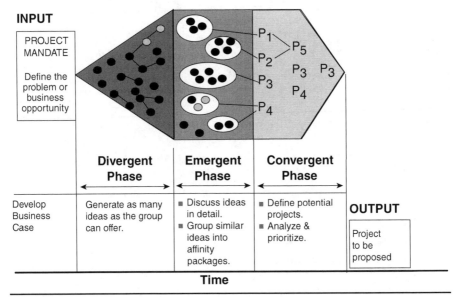

Figure 5.2   P2 LEAN Brainstorming Process for Developing the Business Case

variant of the familiar brainstorming session. This variant is far broader and comprehensive than you may have experienced so far:

Brainstorming Group Operating Rule

When a group member puts an idea on the table for consideration, they surrender ownership of the idea. It becomes the property of the entire group. It no longer makes any difference where the idea came from, and that should not even be part of any later discussions regarding the idea.

- Assemble individuals, whether they are team members, consultants, or others who may have some knowledge of the problem or business opportunity area. A team of 8–12 should be sufficient. They don't need to be experts. In fact, it may be better if they are not experts. You need people to think creatively and outside of the box. They may not be aware of any risks associated with their ideas, and that is good, at this early stage. Experts tend to think inside the box and focus on why something can't be done, rather than on why it should be done. *How* it will be done is a decision better left to the SET-UP and EXECUTION Phases.
- The session begins with everyone recording an idea, reading it to the brainstorming group, and placing it on the table face up so everyone can see it. No discussion (except clarification) is permitted. Silence and pauses are fine. This allows any group member to think about the suggestions that have been submitted and what they have heard and seen, and maybe that will spur another idea. Families of ideas can be generated like those shown linked together in Figure 5.2.
- After all the ideas are on the table and no new ideas seem to be forthcoming from the brainstorming group, the Divergent Phase is declared closed by the facilitator. A Divergent Phase can be completed in less than two hours.

Emergent Phase

The purpose of the Emergent Phase is to collect and consolidate the brainstormed ideas into packages of similar ideas (i.e., affinity packages) as a prelude to defining specific action items:

- Discuss the ideas that have been submitted. Try to combine ideas, or revise ideas based on each member's perspective. Some ideas may not be similar enough to be placed in a package. Don't discard any ideas. They might have value that has not yet been recognized.

- In time, primitive solutions will begin to emerge from these packages. Don't rush this process, and by all means, test each idea with an open mind. Remember that you are looking for a solution that no individual could identify, but that you hope the group is able to identify through their collective efforts. There is a synergy that comes from a well-run Emergent Phase.
- An Emergent Phase can be completed in two to three hours, but don't cut it short if it is still producing good affinity packages. The proposed packages are often grouped into funding categories or aligned to specific corporate strategies.

Convergent Phase

The purpose of the Convergent Phase is to use the affinity packages as the foundation for projects and perhaps group similar packages into projects, and then to analyze, prioritize, and finally, select the project to be proposed. Referring to Figure 5.2, the Convergent Phase consists of these activities:

- Define the P2 LEAN project or projects (P1 through P4).
- Analyze (P1 and P2 become P5).
- Prioritize alternative projects (P5, P3, P4).
- Select the first project to be proposed (P3).

The Convergent Phase is the first time that projects begin to take shape. Even though a single project is chosen, the list still can have residual value if the chosen project does not appear to be delivering business value. You may want to come back to this list for another pick.

Define the P2 LEAN Project or Projects

Whether you use the P2 LEAN Brainstorming Process or some type of feasibility study approach you should have generated a few alternatives, and it is time to explore them in more depth in your search for the best alternative. There are several variables that you might use to profile each alternative project. Here is a suggested approach:

- Order the projects according to expected business value
- Modify the order based on any or all of the following:
  - ✦ Duration
  - ✦ Cost
  - ✦ Team size and skills

Analyze and Prioritize Alternative Projects

The analysis of alternative projects examines their business value. The objective is to prioritize them and select the best. There are several approaches to analyzing the financial aspects of a project. While the sponsor should perform this analysis, it is often done by a project manager. The approaches chosen are easily understood and give enough insight into the financials of the project at this early stage in its life span.

Following are types of financial analyses you may be asked to provide. Keep in mind that the co-managers may not be financial analysts, and providing an in-depth financial analysis may be beyond their ability. We have found these four financial analyses to be easily done by most co-managers:

- Cost and benefit analysis
- Breakeven analysis
- Return on investment (ROI)
- Cost-benefit ratio (CBR)

Cost and Benefit Analysis

Cost and benefit analyses are always difficult to do because you need to include intangible benefits in the decision process. As mentioned earlier in the chapter, things such as improved client satisfaction cannot be easily quantified. You could argue that improved client satisfaction reduces client turnover, which in turn increases revenues, but how do you put a number on that? In many cases, senior management will take these inferences into account, but they still want to see hard-dollar comparisons. Opt for the direct and measurable benefits to compare against the cost of doing the project and the cost of operating the new process. If the benefits outweigh the costs over the expected life of the project deliverables, senior management may be willing to support the project.

Breakeven Analysis

Breakeven analysis is a timeline that shows the cumulative cost of the project against the cumulative revenue and savings from the project. Where the cumulative revenue and savings line crosses the cumulative cost line, the project will recoup its costs. Usually, senior management looks for an elapsed time less than a specific threshold number. If the project meets that deadline date, it may be worthy of support. Targeted breakeven dates are getting shorter because of more frequent changes in the business and its markets.

Breakeven analysis is a technique that is useful to get a good initial input regarding the investment pattern for any project. It involves simply adding up the project's predicted annual cash flows, i.e., the annual income minus expenses for the project in question. The breakeven point for a product is calculated, using the formula:

Breakeven point = (fixed cost)/(selling price – variable cost)

The graph shown in Figure 5.3 will clarify the technique. Breakeven analysis does not add the cash flows for the time period still remaining in the total project once this initial investment has been recovered. It also does not take depreciation into consideration.

Advantages of breakeven analysis:

- It is simple to use
- It is a standard technique used worldwide
- It can be used effectively for high-risk situations

Disadvantages of breakeven analysis:

- Normally ignores the time value of money, i.e., inflation or the discount rate
- Little consideration is taken of the cash flow situation after the breakeven period
- If used by itself, can give rise to poor decision making for investment

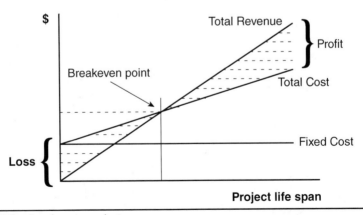

Figure 5.3   Breakeven analysis

Breakeven analysis is a good indicator for initial investment analysis, but it must be used in conjunction with other investment appraisal techniques.

Return on Investment

ROI analyzes the total costs as compared with the increased revenue that will accrue over the life of the project deliverables. Here, senior management finds a common basis for comparing one project against another. They look for the high ROI projects or the projects that at least meet some minimum ROI.

ROI considers only the total cash profit or cash flow (income minus expenses). It does not consider depreciation or the time value of money. To arrive at the project's ROI:

- The cash flow for each year is added without discounting it, and this total cash flow for the complete project is divided by the number of years to get the average return per year
- The average return per year is then divided by the initial investment made in the year 0, and multiplied by 100 to get the project's ROI

Cost-Benefit Ratio

The cost-benefit ratio (CBR) is the ratio of quantifiable benefits to the costs incurred to achieve the benefits. In theory, benefits can be in financial terms covering the revenue generation and cost savings, or they can be the fulfillment of social objectives, intangible, and nonquantifiable, such as improving quality, boosting the morale of the team, etc.

Let us represent benefits as B and costs as C. The CBR is C/B. Inflows can be linked to benefits, and outflows to the costs incurred. Mathematically speaking, a ratio can either be greater than one, less than one, or one itself. If the ratio is less than one, it is much better, as benefits are more than the costs incurred to achieve them. A ratio greater than one will imply that we get fewer benefits in comparison to the costs incurred. A ratio of one implies no gain or loss.

In the case of nonrevenue generating projects, a CBR ratio can be computed by taking the ratio of the total cost savings to costs incurred to affect the savings (for instance, by providing an opportunity for managers to stay with the company by giving them a good compensation package).

Prioritize the Alternative Projects

The list of alternative projects may not lend itself to prioritization when expected business value and the other variables are taken into account. There are a number of prioritization rules that might be applied. They range from the very simple to the very complex. Our experience is that the following four rules adhere to the lean principles we have designed into the P2 LEAN Framework:

- Must do, Should do, Could do, Won't do (MoSCoW)
- Forced ranking
- Risk/benefit matrix
- Paired comparisons

These are roughly ordered from simple to complex. The situation will dictate which is the best fit.

Must Do, Should Do, Could Do, Won't Do

MoSCoW is probably the most commonly used way of ranking. As opposed to the forced rank, in which each individual project is ranked, this approach creates a few categories. The person doing the ranking only has to decide which category the project belongs in. The agony of having to decide relative rankings between pairs of projects is eliminated with this approach. The number of categories is arbitrary, as are the names of the categories.

Forced Ranking

The forced ranking approach is best explained by way of an example. Suppose that five projects have been proposed. Number the projects 1 through 5 so that you can refer to them later. Suppose that the brainstorming team has six members (A, B, C, D, E, F), and they are each asked to rank the five projects from most important (1) to least important (5). They can use any criteria they wish, and they do not have to describe the criteria they used. The results of their rankings are shown in Table 5.1.

Table 5.1   Forced ranking of five solution ideas

Project #	A	B	C	D	E	F	Rank Sum	Forced Rank
1	2	1	3	2	1	4	13	2
2	4	3	2	3	4	3	19	3
3	5	4	1	5	3	1	19	3
4	1	2	4	1	2	2	12	1
5	3	5	5	4	5	5	27	5

The individual rankings from each of the six members for a specific project are added to produce the rank sum for each project. Low values for the rank sum are indicative of projects that have been given high priority by the members. For example, Project 4 has the lowest rank sum, and is therefore the highest priority project.

Ties are possible in forced ranking. In fact, the preceding example has a tie between Project 2 and Project 3. Ties can be broken in a number of ways. For example, the existing rankings can be used to break ties. In this example, a tie is broken by taking the tied project with the lowest rank score and moving it to the next lowest forced rank. For example, the highest rank for Project 2 is 2, and for Project 3 is 1. Therefore, the tie is broken by giving Project 3 a rank of 3, and giving Project 2 a rank of 4.

Forced ranking works well for small numbers of projects, but it does not scale very well. It will work well if a few alternatives (like in a Business Case) are being compared in an effort to pick one to proceed to the project level.

Risk/Benefit Matrix

Another scoring model is the risk/benefit matrix (Figure 5.4). There are many ways to do risk analysis, from subjective methods to very sophisticated

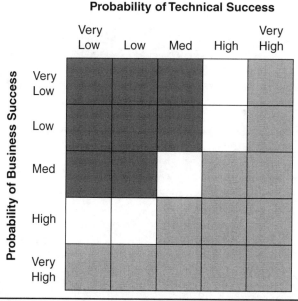

Figure 5.4   Risk/Benefit Matrix

mathematical models. The model that we recommend is a very simple, quasi-mathematical model. The probabilities of success are divided into five levels. Actually, any number of levels will do the job. Defining three levels is also quite common. In this model, you assess two probabilities: the probability of technical success and the probability of business success. These are arranged as shown in Figure 5.4.

Each project is assessed in terms of the probability of technical success and the probability of business success. The probability of idea success is estimated as the product of the two separate probabilities. To simplify the calculation, the graph shows the results of the computation by placing a project in one of the following three shaded areas:

- **Light shading:** These projects should be a high priority
- **No shading:** These projects should be considered
- **Dark shading:** These projects should not be considered unless there is some compelling reason to fund them

When you have a large number of projects, you need to prioritize those that fall in the lightly shaded cells. A good way to do this would be to prioritize the cells starting in the lower right corner and working toward the center of the matrix.

Paired Comparisons

In the paired comparisons model, every pair of projects is compared. Using whatever criteria he or she wishes, the evaluator chooses which project in the pair is the higher priority. The matrix in Table 5.2 shows an example of conducting and recording the results of a paired comparisons exercise.

To use the technique, first of all, list your options. Then draw up a grid with each option as both a row and a column header.

1. List the options you will compare. Assign a letter to each option.
2. Set up a table with these options as row and column headings.
3. Block out cells on the table where you will be comparing an option with itself—there will never be a difference in these cells. These will normally be on the diagonal running from the top left to the bottom right.
4. Also, block out cells on the table where you will be duplicating a comparison. Normally these will be the cells below the diagonal.
5. Within the remaining cells, compare the option in the row with the option in the column. For each cell, decide which of the two options is more important. The more important one scores 1, the lesser important scores 0.

Table 5.2   An example of paired comparisons

Project #	A	B	C	D	E	Sum	Rank
A	X	1	1	0	1	3	2
B	0	X	0	0	1	1	3
C	0	1	X	0	0	1	3
D	1	1	1	X	1	4	1
E	0	0	1	0	X	1	3

Select the Project to be Proposed

This step ends with the selection of a project to take to the next step, in which the Project Product Description is developed (Chapter 6). The decision will be based on both quantitative and qualitative data. In the final analysis, these data are guidelines for a decision that is *first* a good business decision. It would be unusual if all prioritized lists have the same project as highest priority, but it has happened.

> The Business Case is the foundation for all project decisions in both P2 and P2 LEAN projects. It maintains alignment of the project to the expected business value validated for the project.

PUTTING IT ALL TOGETHER

At this point in the life span of the project, we have reached a significant decision point. Does the Business Case validate going forward into a more detailed description of the suggested project? The executive is empowered to make this decision based on the current version of the Business Case. There will be situations where adjustments may be required to the Business Case before reaching a positive decision from the executive. That positive decision moves the project to the Requirements Elicitation Process where an acceptable solution is defined and a Project Brief prepared.

6

CREATING THE PROJECT PRODUCT DESCRIPTION

The great art in writing well is to know when to stop.
—Josh Billings, American writer and auctioneer

This report, by its very length, defends
itself against the risk of being read.
—Winston Churchill, English Prime Minister, author, and soldier

CHAPTER LEARNING OBJECTIVES

This chapter will provide readers the knowledge or ability to:

- Know the challenges of identifying a complete product description in a complex project
- Understand the PRINCE2 (P2) LEAN definition of high-level requirements
- Establish a mindset that the product description will evolve through several stages

The P2 LEAN Project Product Description Document states the conditions that an acceptable solution must meet. The term *requirements* is in common use in the U.S., but is not used in P2—*Product Description* is the closest synonym. In the complex project landscape, the project management thought leaders agree that only in the simplest of projects is it possible to completely describe the product. To circumvent the impact that an incomplete specification can have on managing the project, the P2 LEAN Framework is based on a new definition of requirements that will be used to generate the Project Product Description. However, the P2 LEAN Framework includes an understanding of how requirements are defined, elicited, and implemented in the life span of a complex project. Having this understanding is a valuable addition to the P2 LEAN practitioner's and professional's tool kit as they accommodate the uncertainties and complexities of contemporary projects. Using this new definition of requirements pushes the resolution of the uncertainties and complexities into the later Stages. Probative Swim Lanes (Artifact #6) are designed to remove uncertainty and complexity, and establish a pathway to the discovery of an acceptable solution. Within those constraints, the Project Product Description and the product breakdown structure (PBS) are developed.

P2 LEAN PROJECT PRODUCT DESCRIPTION PROCESS FLOW

The Project Product Description is created during the Starting Up a Project Process—right at the beginning of the project and before the Initiation Stage, where we will create the Project Plan. To differentiate what we are doing here from the Project Plan, we are using the term PBS, which only applies to this early view of what major products are needed.

In complex projects, complete and defined requirements (Figure 6.1) have not been forthcoming during the Starting Up Process. As a result, requirements elicitation is compromised and the lean principles challenged. A new approach is developed for the P2 LEAN Framework that averts those compromises.

What Is a P2 LEAN High-level Requirement?

A continuing problem with requirements elicitation in complex projects derives from not knowing what an acceptable solution contains from a complete statement of requirements. Beyond knowing the requirements, there is the associated problem of how those requirements will be achieved. The root cause of that problem is partially based in an unclear definition of the solution and partially based in not knowing how to achieve the solution. The P2 LEAN Framework defines a two-step process of Requirements Elicitation (Artifact #2). The first step defines the high-level requirements that every acceptable solution must contain. That is the step that we take in creating the Project Product Description. The second step is imbedded in the Stage Process that will be used to iteratively learn and discover the details of

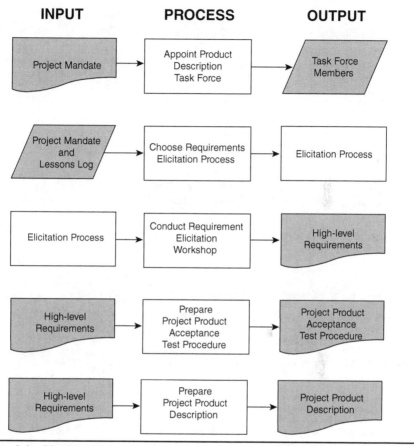

Figure 6.1   P2 LEAN Project Product Description Flow Diagram

those high-level requirements. Those details will be a finer definition of the requirements and how they might be achieved.

Definition: P2 LEAN High-level Requirement

A P2 LEAN requirement is an end-state condition whose successful integration into the solution delivers specific, measurable, and incremental business value to the organization.

The set of P2 LEAN requirements forms a necessary and sufficient set for the attainment of all project acceptance criteria including the delivery of the expected business value.

This definition postpones the challenges associated with incomplete requirements and moves them to the stages and the process of learning and discovery.

Requirements define the properties and characteristics of the products, processes, or services that are the deliverables of the project. The P2 LEAN Framework adopts the P2 term *product* for all of these deliverables. These requirements are the basis for analyzing the effect of any changes to a current situation that your client is seeking. A requirement exists either because the product demands certain functions or qualities not present in the current solution. Product definition begins with what the customer really needs, and ends when the product evolves into a deliverable that satisfies those needs. (Note that we are saying *needs*, not *wants*.) This often leads to nonessential or over-specified requirements. You are cautioned to be very careful about assuming who knows *what* and who understands *what*. The P2 LEAN Framework is designed to ensure that all project team members know and understand *what*.

> What the client wants may not be what the client needs. The co-managers' jobs are to make sure that what is wanted is what is needed and that what is needed is what is delivered.

This definition of a P2 LEAN Requirement is quite different than the International Institute of Business Analysis (IIBA) definition of a requirement, but in its simplicity and uniqueness, it puts the connection between requirements and the project in a much more intuitive light. The P2 LEAN Requirements are very similar to an *Epic*, which is defined in P2 Agile where the term *requirements* is first used in a P2 publication (AXELOS, 2015). P2 LEAN Requirements will be the causal factors that drive the attainment of the acceptance criteria, as stated in the Project Brief. Every P2 LEAN Requirement should be clearly related to one or more of the project acceptance criteria. This definition results in a small number (8–12) of requirements at the beginning of the project, whereas the IIBA definition generates hundreds of requirements, which can never be considered a complete set at the beginning of the project. The mind could not grasp completeness, anyway.

Subject to the learning and discovery that may uncover other requirements, the list generated using the P2 LEAN Requirements definition can be considered complete at the beginning of the project. The decomposition of those requirements is not fully known at the beginning of the project, however. A P2 LEAN Requirement is a more business-value-oriented definition than the IIBA definition.

The learning and discovery derived from completed project stages will clarify the P2 LEAN Requirements through decomposition to the function, subfunction, process, activity, and feature levels. The first level decomposition of a P2 LEAN Requirement is to the functional level, and can be considered equivalent to IIBA requirements. So, while you can identify all high-level P2 LEAN Requirements at the beginning of the project, you cannot describe the details of the requirements at the functional, subfunctional, process, activity, and feature levels. This detail is learned and discovered in the context of the stages that make up the project. This two-step process for Requirements Elicitation is also consistent with lean principles (Poppendieck and Poppendieck, 2003).

The P2 LEAN definition of high-level requirements should be preferred to the IIBA definition because it ties requirements directly to the project success criteria, which is not the case with the IIBA definition. That makes it possible to prioritize P2 LEAN Requirements, whereas no similar case can be made for prioritizing IIBA requirements. Under the IIBA definition, setting priorities is more of a technical assessment than a business assessment.

The choice of a single project to propose can be made based on the high-level requirements. Since the requirements describe an acceptable solution, the decision can be driven by the degree of fit between a proposed project and the effectiveness it will have in producing deliverables that satisfy the requirements. Reaching this decision is subjective—not objective.

Appoint Product Description Task Force

The primary purpose of the Task Force is to create the set of necessary and sufficient high-level requirements that any acceptable solution must meet. In meeting that purpose, the Task Force will develop some detail regarding the certainty of those high-level requirements through an initial view of the decomposition of those requirements. This is valuable insight for the SET-UP Phase to follow. To do this effectively, the Task Force membership must contain the co-managers, the Core Team, and any other subject matter expert (SME) whose skills and competencies span the business processes and development processes needed to deliver an acceptable solution. A facilitator should be assigned to direct this process. Our recommendation is that this should not be either co-manager, but rather a senior project manager with no connection to the project, or to an outside consultant with the requisite experience. This strategy keeps the co-managers free from any facilitation responsibilities and allows them to focus on Requirements Elicitation and Product Description.

> **Definition: Product Breakdown Structure (PBS)**
>
> The PBS is a hierarchical decomposition of all product requirements that must be present in the solution in order for the product to be acceptable and deliver the business value expected.

Choose Requirements Elicitation Process

Requirements have always been a sticking point in the process of deciding how to manage a complex project. There will be those situations where the project has been done several times, and there is a documented history of those efforts. All requirements should be known. At the other extreme are projects that have never been done before, so most requirements will not have a history that can be used as a template for the current project. When that history is not available, the project will be a high-risk project and most likely complex, too. The unknowns may dominate attempts to discover an acceptable solution.

Approaches to Requirements Elicitation and Decomposition

Requirements have to be defined through a carefully planned engagement with the client. Of all the requirement gathering approaches, there are four methods that work particularly well within the P2 LEAN world. These are widely used methods for generating requirements. More than one method may be chosen to generate the requirements on any project. Selection of the best methods to generate potential requirements for the project is the responsibility of the project co-managers, who must evaluate each method for costs, ease of implementation, reliability, client comfort level with the chosen process, and risks. Certain methods have been proven effective for specific industries and products. An example of this would be using physical, three-dimensional wireframe models in product design or solid models in bridge construction.

Requirements elicitation is the first task that the co-managers will face in the life of a complex project. The co-managers will have to be prepared to engage in the elicitation, decomposition, and documentation process. Their attitude, commitment, and willingness to be meaningfully involved are major determinants in the choice of approach. This preparation will include the choice of approach to be used and perhaps some preliminary training of the client and the Core Team. Some clients will be open and proactively participate; others will not. Some will be sure of their needs; others will not. Some will be expressing their wants, which may be very different from their needs. Be careful with the wants-versus-needs dilemma because wants are often a client's expression of what they believe to be the solution to an unstated problem.

There are many techniques that have been used successfully to decompose and document requirements. We have had good success using brainstorming, user stories, prototyping, and requirements workshops. All of these should be in your P2 LEAN vetted portfolio (see Chapter 15).

The steps to generate requirements begin by looking at the business function as a whole. This is followed by the selection of a method or methods for gathering requirements. This effort must be planned. The recommended approaches (listed at the end of this paragraph) are arranged from least formal to most formal. These are usually understood or easily adopted in less-sophisticated environments. (A comprehensive reference on all the popular methods for gathering requirements is given in Robertson and Robertson, 2012.) These are our recommendations:

- Brainstorming
- User Stories
- Prototyping
- Requirements Workshop

We single out these four methods because they work best when translating business requirements into business deliverables. Across the history of the Effective Complex Project Management (ECPM) Framework, these methods have consistently been the most successful. They can also be used to decompose requirements and generate the PBS. Regardless of the method you use to generate the PBS, we strongly advise creating a PBS for every project for the following reasons:

- The PBS is housed in the client's language
- The PBS is a deliverables-based approach
- The PBS is consistent with the *Project Management Body of Knowledge (PMBOK® Guide)*
- The PBS remains client-facing as long as possible

The four methods listed previously share these reasons and will help keep the client well within their comfort zone:

> **Brainstorming:**

This has been extensively covered in Chapter 5. Brainstorming is a technique that can stimulate creativity and help the team discover solutions. In some situations, acceptable ideas and alternatives do not result from the normal team deliberations. In such cases, the co-managers might suggest a brainstorming session. A brainstorming session is one in which the team contributes ideas in a stream-of-consciousness mode, as described in the next paragraph. Brainstorming sessions have been quite successful in uncovering solutions where none seemed present. The team needs to know how the project manager will conduct such sessions and what will be done with the output.

> **User Stories**

Utilize user stories on occasion, but very informally. Basically, a user story is just that. Pick some piece of a business process and have the user tell you how it does or should operate—who does what and when. The story can be used as a jumping-off point for a discussion of what does not work well and why, as a prelude to process improvement. This keeps the user well within their comfort zone and does not require them to have any special knowledge about user stories and how to document them.

The process of writing user stories follows a top-down process. At the top of the process is the identification of the steps that capture the user story. These can be displayed on a linear sequence of sticky notes as shown in Figure 6.2. With that level, each step is further explained with the lower level details of each of the high-level steps. Those are also shown in Figure 6.2 below each Epic.

Epics, stories, and tasks are a product-focused decomposition not unlike the boulder/rock/pebbles metaphor introduced by Jeff Patton (Patton, 2014). Epic is a term not used in P2 but it is used in P2 Agile (AXELOS, 2015). An Epic is virtually the same as a high-level P2 LEAN Requirement. But in the case of P2 LEAN, the collection of high-level requirements is a necessary and sufficient set for the attainment of an acceptable solution. Furthermore, the decomposition of Epics into Stories and Tasks follows a specific set of rules that define a complete decomposition. This complete decomposition defines the list of tasks that are the building blocks of the project schedule. See Chapter 11 for more details on how to build the PBS.

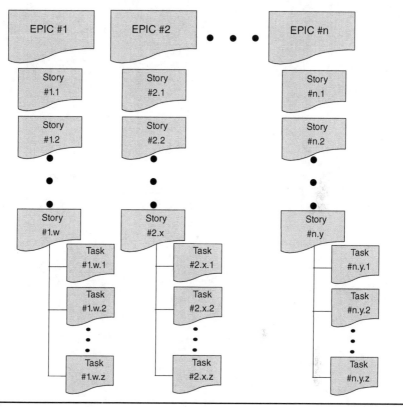

Figure 6.2   Explaining user stories

For some clients who are more visually stimulated and when the project involves business process improvement or design, P2 LEAN begins the Requirements Elicitation with a graphical representation that collectively includes these stories rather than a written presentation. This alternative approach is also useful for prototyping. A typical presentation is shown in Figure 6.3, which was constructed using MS Visio.

➢ **Prototyping**

Many clients cannot relate to a narrative description of a system, but they can relate to a visual representation of a system. For requirements decomposition purposes, the idea of a prototype was conceived several decades ago. Its original purpose was to help clients define what they wanted. By showing them a mock-up of a solution, they could comment on it and give the developers more insight into what constitutes an

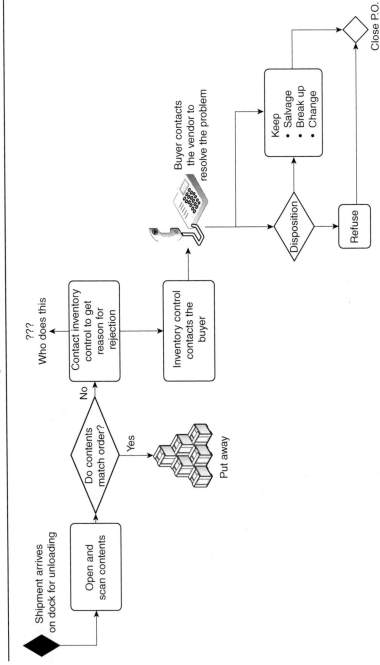

Receiving Inspection Process

Figure 6.3   Business process flow diagrams as an alternative to writing user stories

acceptable solution. The prototype is revised and the process repeated until the user is satisfied that an acceptable solution has been found. Originally these prototypes were storyboard versions, not production versions. Later prototypes did become production versions of the solution when used in complex projects.

➢ **Requirements Elicitation/Decomposition Workshop**

The aforementioned approaches work well for smaller projects. But a more formal process approach will be required for larger, more complex projects, especially if the clients come from different business units in the organization, or different organizations altogether. At the same time, it is good practice to be prepared to work with a client who has not previously experienced the Requirements Elicitation/Decomposition Process. From our experiences, the best results often come when training is offered concurrently with the application of that training on a real project. It puts the training in the context of real work and not just an exercise. Clients tend to remain motivated throughout the workshop because they have an immediate need to be satisfied. With first timers, the quality of the results tends to improve over other approaches. A typical workshop is a structured event. Here is a template that can get your co-managers started with the planning of that workshop:

- Co-managers have been selected
- Select attendees (Core Team, SMEs as appropriate, senior and junior users)
- Select workshop facilitator (discussed later)
- Distribute copies of the Project Mandate and Business Case to attendees and the facilitator
- Launch the workshop:
    + Discuss Project Mandate and Business Case
    + Profile and agree on the Desired End State
    + Brainstorm High-level Requirements needed to achieve the Desired End State
    + Discuss and agree on High-level Requirements as the necessary and sufficient set for achieving the Desired End State
    + Incorporate known requirements decompositions (no guessing allowed)
- Co-managers prepare the Project Product Description Document

The Project Product Description Document is deposited in the Scope Bank (Part 4, Artifact #4) and will be updated as part of the Stage Management and Planning activities. High-level requirements are fixed and rarely change. Decomposed requirements are learned and discovered as part of stage deliverables.

Which Approach Should We Use?

There are several things to take into account when deciding which of the above approaches to utilize:

- **The experience of the client team**—If the client team has memorable and effective experiences with any of the requirements gathering approaches, try to select from among them. To the greatest extent possible, put the client in their comfort zone so that they can focus on the work of defining requirements.
- **The experience of the development team**—If the development team has memorable and effective experiences with any of the requirements gathering approaches, try to select from among them. Given the choice of two or more approaches, choose the one that favors the client.
- **The complexity and nature of the project**—The more complex the project, the more you would want to use approaches that give detailed information and are less likely to overlook anything. A formal process should be preferred to an informal process.
- **The experience of the session facilitator**—First of all, the session facilitator should not be a member of the client team or the development team. This may come as a surprise, but there are good reasons that back it up. The facilitator's job is so critical that you need someone with experience and with no bias toward the project. Their job is to facilitate, not to play politics. The co-managers need to focus their attention on the deliverables from the requirements gathering exercise, not on the process of getting them, and so they are not good choices for facilitator. If there is no one internal to the organization that meets the criteria, hire an outside consultant. This is no place to cut expenses. The more critical and complex the project, the more you should favor the use of an outside facilitator.

Conduct Requirements Elicitation Workshop

With the preliminary work done, the facilitator assigned, and the choice of approach made, the workshop can begin. A one-day workshop should be sufficient except for the largest and most complex of projects.

Elicitation and Documentation Requirements

Complete and clear document requirements at the beginning of a project have never really happened. It just isn't possible, except in the simplest of projects. (Infrastructure projects are an example because they tend to be isolated from the outside world.) A few *cowboys* would claim to have done so, and launched into project planning under the assumption of having a complete Requirements Document. Later, to their dismay, they are deluged with scope change requests from the client: "What happened? I thought we had all of this nailed. You told us you were satisfied and that we had done an exemplary job of gathering and documenting your requirements." The problem is not with the process. The problem is not with the initial documentation. The problem is that the world is not a static place. It never has been and never will be. So, why should you expect your Requirements Document to stand still while you do the project? Change is inevitable, regardless of how well the project was organized at the outset. There must be better ways—and there are!

Create a PBS for every P2 LEAN project because it:

- Is expressed in the language of the client
- Promotes client ownership and eventual buy-in of the solution
- Is a deliverables-based approach which is in the client's comfort zone
- Can be used to measure progress toward solution discovery
- Can be used to measure project performance
- Is consistent with the *Project Management Body of Knowledge (PMBOK® Guide)*
- Remains client-facing as long as possible into the planning process

In complex projects, an incomplete PBS is the rule rather than the exception. It would be unusual to have a complete PBS at the start of a complex project. Some functions and features may not be known, and their absence may not be known at this early stage, either. These are the unknowns and they are part of every complex project. Being able to say that the PBS is complete is based more on a feeling than on hard fact. The P2 LEAN Framework stages are designed to learn and discover the complete PBS, and hence the solution, through iteration.

> Conventional wisdom says that a complete PBS is not possible at the start of a complex project, but can only be defined through a sequence of dependent stages, where each stage is designed to add more detail to the PBS. There may be exceptions for projects that are often repeated.

Prepare Product Acceptance Test Procedure

The Acceptance Test Procedure (ATP) is a checklist of functions, features, and performance requirements that the project product must do in order to be acceptable to the client. It is developed for the Project Product Description Document. The task of writing the ATP begins during the Requirements Elicitation Process and is completed during the writing of the Project Product Description Document. The ATP is created early in the project life span to avoid any eleventh hour disputes over the suitability of the final project product. The ATP is updated at the completion of each stage and is the criteria that will be used to declare the project complete and to enter the closing activities.

Project Product Description Document

The P2 LEAN Project Product Description Document describes a product that is only partially known. The document itself will evolve through the learning and discovery that results from completed stages. What are known at the outset are the High-level Requirements—and those will be introduced in the initial version of the Project Product Description. That document can be outlined as a guide for the co-managers.

Project Product Description Document Outline

This document evolves through the stages:

- Title of the project
- Overall purpose of the end product
- A description of the major products to be delivered by the project
- Who will use the end product
- Source of the requirement; examples might be:
  + Existing products that need modification
  + A feasibility study
  + A business strategy document
  + Reference to a program of which the project is part
- Skills required to develop the end product
- Client's quality expectations
- ATP for the end product; a list of criteria that the end product must meet in order to be acceptable to the client

Who Should Prepare This Document?

The document will be signed by the co-managers and they should facilitate its preparation supported by the Core Team.

PUTTING IT ALL TOGETHER

Requirements Elicitation and Decomposition is the heart of any ECPM approach. Change is inevitable in the dynamic environment of a complex project. It can change at any time and in unexpected ways, and it directly impacts requirements. The only steady state in all of this change is the Business Case that initially was the justification for authorizing the project. The alignment to that, and the expectation of the validating business value being realized is the justification for continuing or modifying the project.

To the extent possible, the requirements infrastructure must be such that it brings as much stability to the project as is possible. The definition of requirements, as provided by the P2 LEAN Framework, delivers that stability. The iterative definition of the requirements breakdown structure is the enabling tool.

Web
Added
Value™

7

PREPARING FOR THE INITIATION STAGE

Goals should be specific, realistic, and measurable.
—William G. Dyer, Brigham Young University

*If I understood too clearly what I was doing, where I was going,
then I probably wasn't working on anything very interesting.*
—Peter Carruthers, Physicist

*Objectives are not fate; they are direction. They are not
commands; they are commitments. They do not determine
the future; they are means to mobilize the resources and
energies of the business for the making of the future.*
—Peter F. Drucker, Management consultant and writer

CHAPTER LEARNING OBJECTIVES

This chapter will provide readers the knowledge or ability to:

- Explain the purpose of the Project Brief
- Understand the component parts of the Project Brief
- Write the one-page Project Brief
- Understand the component parts of the Initiation Stage Plan
- Prepare the Initiation Stage Plan

The PRINCE2 (P2) LEAN Framework utilizes an intake process that has few constraints. The intent is to welcome ideas and suggestions for business improvement. Those suggestions might include a problem that has avoided any resolution, or could reveal an untapped business opportunity. The suggestion should have arrived in the form of a Project Mandate, which was then translated into a Project Product Description. (Chapter 6 discussed this in full detail.) At this point, enough detail has been developed to define a project that addresses the original Project Mandate, along with a Business Case to support it. That project is formally introduced to the Project Executive with a Project Brief. Accompanying the Project Brief is the Business Case and a plan for conducting the Initiation Stage. (Chapter 5 presented full details of the Business Case and its preparation.)

All of these documents are presented to the Project Executive in order to gain approval to enter the SET-UP Phase. That approval is the next step in the process of preparing a detailed proposal, called the Project Initiation Documentation (PID) whose approval is the authorization to do the project (i.e., enter the EXECUTION Phase).

INTRODUCTION

The deliverables from the IDEATION Phase are three critical products that define the project in increasing levels of detail and that provide the Project Executive with the information needed to get the project into the corporate plan. Figure 7.1 is the recommended process flow for those documents to gain the necessary approvals to proceed to the SET-UP Phase of the project.

APPOINT THE PROJECT BRIEF TASK FORCE

The Project Brief Task Force will be charged to create the Project Brief, Business Case, and Initiation Stage Plan. Its members will be the co-managers plus any likely Core Team members whose expertise will be needed for the more technical and business process areas. Exceptions will occur for projects that are very complex and the goal and/or solution is largely unknown or unclear. This is a judgment call by the co-managers to secure additional subject matter experts (SMEs) if needed. Having these professionals assembled from the start minimizes the briefings and orientations that will be required for those team members who are added later. While it may be considered overkill initially, the long-term benefits will outweigh the resource use.

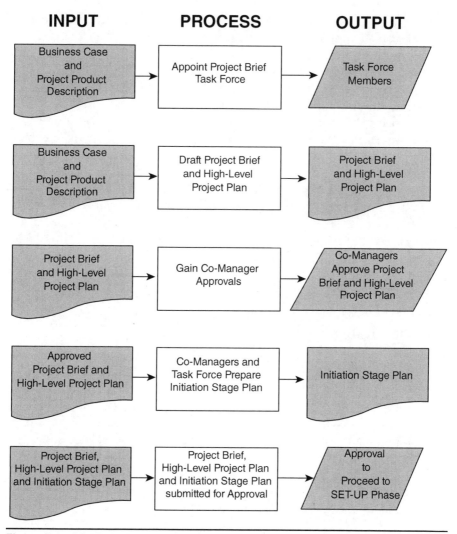

Figure 7.1   P2 LEAN Framework IDEATION Phase Deliverables IPO Diagram

DRAFT THE PROJECT BRIEF

The Project Brief is the first formal document that describes the proposed project at a high level. In most cases, it will have wide circulation among the management team. P2 LEAN constrains the Project Brief to the equivalent of one printed page. Furthermore, it should be written in the business language of the enterprise, so that anyone who has the occasion to read it will understand it. Technical jargon and terminology should not be used unless it is in the common parlance of the enterprise.

The P2 LEAN Framework invites project ideas from anyone in the organization. Protocols may require that these are submitted up through the organizational hierarchy to a senior manager or executive and then forwarded for input into the project/program/portfolio process. Because there is no formal process for submitting a Project Mandate, it may be a statement that describes a desired end state that has not been thought out, or it may be quite detailed, even to the point that a solution is recommended. The P2 LEAN Framework is such that the constraints on this intake process are minimal. Back-of-the-napkin scribbles, as well as detailed specification documents, are all acceptable submissions. To encourage submissions, few constraints or content requirements should be in place. The submissions are allowed to come as they arise, although they might be recognized, held, and formally processed on a scheduled basis—say, quarterly.

Purpose of the P2 LEAN Project Brief

In addition to bringing a business situation to the attention of senior management, the P2 LEAN Project Brief has the following purposes:

- To secure the Project Executive's approval to Initiate a P2 LEAN Project
- To provide a general statement of a proposed P2 LEAN Project
- To establish a basis for future planning and execution of the P2 LEAN Project
- To be used as a reference document for project team members, new members, and future decision making

Drafting the P2 LEAN Project Brief

The appropriate members of the Task Force prepare a draft of the P2 LEAN Project Brief and submit it to the co-managers for their approval. In some cases it might be appropriate for just the co-managers to draft the document and avoid the approval step.

Definition of the P2 LEAN Project Brief

A P2 LEAN Project Brief is a preproject statement of an unsolved problem or untapped business opportunity that should be pursued, the reasons why, and the potential benefits to the enterprise. It is a lean derivative of the P2 Project Brief, and consists of five interrelated parts:

- Problem/Opportunity statement—the reason for doing the project
- Goal statement—what will generally be done
- Statement of objectives—what the product deliverables will do
- Acceptance criteria—quantitative metrics of expected business value
- Risks, assumptions, and obstacles to project success—high-level only

These five parts of the P2 LEAN Project Brief are described in the following sections.

Problem/Opportunity Statement

A well-defined need, and a clear solution pathway to meet that need, define a project that the traditionalist expects. A rather vague idea of a *want*, coupled with a vague idea of *how* it will be satisfied, defines a P2 LEAN Project that complex Project Co-Managers expect. The problem or opportunity that this project is going to respond to must already be recognized by the organization as a legitimate problem or opportunity that must be attended to. If anyone in the organization were asked about it, he or she would surely answer, "You bet it is, and we need to do something about it." In other words, it is not something that needs a defense. It stands on its own merits. Furthermore, the problem or opportunity statement must be expressed in terms that anyone in the organization who would have a reason to read the statement could understand without the need for further explanation.

Goal Statement of This Version of the Solution

Version deserves some comment. In the agile project landscape, solutions are seldom universal solutions. They are the best that can be done, given the current understanding of a complex situation. As experience is gained with this version of the solution and as technology continues its relentless march, better solutions will be suggested. That leads to Version 2, etc.

The goal will be a simple yet definitive statement about what this project intends to do to address the problem or opportunity. It might be a total solution, but to be more realistic, it would be a solution that addresses a major segment of the problem or opportunity. In the spirit of the P2 LEAN Framework, caution is given to not reach beyond the extent of your grasp. All too often, projects are defined that are far too large in scope. Maybe a more realistic approach would be to solve the parts of the problem that will have a major impact on the business; to be followed quickly with a project to deliver solution components of lesser business value. Sure, curing all forms of cancer would be great, but be realistic. Maybe curing one form of cancer would be a lofty enough goal.

Having a goal that is too ambitious will open the project to added risks over a more conservative goal and scope reduction as the project becomes framed in a more attainable way. Furthermore, there can be changes in the environment that render a too-ambitious goal ineffective or unattainable. So, a project with a long delivery time is exposed to cancellation before it can deliver any business value. By defining the goal of this version to be a reachable target, rather than a lofty or unattainable ambition, we protect the client and the team from scope reduction and significantly increase their chances of delivering business value. We are sure that being too ambitious has a lot to do with the high incidence of project failure. It may sound pedestrian to some, but slow and steady will be far more successful in the long run.

Writing the Objectives of This Version

By way of analogy, think of the goal statement as a pie and the objective statements as slices of the pie. All of the slices that make up the pie are the objective statements. If you would rather have a mathematical interpretation, think of the objectives as necessary and sufficient conditions for the attainment of the goal. In either case, the objective statements give a little more detail on how the goal will be achieved. They are the boundary conditions, if you will. Six to ten objective statements to clarify your goal statement would be typical. Together, the goal statement and the objectives statements collectively define the deliverables that the project will produce. We will see that High-level Requirements (Chapter 6) can also be used as objective statements.

Defining the Acceptance Criteria

The acceptance criteria (or explicit business outcomes) are quantitative statements of the results that will be realized from having successfully completed this project. They are formulated in such a way that they either happened, or they did not happen. There will be no debate over attainment of the acceptance criteria. Statements like: "pre-tax profit margins will increase from their current average of 23 percent per month to an average of at least 34 percent per month by the end of the second quarter of operations using the new system" are acceptable. Statements like "increase customer satisfaction" are not. Expect to see two, or perhaps three, acceptance criteria for your project. If High-level Requirements have been used as objectives, expect to see at least one acceptance criterion attached to each High-level Requirement. Acceptance criteria generally fall into one of three categories:

- A quantitative metric related to increased revenues (IR)
- A quantitative metric related to avoidance of cost (AC)
- A quantitative metric related to increased service levels (IS)

This list is identified with the acronym IRACIS.

Listing the Major Assumptions/Risks/Obstacles

Put yourself in the shoes of the financial analyst who might ask, "I am being asked to invest $10 million in a new process that is supposed to cut operating expenses by 5 percent per month for the next five years. What risks are we exposed to that might prevent us from achieving that return on investment?" What would you tell the analyst? That answer is what you would list as major risks or obstacles. As another example, you might make senior managers aware of the fact that certain staff skill shortages are going to be a problem, or that the ongoing reorganization of sales and marketing will have to be complete or there will be serious consequences during system implementation.

Gain Co-Managers' Approvals

Because of the SMEs on the Task Force, this approval may require one or more iterations, but these should be more for clarification than content revision.

An Example P2 LEAN Project Brief

PROJECT BRIEF	Project Name **Common Cold Prevention Project**	Project No. **16 - 21**	Co- Project Managers **Earnest Effort** **Hy Podermick**

Problem/Opportunity

There does not exist a preventative for the common cold.

Goal

Find a way to prevent the common cold.

Objectives

1. Find a food additive that will prevent the occurrence of the common cold.
2. Alter the immune system to prevent the occurrence of the common cold.
3. Define a program of diet and exercise that will prevent the occurrence of the common cold.

Success Criteria

The solution must be effective for at least 90% of persons of any age.
The solution must not introduce any harmful side effects.
The solution must cost the consumer less than $20.00 per dose.
The solution must be accepted by the U.S. FDA.
The solution must be obtained over the counter at any pharmacy.
The solution must return at least 20% gross profit.

Assumptions, Risks, Obstacles

Assumption: The common cold can be prevented.
Risk: The solution will have harmful side effects.
Obstacle: Drug manufacturers will hinder the search for a cure.

Prepared By **Earnest Effort** **VP Project Management**	Date **6-14-2016**	Approved By **Hy Podermick** **VP Research & Development**	Date **6-16-2016**

Figure 7.2   Example P2 LEAN Project Brief

Prioritize the Scope Triangle Parameters

You might be asking: "Why prioritize the scope triangle parameters?" and "Why now?" Those are fair questions. Here is the rationale—you want to avoid having to make these decisions when you are in the heat of battle; that seldom gives a good result. You will have to assign these priorities anyway, so do it now, while in calmer times and when you can think clearly. A trade-off matrix like that shown in Figure 7.3, is a simple, yet elegant tool for facilitating the prioritization discussion, and can be a good reference when such information is useful for decision situations that will arise later in the project.

There are five parameters that define the P2 LEAN Scope Triangle. They are prioritized into a list with no ties. The list is used primarily as part of the decision support for processing changes during Stage Planning. It is important to have these priority discussions as part of Version Planning. Postponing such decisions is not a good practice for complex project management.

CREATE THE P2 LEAN INITIATION STAGE PLAN

This is basically the plan for conducting the P2 LEAN SET-UP Phase and the activities in IP (Initiating a Project). It is done only once, as it is a plan for the SET-UP Phase, which is also done only once per project. The SET-UP Phase includes:

- Select the project Core Team
- Design the project approach

Priority Variable	Critical (1)	(2)	(3)	(4)	Flexible (5)
Scope				**X**	
Quality			**X**		
Time	**X**				
Cost					**X**
Resource Availability		**X**			

Figure 7.3   P2 LEAN Scope Triangle Example Prioritization Matrix

- Create the High-level Project Plan
- Prepare the PID

The Initiation Stage Plan must address how these four activities will be done. The Initiation Stage Plan is a product of the IDEATION Phase and is an exercise to decide *if* and *how* a project can be justified to address the Project Mandate. The purpose of the Initiation Stage is to decide if the project should be approved and funded. The contents of the Initiation Stage Plan are:

- Project description
- Prerequisites
- External dependencies
- Planning assumptions
- Lessons incorporated
- Monitoring and controls
- Budgets
- Tolerances
- Stage Product Descriptions

AUTHORIZING THE SET-UP PHASE

The Project Brief, Business Case, and Initiation Stage Plan form the package that is forwarded to the Project Executive to seek approval to enter the SET-UP Phase. It would not be unusual for the Project Executive to return the submission with questions to be answered before that authorization is granted. The questions might be for clarification, but might also require revision of the package. For example, some of the questions the Project Executive will want to answer include:

- How important is the problem or opportunity to the enterprise?
- How is the project related to the corporate strategic plan?
- Does the goal statement follow logically from the problem or opportunity statement?
- Are the objectives a clear representation of the goal statement?
- Is there sufficient business value as measured by the Business Case to warrant further expenditures?
- Is the relationship between the project objectives and the acceptance criteria clearly established?

- Are the risks too high and the business value too low to justify continuing with the project?
- Can senior management mitigate the risks identified?

The answers will support the decisions.

PUTTING IT ALL TOGETHER

StageGate #1 is the end stage assessment for senior management approval to proceed to the P2 LEAN SET-UP Phase. Along with this approval is the release of the resources that will be needed for that phase. Since requirements elicitation can be a labor-intensive activity, it is not done until StageGate #1 approval is granted. There is still a lot about this project that has to be defined before any version planning work can be done, and one more approval step (StageGate #2) before the actual work of the project is authorized and budgeted by senior management.

There will be occasions when the Project Brief is not approved. This usually means that the sponsor and co-managers have not made a compelling argument for the business viability of their intended approach to the problem or opportunity. Despite the fact that the business need may be critical, the risk of failure is weighed against the expected business value of the solution. Expected business value may not justify the cost of the project. It does not mean that the project is not important to the senior executives, just that the approach chosen does not make good business sense—some other approach is needed. The sponsoring business unit is invited to revise and resubmit the Project Brief. Alternatively, the Project Brief may be rejected without further consideration.

In the IDEATION Phase, an idea has been brought from a very informal statement of need or opportunity to an initial definition of one or more prioritized projects, and finally to a choice of the initial project to be pursued. The IDEATION Phase is ended with a one-page statement of that project, and is then forwarded for senior management approval. The IDEATION Phase is an essential first step to defining a project and seeking the resources and authorization to proceed to the Project SET-UP Phase.

PART 3: PRINCE2 LEAN AND THE SET-UP PHASE

The objective of Part 3 is to take the Project Product Description and Project Brief as input to a four-step process in which the output is the project management approach that will initiate the EXECUTION Phase. We say *initiate* because the unpredictable dynamics of a complex project may suggest a revision to that project management approach. This SET-UP Phase is unique to PRINCE2 (P2) LEAN. It is a powerful tool that strictly adheres to the 7 Lean Principles. At the same time, it easily adapts to the P2 Framework and should not create any issues. It has no equivalent in P2 other than the fact that P2 is an adaptive framework and could include a similar process without any suggestion as to what that process might entail.

The SET-UP Phase overlaps both the Starting Up (SU) and Initiating a Project (IP) Processes. The Project Executive and Project Co-Managers would have been appointed as part of the SU Process and the project approach; and Core Team members from the IP Process. The P2 LEAN SET-UP Phase involves four steps and a Stage Gate:

- Determine Project Quadrant
- Choose best-fit Project Management Life Cycle (PMLC) Model Type
- Assess project characteristics
- Choose and modify specific PMLC Model Template
- StageGate #2

PLANNING FOR THE SET-UP PHASE

The Project Co-Managers are appointed once the authorization for the SET-UP Phase has been given. It is their job to plan for the SET-UP Phase.

8

SELECTING THE PROJECT CORE TEAM

---

*The hammers must be swung in cadence, when
more than one is hammering the iron.*
—Giordano Bruno, Italian philosopher and astronomer

*Very small groups of highly skilled generalists
show a remarkable propensity to succeed.*
—Ramchandran Jaikumar, Harvard Business School

*The organization makes demands on the individual to learn something
he has never been able to do before: to use organization intelligently,
purposefully, deliberately, responsibly ... to manage organization ... to
make ... his job in it serve his ends, his values, his desire to achieve.*
—Peter F. Drucker, Management consultant and writer

CHAPTER LEARNING OBJECTIVES

This chapter will provide readers the knowledge or ability to:

- Understand that the PRINCE2 (P2) LEAN project team contains all of the skills and competencies that the project requires
- Understand that the P2 LEAN project team is self-directed and self-managed

- Meaningfully apply the decision-making authority of the co-managers to maximize the probability of project success and the delivery of expected business value

The P2 LEAN project team is a unique entity. In the spirit of agile, it is a self-managed and self-directed team. Some would even argue that such a team doesn't need a project manager. That is not the case with a P2 LEAN project team, however. The Co-Manager Model is a critical success factor for complex project execution and for the delivery of the expected business value in a high-risk project that has no assurance of success. All that can be promised is the best effort possible, given the constraints. From a process perspective, many of the management and decision-making constraints have been removed. The P2 Project Board is not present in the P2 LEAN Framework. Instead P2 LEAN Project oversight is under the advice and counsel of a Project Review Board. From a product perspective, the Co-Manager Model gives the client and the typical project manager equal authority and decision-making responsibility. In the spirit of lean, it is self-contained in that it includes all of the skills and expertise that will be needed throughout the project life span. Furthermore, all non-value-added work has been removed. The result is a P2 LEAN Framework that embodies the best processes and practices possible. The P2 LEAN Framework creates a robust management environment that thrives on business challenges and the creativity of the team—with the change process as the driver to solution discovery.

THE P2 LEAN PROJECT TEAM TEMPLATE

The P2 LEAN Framework provides a project team template. It is the beginning of the process to define the team architecture that will be used for a specific project.

The important characteristic to note in Figure 8.1 is the degree to which the members are interlinked. It is very much like a nonhierarchical structure. This is a mirror image of the typical agile project team. An open and honest working relationship among all of the members is essential. The problem being solved or the business opportunity being exploited is complex, and an acceptable solution is not guaranteed—the more complex the project, the higher the risk of failure. Any barriers to success are unacceptable, and that includes the project team organization. So this team structure is very supportive of the interactive nature required for the successful execution of a complex project.

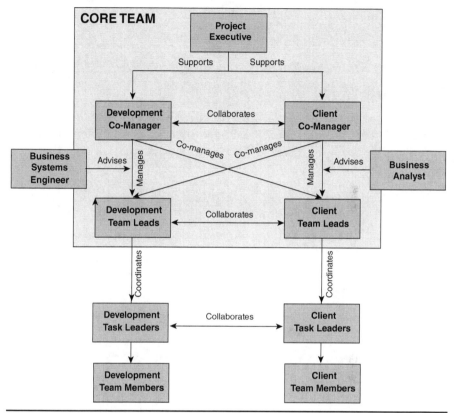

Figure 8.1   The P2 LEAN Project Team Template

Project Executive

The P2 LEAN Project Team does not have a Project Board in the sense that a P2 project does. In place of the Project Board, the P2 LEAN Project Team is accountable to the Project Executive, who can be the Sponsor or a Program Manager if the project is part of a larger program; or a Portfolio Manager if the project is part of a portfolio. The Project Executive could collectively stand for all three of these senior managers. It all depends on how the project fits within the corporate strategic plan. The role of Project Executive is to make up or down decisions regarding the project or a stage of the project. The remaining roles and responsibilities of the P2 Project Board are assigned to the co-managers. The centralization of these roles and responsibilities is in line with the lean principles of the P2 LEAN Framework. The communication interfaces between Project Executive and the co-managers has been minimized in the P2 LEAN Framework. This directly impacts non-value-added work time and protects the lean principles of the project.

Co-Manager Model

The Co-Manager Model is the most effective management model for achieving and sustaining meaningful client involvement in the complex project space. It has been used in the U.S. since 1991 on a number of complex projects. It has become a requirement for several reasons:

- Improved scope planning and requirements management at Client Checkpoints
- Early realization of business value through incremental product/service delivery
- Leverages client product/service expertise and create client ownership of deliverables
- Efficiently supports iterative solution discovery and maintains lean principles

Any reference to the *Complex Project Team* is a reference to the team shown in Figure 8.1.

The first and perhaps most important advice we can offer is to adopt the Co-Manager Model, where the complex project is co-managed by a client representative with decision-making authority equal to that of the Development Co-Manager. That includes the design and implementation of the Complex Project Methodology and all the projects that utilize the methodology. For that to succeed, the co-manager should be a high-level manager from the client side of the enterprise. That person must be capable and willing to get meaningfully involved on a day-to-day basis. Token representation is not going to work. Unfortunately, the higher you go in the enterprise, the greater the risk that you will end up with token representation. That would be the death of a complex project. Treat each case as unique and proceed accordingly. You need someone who can provide ideas and visible support. This Co-Manager Model is fundamental to successful complex project management. One manager is from the developer side, and the other is a high-level manager from the client side. Line-of-business managers, functional managers, and resource managers are often good choices as well. Both managers are equally involved and authorized to make all decisions and share in the success and failure that flow from their decisions. If you put your reputation on the line in a project, wouldn't you participate in the project to protect your reputation and your business interests? You bet you would.

So the project is technical and the client is not, and they want to know why you want them as your co-manager. That's easy. Before the project was a technical project, it was a business project, and it needs a business person as a major partner and decision maker. The project team should not be forced to make business decisions. As the technical project manager, you want every decision to be the best business decision possible, and your client is in the best position to make that happen.

Keep the client in the best possible position to make those business decisions in a timely way. Given the need for a business decision, the project team can often present alternatives, maybe rank them, and even offer costs and benefits. Give the client whatever information you can to help them decide. Then step back and let them decide, based on whatever business criteria they wish to use.

In the complex project world, holistic decisions—those that balance task feasibility and business value—are even more important and critical. In these projects, either the goal or solution (or both) cannot be clearly defined at the beginning of the project. The search for an acceptable business outcome drives the project forward. Again, the client is in the best position to choose the alternative directions that lead to the deliverables that produce acceptable business value. Present the feasible technical alternatives to the client and let them choose the best alternative. These iterations are repeated until there is convergence on a goal and solution that achieves the expected business value, or until the client terminates the project because it isn't heading in a fruitful direction. The remaining time, money, and resources can be redirected to a more likely goal and solution. This strategy speaks of a team/client partnership. Without it, success is unlikely.

The complex project is a high-risk project. The client is the best subject matter expert (SME) for an overall mitigation plan to manage and contain that risk. Integrating agile practices such as the Effective Complex Project Management (ECPM) Framework benefits the P2 LEAN Method in a number of ways:

- Improved scope planning and requirements management at Client Checkpoints
- Early realization of business value through incremental product/service delivery
- Leverages client product/service expertise and create client ownership of deliverables

- Efficiently supports iterative solution discovery and maintain a lean process

The lessons from the Co-Manager Model are clear. No one can claim a corner on the knowledge market (i.e., more than one SME may be needed), and the client and every team member must be given a chance to contribute openly, in a brainstorming fashion, to the solution. Creativity is a critical component and must be openly encouraged and practiced. The development team and the client team can form a formidable partnership, if given the chance, and exploit the synergy that results. Ownership of the resulting solution can only come from giving all of the stakeholders an equal opportunity to meaningfully participate in the development of the solution. Ownership of the solution, leads to ownership of the implementation. Since it was their solution, they wouldn't let it fail. The client took the lead. How often can you claim that?

Business Systems Engineer and Business Analyst

The Business Systems Engineer and the Business Analyst roles are consultative to the project team. These are the SMEs in most complex projects. These roles can be filled by one or more professional staff. Both of these roles are familiar with the parts of the business that affect or are affected by the project deliverables.

Development Team and Client Team

The development team needs no further explanation at this point, but the client team can be more complex than you might first envision. The client team can consist of those in a single business unit or multiple business units, and the activities of those teams are quite straightforward. Where multiple business units are involved in the same project, the situation can become far more complex. The complexity begins at the Requirements Elicitation Phase and continues to the end of the development efforts. Competing and contradictory requirements often arise. In extreme cases, multiple interfaces or user views in the solution can resolve contradictory requirements. It takes a village to successfully deliver a complex project.

An Overall View of the P2 LEAN Framework Project Team

Implementing these practices takes project manager leadership and courage. For some clients, that requires selling the idea because they were the ones who responded to the request to participate by saying they were not technical and couldn't contribute to a technical project. The selling proposition is that even though they may not be technical, the developer is not an expert in their line of business or business function. So by combining their separate kinds of expertise, they can produce an effective solution and create the expected business value that justified approving the project in the first place. They bring the business knowledge and experience to the table, and the developer team brings the technical knowledge and experience. Together, they create the synergy needed to find creative solutions in the midst of a complex project world.

As emphasized in the earlier text, involvement of the client and the users of the end product is essential. Let's see how the standard P2 project organization deals with this. As Figure 8.1 shows, the client (customer) is involved at the top in deciding who should take on the various roles. The Project Board contains the three decision-making roles for the project. The Project Executive holds the budget and is ultimately responsible to the client for the successful delivery of the end products. In almost all cases, this role is filled by a manager of suitable seniority from the client. The role corresponds exactly with the ECPM Sponsor role.

The Senior User role is a manager from the client area where the end products will be used. This role confirms that the specification accurately describes the user needs and at the close confirms that the end product meets that specification and the acceptance criteria. There is a strong link between this P2 role and the ECPM Client Co-Manager.

The P2 project team has a Project Assurance role. This, in fact, is a "team" of roles: Business Assurance, User Assurance, and Supplier Assurance. It is the job of User Assurance to monitor the project on behalf of the user, and can directly relate to the Business Analyst role in ECPM. The User Assurance role works with the project manager, but reports to the Senior User. Between them, the roles of Senior User and User Assurance combine the ECPM roles of Client Co-Manager and Business Analyst. On the surface, the P2 role of Senior User has more authority and may be more remote than the ECPM Client Co-Manager, but sensible professionals can establish a good working relationship.

The ECPM role of Business System Engineer matches the PRINCE2 role of Supplier Assurance. There is, of course, no barrier to including business systems engineers as development team members.

The P2 role of Team Manager corresponds directly with the ECPM role of Task Leader. P2 has teams, and it is normal in complex projects to have a client team working on the specification, working with the development teams in creating a design that will meet the specification, and co-operating in all work. Whereas Figure 8.1 shows separate teams for developer and client, P2 simply looks at them as teams. They could be separate client and developer teams, as in ECPM, or they could be combined into one team. Keeping them separate, as in ECPM, means fewer management problems.

Looking at the ECPM argument for SMEs, P2 offers the roles of Senior User and User Assurance to provide SMEs for all user tasks, such as product specification, migration planning, and quality verification.

SELECT THE P2 LEAN PROJECT TEAM PROCESS FLOW

The co-managers and Core Team were selected during the IDEATION Phase and have participated in the Starting Up a Project (SU) and Initiating a Project (IP) Processes. Defining and populating the remaining roles is straightforward, as described in Figure 8.2.

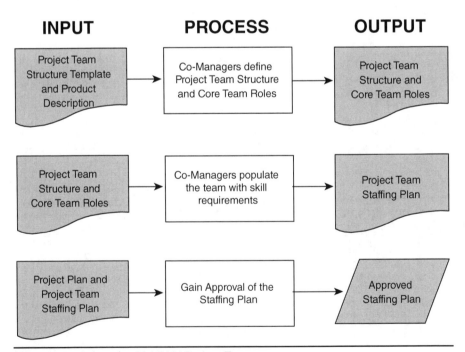

INPUT   **PROCESS**   **OUTPUT**

| Project Team Structure Template and Product Description | → | Co-Managers define Project Team Structure and Core Team Roles | → | Project Team Structure and Core Team Roles |

| Project Team Structure and Core Team Roles | → | Co-Managers populate the team with skill requirements | → | Project Team Staffing Plan |

| Project Plan and Project Team Staffing Plan | → | Gain Approval of the Staffing Plan | → | Approved Staffing Plan |

Figure 8.2   Select the P2 LEAN Project Team

Co-Managers Define Project Team Structure and Core Team Roles

Identifying P2 LEAN project team roles is a challenge simply because there are any number of unknown unknowns that only the stages can uncover. Choosing the Core Team is the beginning of the activities that will result in defining not only the roles that will be needed, but also the specific positions that can fill those roles. So the infrastructure has to provide not only the position family but also the career and professional development program to create an inventory of current and future positions.

Figure 8.3 describes the inputs to conducting this activity. The Lessons Log is a historical account of previous experiences defining such teams based on comparisons to previous and similar projects. In those accounts, specific individuals may have demonstrated a skill and competency that will be valuable to the present staffing needs. In addition to the co-managers, the Core Team will have been formed, and they will have particular insights into what will be required of the project team structure they developed.

In general, the Core Team roles include:

- Risk Management
- Issues Management
- Scope Bank Management
- Bundled Change Management
- Vetted Portfolio Management
- Project Review Management

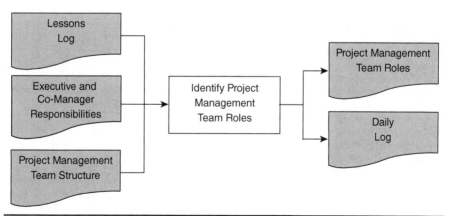

Figure 8.3   Identify Project Management Team Roles

- Communications Management
- Project Notebook Management

These roles need to be assigned to a team member or retained by the co-managers. The assignment could be rotated or fixed for the project life span.

Co-Managers Populate the Roles with Skill Requirements

Roles, plus specific skills, will eventually translate into position titles; and after schedules are available, specifically named individuals will be appointed to the P2 LEAN Project Team. Some of these individuals will be assigned full-time to the project; others for only the window of time for which their expertise is needed.

Performing this activity effectively requires an infrastructure and several support functions. The Project Support Office is the organizational entity that will provide those support functions. At a minimum:

- A P2 LEAN Position Family must be defined and operational
- A Career and Professional Development Program must be in place
- A training curriculum must be readily available in both real time and in online delivery formats
- A Human Resource Management Process must be in place

These are not optional—they are required. (See Chapters 15 and 16.)

Gain Approval of the Staffing Plan

At this point the staffing plan can only be defined at the position title level. This information is in the Project and Stage Plans. Specific individuals cannot be named until a Project and Stage Schedule is in place. Resource Availability is a critical variable in the P2 Lean Scope Triangle. The Core Team of the P2 LEAN project team has been named because their participation is needed during SET-UP Phase Activities.

The Staffing Plan is submitted for approval along with the already approved High-level Project Plan. Staffing requirements are identified by position title and, to the extent possible, are filled when those positions will be needed in the project schedule. All of this schedule information is contingent on what actually happens during the project up to the point where those resources are needed. The Resource Managers will have all of the data they need to allocate specific individuals to the project, either as members of the Core Team or assigned to specific stages.

PUTTING IT ALL TOGETHER

The P2 LEAN Project Team is unlike teams that you have seen in the past. In the agile world, such teams are self-directed and self-managed. This is possible because the team includes all of the skills and competencies needed to successfully execute the project. The P2 Team is co-managed, which is unlike any other team you will have encountered. That co-management assures the delivery of the best solution from a delivered business value standpoint than any other team structure. But, as we pointed out, it cannot succeed without having the infrastructure and support services in place.

9

DESIGNING THE PROJECT APPROACH

To do easily what is difficult for others is the mark of talent.
To do what is impossible for talent is the mark of genius.
—Henri Frederic Amiel, Swiss journalist and critic

She is efficient in doing things right, and ef-
fective in doing the right things.
—Anonymous

CHAPTER LEARNING OBJECTIVES

This chapter will provide readers the knowledge or ability to:

- Classify a project into the four-quadrant landscape; categorize the project as Linear, Incremental, Iterative, Adaptive, or Extreme; and choose a specific Project Management Life Cycle (PMLC) Model for project execution
- Know how project characteristics as well as internal and external environmental conditions will alter the chosen PMLC Model for a better fit to improve the likelihood of generating the expected business value
- Create the project approach using the vetted portfolio of tools, templates, and processes

The Project SET-UP Phase of the PRINCE2 (P2) LEAN Framework is unique. That uniqueness gives the P2 LEAN Framework a powerful and effective process for successfully managing any type of project from IDEATION to the end of its product's useful life. First, few project management books discuss the decision processes and practices over the entire project life span. Second, and most important—but often overlooked—the P2 LEAN Framework is based on the fact that every project is unique and to a certain extent, the best approach to managing it will also be unique. Finally, a project is a dynamic entity that changes for all sorts of reasons—both predictable and unpredictable—and for that reason the best management approach will also be dynamic and change along with the changing project conditions that arise during the Project EXECUTION Phase. These three reasons place several challenges on the Development Co-Manager, the Client Co-Manager, the development team, and the client team. They must be constantly vigilant, work as a unified team, and be always ready to accommodate change.

P2 states that it can adapt to any type of project, but offers no details on how that might happen. The P2 LEAN Framework provides several decision models and processes to tailor the project approach to any type of project. These are introduced and discussed in detail in this chapter.

Once developed, a project management plan responds to change by changing the plan. While that may work in most cases, the complex project landscape is such that a change in the PMLC Model may be the correct response. The P2 LEAN Framework is designed to accommodate that type of change, too. It is unique in that respect.

The P2 LEAN SET-UP Phase is unique to the Effective Complex Project Management (ECPM) Framework and to the P2 LEAN Framework, as well. You will not find anything resembling it in any other PMLC Model. It contains the analytic tools and decision models the team will need to build and maintain the *recipe* for the success of a specific complex project.

P2 LEAN COMPLEX PROJECT SET-UP PHASE

The Project SET-UP Phase begins with a definition of the business problem or untapped business opportunity, and the high-level definition of solution requirements as described in the Project Brief and Project Product Description. These are input from the IDEATION Phase. The SET-UP Phase proceeds to choosing and adapting the best-fit management model to effectively discover, develop, and deploy a solution to the specific business problem and/or untapped business opportunity. These management models include project management, and may also include systems development, business process design, and process improvement. Chapter 16 discusses the vetted portfolio of tools, templates, and processes for those details. Figure 9.1 illustrates the steps that are executed during the Project SET-UP Phase.

The P2 LEAN Framework leads the Project Executive and Project Co-Managers through a decision model to define that management process and implement any adaptations to better align with the project situation. The SET-UP Phase consists of Steps 4–7, shown in the shaded SET-UP Phase boxes in Figure 9.2. These steps define a comprehensive process

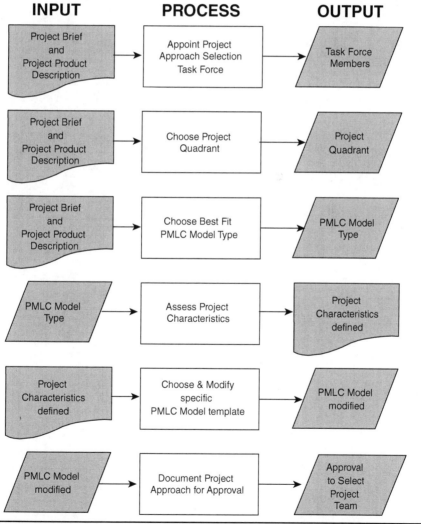

Figure 9.1   P2 LEAN Project SET-UP Phase to Select Project Approach

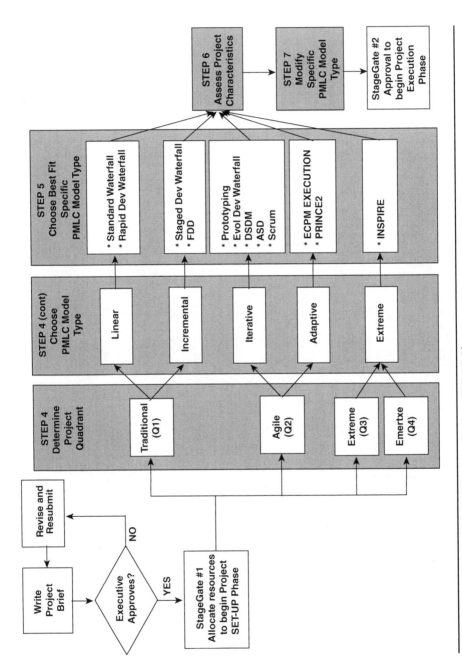

Figure 9.2   A look inside the P2 LEAN Project SET-UP Phase

embedded in the organization's P2 LEAN Framework. We are going to limit our discussion to the specific P2 LEAN Framework that derives from a P2 foundation. In other words, our selection process is limited to a P2 environment; but keep in mind that the project management environment is far more encompassing.

The definition of the P2 LEAN Framework project management approach has come a long way with the approval of the Project Brief and Project Product Description, but there are still several questions to be answered before we can request approval to enter the EXECUTION Phase of the project.

- What type of project is this?
- What is the best-fit PMLC Model type from among the five choices?
- What specific PMLC Model should we use?
- What modifications will be needed to align with the project characteristics and its total environment?

These questions will be answered in Steps 4–7 (the shaded portions of Figure 9.2) with the constraint that we are embedded in a P2 project management foundation.

Appoint Project Approach Selection Task Force

The business definition of the project is done, but the technical aspects of the management approach are yet to be defined. This task force is a technical task force, but it does include client representation through the Client Co-Manager and other product-facing members of the Core Team. That definition requires the special process and product expertise of the co-managers supported by the technical skills of the developers and product skills of the client. These will be identified as the Core Team and its members, as shown in Figure 9.3. (See Chapter 8 for a detailed discussion of the P2 LEAN Project Team.)

The Core Team includes both generalists (the Project Executive and Project Co-Managers) and specialists (Business Systems Engineer, Business Analyst [BA], Development Team Leads, and Client Team Leads). The co-managers and specialists form the Project Approach Task Force. These team members have been identified by position and by name. This task force is self-contained and includes all of the expertise needed to conduct Steps 4–7 in Figure 9.2. The Core Team members participate in the project over its entire life span. They can be 100% assigned to the Core Team but that is not a requirement for membership. Such would be the case with the specialists.

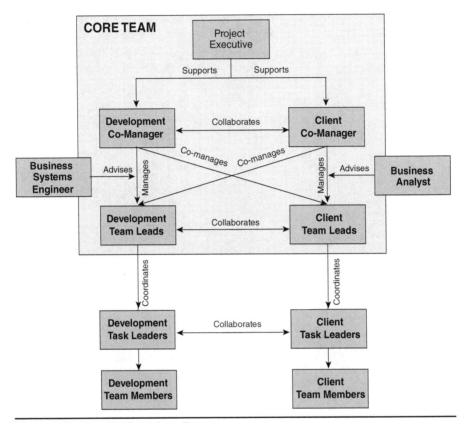

Figure 9.3   The P2 LEAN Core Team

Choose Project Quadrant

Recall from Chapter 2 that the project landscape was a four-quadrant landscape, as shown in Figure 9.4.

The purpose of the project landscape is to provide a simple structure that the co-managers could use as the beginning point as they searched for the best-fit PMLC Model. Once they had assigned the project to a quadrant, they could determine the best-fit PMLC Model Type within that quadrant. That choice will be based on a subjective assessment of the degree to which the current but incomplete product breakdown structure (PBS) has been documented. Once the best-fit PMLC Model has been chosen, the specific model choice and its modification will be a function of the project's characteristics as well as its internal and external environment.

The choice of quadrant should follow directly from the Project Brief and the Project Product Description Document. In these documents the

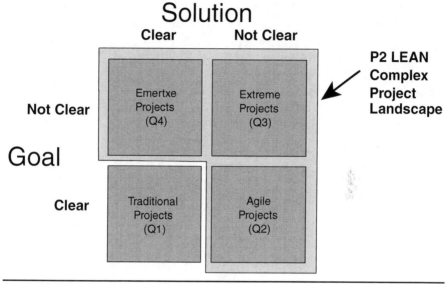

Figure 9.4   The Complex Project Landscape

necessary and sufficient set of high-level requirements will have been defined as well as the acceptance criteria. As part of the elicitation process, there will be some visibility into the level of detail associated with each of those requirements and how they might be delivered. Some progress will have been made with respect to decomposition. We don't expect that to be complete but we do expect to gain some visibility into how near or far that complete decomposition is known.

The decision is based entirely on goal and solution clarity or lack thereof. The most important part of that decision is whether or not the project belongs in Q1. If you aren't sure, don't guess; place the project in Q2 or Q3, as appropriate. That is perfectly acceptable and will not negatively affect the outcome. In fact, it will usually positively affect the outcome. This initial decision is based on the best information available at this early stage and is used to choose the project quadrant.

Choose the Best-fit PMLC Model Type

At this point, the project has been classified into one of the four quadrants of the project landscape. Within the quadrant, we now have to choose a PMLC Model Type from among Linear, Incremental, Iterative, Adaptive, and Extreme to manage the project. Once the PMLC Model type is determined, the next step is to choose a specific PMLC Model as the best fit.

Five types of models populate the project landscape as defined in Figure 9.4. These are shown in Step 5 in Figure 9.2. Note that the only substantive graphical differences between the five PMLC Models are the feedback loops shown in Figure 9.5. In the Linear case, there is no feedback. In the Incremental case, the feedback loop is to the next increment with the scope and plan remaining intact. In the Iterative and Adaptive cases, both feedback loops are to the next just-in-time plan. However, at the detailed level, the purposes and interpretations are quite different. For the Extreme case, the feedback loop is to the scoping phase, where both the goal and solution can be reset.

Within the chosen PMLC Model Type, the portfolio of PMLC Models is in the organization's P2 LEAN vetted portfolio. Using Figure 9.4 as an example, there are 14 specific PMLC Models in the recommended P2 LEAN vetted portfolio (Figure 9.6). These models form the starting PMLC Model Portfolio. Your organization will have their own PMLC Model Portfolio, which will cover the types of projects in their landscape. The contents of an organization's portfolio will be a matter of the industry in which it practices project management; the history of project management in the organization; the types of projects encountered; and, the human resource base modified by its experiences and preferences.

Assess Project Characteristics

So far the selection process has chosen an out-of-the-box model, but the process is not yet complete. That selection is presented to the task force as a predefined recipe to be followed. In some organizations, deviations are not allowed. This *one-size-fits-all* approach will frequently fail, especially in the complex project world. The data bears this out.

One of the first projects that started the journey to ECPM Framework design was a 1994 implementation of the Effective Project Management Model, 3rd Version (Wysocki and McGary, 2004), but with a twist. Beginning with this model as the starting point, the client defined 42 processes for their version of the implementation. Of the 42 processes, only 11 were required for every project. The others were optional, and could be used or modified at the discretion of the co-managers. As we began sharing these processes with the co-managers, they pointed out projects they had managed where they felt that exceptions to the 11 required processes should be allowed. In some cases, those exceptions would involve varying how the

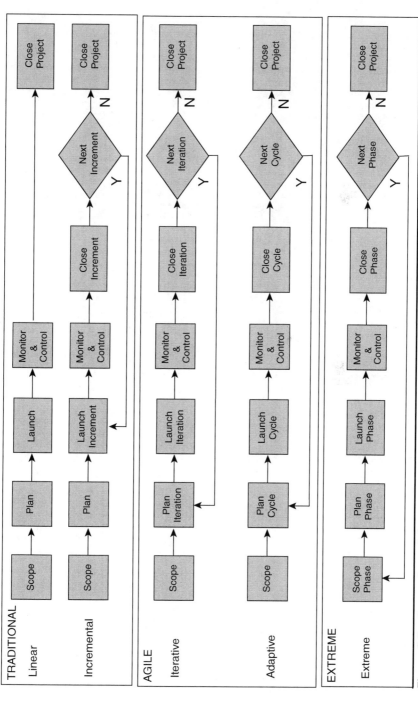

Figure 9.5   Comparison of the 5 PMLC Model Types

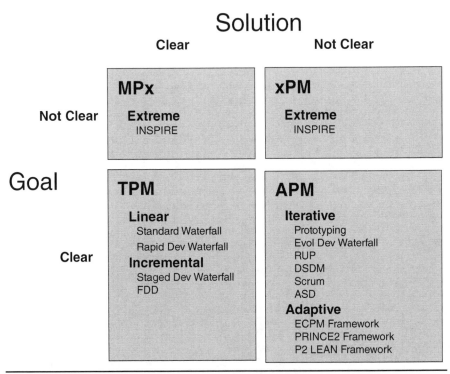

Figure 9.6   Specific PMLC Models in the vetted portfolio

defined process was designed; in other cases, the exceptions would be to not do the process at all. The final version of the client's methodology included the required 11 processes, and allowed the co-managers to deviate, but only with an accompanying justification and rationale for their actions. Almost immediately, team morale increased and the co-managers were thankful for their new authority. In time, project failure percentages began to decrease. That result was taken to the next level, deciding that no project management methodology could possibly account for all contingencies and that flexibility and adaptability would be a critical success factor in the ECPM Framework. That became a requirement in the P2 LEAN Framework and has been met without compromise.

Once the best-fit methodology has been chosen, it will need to be modified to meet the constraints and conditions imposed on the project by the project's characteristics; and it will need to be continuously adjusted as the project work commences and those conditions change. The characteristics that suggest modifications to the best-fit methodology and that have had an impact on the chosen PMLC Model in client engagements are:

➤ Project Characteristics:

1. Risk
2. Cost
3. Duration
4. Complexity
5. Goal and solution clarity
6. Team skills and competencies
7. Completeness of requirements

➤ Internal Characteristics:

8. Business value
9. Technology used
10. Client involvement
11. Organizational stability
12. Organizational velocity
13. Number of departments affected

➤ External characteristics:

14. Market stability
15. Business climate
16. Competitor behavior
17. Breakthrough technologies

For example, the best-fit PMLC Model for your complex project might be to use Scrum with the addition of a senior project manager, instead of a Scrum Master directly participating as a member of the Scrum team, and a senior level BA or Business Process Manager in the role of product owner. All of these adjustments to the standard Scrum Model will have been driven by the project characteristics and the environment in which the project is to be conducted. So, to be successful, your project management approach is unique to the details of the project and its internal/external environment.

Every project is continuously impacted by one or more of these characteristics, and therefore, the best-fit project management approach is likewise impacted. Furthermore, it is not a *once-and-you-are-done* impact. As the project changes, the solution begins to emerge, and any one or more of the internal or external characteristics changes, so could the best-fit project management approach also change. If we are to effectively manage this ever-changing environment, we need a framework to guide our decisions on choosing and adjusting the best-fit approach. That framework is the P2 LEAN Framework.

Choose and Modify the Specific PMLC Model Template

The choices for a specific PMLC come from among approaches such as Waterfall, Scrum, P2, and many others. We have included specific PMLC Models (see Figure 9.6) in the P2 LEAN/kit. Organizations will have a preference, along with skilled and experienced potential team members to adequately staff their preferences. Scrum is an extremely powerful and popular choice in many organizations, but it requires a senior-level developer, who can work without supervision in a self-managed situation. That puts a strain on many organizations, whose developers are often less experienced.

Our emphasis in this book is on P2, so we are building a P2 LEAN Framework within the PMLC Model Template choices. However, for completeness, the organization should include PMLC Model Templates for their P2 LEAN Framework.

Which Specific PMLC Model Is the Closest Fit?

Based on the project characteristics, which specific PMLC Model is the closest fit? The initial decision is made without a consideration of the environment in which it will be implemented. It is based solely on goal and solution clarity.

Should the Chosen PMLC Model Be Adjusted for Better Alignment?

Based on the internal and external characteristics, the chosen PMLC Model may need to be adjusted for better alignment. A consideration in regard to this adjustment is: *what is the best way to convey this information?* Suppose the project is in the adaptive category, and Scrum is the PMLC Model choice. Scrum requires meaningful client involvement through their representative, the Product Owner, but such an individual cannot be identified. As an alternative, an iterative approach, such as the Rational Unified Processs or Evolutionary Development Waterfall Model might be used, the difference being that the project manager and a senior-level business analyst can function as co-project managers. Together, they can take a more proactive role than otherwise would have been done by the Product Owner.

What if There Isn't a Good Fit with a Specific PMLC Model?

The choice of a specific PMLC Model is not an absolute requirement. There have been cases where the vetted portfolio of PMLC Models does not offer a good fit, or the closest fit will require so many adaptations that it loses all identity with the original PMLC Model.

Advice for Complex Project Co-Managers

The best advice for the complex project co-managers is to *do what makes sense*. After all, complex project management is nothing more than organized common sense.

The objective is to deliver expected business value, not to be compliant with an existing recipe.

In those cases, it serves no useful purpose to force fit the approach into an existing recipe. The P2 LEAN Framework offers a bottom-up process to design a custom approach. The creative skills of the chef are needed here.

While every situation will be unique, we can offer some guidance on how that exercise might be conducted. The P2 LEAN Framework is defined by 7 processes and 44 activities. Of those 44 activities, 27 are labeled "A." The labels A through D are ordered from most significant to least significant, so that the A activities are required of even the smallest and simplest of projects. As the project becomes larger, more complex, or uncertain, "B" Activities are added, then "C," and finally "D." This classification scheme is based on the MoSCoW method of *must do, should do, could do, won't do*. Many of these 27 activities will have more than one version that the co-managers could use, but they have to use one of them or offer a reasonable alternative. The Core Team should walk through each of the 7 processes to build the *recipe* for managing their P2 LEAN Project. The vetted portfolio will assist with the construction of the *recipe*.

➤ **Starting Up a Project (SU)**

- A   Appoint Project Executive and Project Co-Managers
- D   Capture previous lessons
- A   Prepare the Business Case
- A   Identify High-level Requirements (Epics in P2)
- A   Write the Project Brief
- A   Plan the Initiation Stage

➤ **Initiating a Project (IP)**

- A   Authorize the Initiation Stage
- A   Appoint the Core Team
- C   Select the project approach
- A   Choose and adapt the best-fit PMLC Model
- B   Prepare the Risk Management strategy
- B   Prepare the Quality Management strategy
- C   Prepare the Communication Management strategy
- C   Set up project controls
- A   Create High-level Project Plan
- A   Create Benefits Realization Plan
- D   Refine Business Case (if needed)
- A   Assemble Project Initiation Documentation

➤ **Controlling a Stage (CS)**

- B   Capture, examine, and escalate issues and risks
- D   Review Stage status
- A   Take corrective action
- A   Conduct Bundled Change Management
- A   Authorize Work Packages
- C   Review Work Package status
- A   Receive completed Work Packages

➤ **Managing Product Delivery (MP)**

- B   Accept Work Package
- B   Execute Work Package
- A   Deliver Work Package

➤ **Managing a Stage Boundary (SB)**

- A   Update Project Scope Bank
- A   Plan Next Stage
- C   Update Project Plan
- C   Update Business Case
- C   Update Benefits Realization Plan
- A   Report Stage end

➤ **Closing a Project (CP)**

- A   Recommend project closure
- A   Create End of Project Plan

- A   Hand over products
- D   Evaluate the project
- A   Prepare End of Project Report

➢ **Planning a Project (PL)**

- A   Initiation Stage Plan
- A   High-level Project Plan
- B   Team Plans
- A   Next Stage Plan
- A   End of Project Plan

Document Project Approach for Approval

StageGate #2 is the approval of the project management approach for the given project. It is the authorization to execute the Project Plan. The need for this approval will be new to sponsors and clients because they will not have encountered it in any other PMLC Model. Those who participate in this approval will need to understand that this is not just a formality. The approval includes the allocation of the infrastructure resources needed to support the adapted or custom-built PMLC Model. It is also a signal to the resource managers that they will be called on for that support as well.

PUTTING IT ALL TOGETHER

The four steps in the SET-UP Phase start with an approval to begin planning the project. No detail of how the project will be done has been discussed. The project must be classified in the appropriate quadrant of the project landscape (Step 4). Within that quadrant there will be several PMLC Models to choose from. That decision process is embodied in Step 5. The ECPM Framework does not assume that the chosen PMLC Model will be an off-the-shelf solution to the project management approach. Rather, the chosen PMLC Model might have to be adjusted based on internal and external characteristics within which the project will be executed. Those characteristics are assessed in Step 6, and any adjustments made in Step 7.

The SET-UP Phase is a unique part of the P2 LEAN Framework. It has been labeled the *create the recipe* phase of a P2 LEAN Project. It is unlike anything you will find in a commercial project management model. In its uniqueness, the SET-UP Phase brings a flexible and creative dimension to ECPM. But it comes with some baggage, too. The P2 LEAN/kit defines the tools, templates, and processes available for the recipe—it is your *pantry*; that is fixed. The creative part is how you use that pantry.

The complex project characteristics that will influence the recipe have been identified. Some characteristics are known at the outset of the project and can be accommodated with the contents of the pantry. Other characteristics are dynamic and can change during project execution. That change brings into play a series of decisions that you will not have made from using any other PMLC Model. Do not expect these to be yes/no decisions. Expect to identify a number of possible actions from which a choice must be made. In most cases, expected business value will be the criteria for making the choices.

10

PREPARING THE PROJECT INITIATION DOCUMENTATION

Learn to write well or not to write at all.
—John Dryden, English poet

*How well we communicate is determined not by how well
we say things but by how well we are understood.*
—Andrew S. Grove, CEO, Intel Corporation

CHAPTER LEARNING OBJECTIVES

This chapter will provide readers the knowledge or ability to:

- Understand the uniqueness of the SET-UP Phase with respect to its contribution to the PRINCE2 (P2) LEAN Framework and the proposed project
- Create the High-level Project Plan
- Refine the Business Plan using the High-level Project Plan
- Create the First Stage Plan
- Create the first pass at the Benefits Realization Plan (BRP)
- Prepare the Project Initiation Documentation (PID) as a convincing argument for Project Executive approval of the project for the P2 LEAN EXECUTION Phase

The Project Mandate has been further analyzed and a Business Case developed that produced a feasible project that has since been approved by the Project Executive. The project now enters the SET-UP Phase, and the deliverable is the PID. The PID contains all of the information that is needed to authorize project execution. The purpose of this chapter is to establish the PID and gain Project Executive project approval for the first entry into the EXECUTION Phase. At the completion of each stage, the PID is updated. The update is discussed in Chapter 11.

Preparing the initial PID includes these activities:

- Prepare the Risk Management Plan
- Prepare the Quality Management Plan
- Set up project controls
- Create the High-level Project Plan
- Create the BRP
- Refine the Business Case, if necessary
- Assemble the PID
- Submit PID for Project Executive authorization to enter the SET-UP Phase

THE PROJECT INITIATION DOCUMENTATION

The P2 LEAN Project Brief and Initiation Stage Plan have been approved by the Project Executive and the project has entered the SET-UP Phase. During the SET-UP Phase a number of documents will have been prepared and packaged for submission to the Project Executive to obtain authorization to enter the EXECUTION Phase. That packaging is called the PID. All of this detail will be reported in the PID along with a request to approve entry into the P2 LEAN EXECUTION Phase.

The PID is the input to the Project Executive for an up or down decision authorizing the EXECUTION Phase. The first stage execution completes the activities described in the PID. The Next Stage Plan is developed at or near the completion of the first stage activities and submitted for approval. This second stage is actually the beginning of the sequence of stages that discover and integrate solution components. If the project is part of a program or portfolio, it is prioritized and scheduled. The scheduling commits the resources to the schedule dates.

The PID is a comprehensive description of the project and its solution, based on what is known at the completion of the previous stage. First, it provides the Project Executive with the information needed to authorize the EXECUTION Phase. Second, it is a documentation package that is continually updated at the completion of each stage so that the Project Executive is not only abreast of project performance and progress but also is provided with the information needed to continue the project to the next stage.

The Input-Process-Output diagram for creating the PID is simple and is shown in Figure 10.1.

The purpose of the Initiation Stage is to offer the details of how the project will be executed to produce the expected benefits. In a sense, it is an intermediate step to assess the feasibility before significant resources are

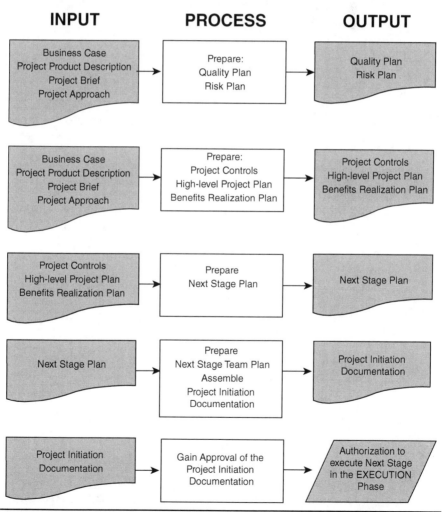

Figure 10.1 Prepare and assemble the Project Initiation Documentation

committed. Risk, quality, configuration, and communications are important parts of that assessment. The Initiation Stage is approved based on the Project Brief, the High-level Project Plan, the Business Case, and the PID. The PID is a collection of documents that describes the business and technical details of the product and the High-level Project Plan for delivering that product. Keep in mind, however, that the actual product that will be delivered is somewhat speculative. Either the goal or solution, or both, may not be clearly defined at the outset. What are clearly defined are the performance requirements that the delivered product must satisfy. Whether those requirements can be fully met is not guaranteed. So the P2 LEAN Project is a high-risk project. With that as a given, the PID is the proposal that the Project Executive will use to authorize the EXECUTION Phase.

The P2 LEAN PID Table of Contents (TOC) is slightly different than in the P2 PID, because it is tailored to agile projects where either the goal or solution, or both, are not clearly known at the outset of the project. The input documents that have already been developed are listed below and the further Initiating a Project (IP) activities that are needed to prepare the P2 LEAN PID TOC are listed in chronological order below:

➤ **Existing documents**

- Business Case (Chapter 5)
- Project Product Description (Chapter 6)
- P2 LEAN Project Brief (Chapter 7)
- Project Team Structure and Role Descriptions (Chapter 8)
- Project Approach (Chapter 9)

➤ **IP Activities**

- Define Quality Management Strategy
- Define Risk Management Strategy
- Establish project controls
- Create High-level Project Plan
- Define Benefits Realization Strategy (BRS) and Create Plan
- Create Next Stage Plan
- Create Next Stage Team Plan
- Assemble PID

The IP activities are described in the following text. Note that the P2 LEAN PID does not contain a Version Control activity. In a P2 LEAN Project, issues are brought up as they arise and their resolution assigned during daily 15-minute team meetings. Some of the issues impact the current stage and their resolution is required, others are longer term. This is standard procedure in the Effective Complex Project Management (ECPM) Framework and highly recommended for the P2 LEAN Framework. The activity is totally verbal. There are no written reports. There will be situations where the issue cannot be resolved within the scope of authority of the co-managers. These issues are referred to the Project Executive with a suggested resolution. Such occurrences are rare and early termination of a stage will often be the best resolution. Lean principles always apply.

Quality Management Plan

Quality is a critical success factor in every P2 LEAN Project:

- **Process quality** is monitored and adjusted using a Project Review Board. The Project Review Board is chaired by the Project Executive and staffed by two to three senior-level project managers who have no vested interest in the project except that its processes achieve certain performance standards. Some level of detail is discussed in the PID. The ECPM Framework includes a continuous process improvement program that runs concurrently with every complex project. We highly recommend the same for the P2 LEAN Framework.
- **Product quality** is continuously monitored by the Client Co-Manager. Product quality is measured against product performance criteria that are defined in the Project Brief. The Project Brief includes quantitative and measurable success criteria against which the acceptability of the solution is continuously evaluated.

The Quality Management Plan includes a process component prepared under the direction of the Development Co-Manager Core Team and a product component prepared under the direction of the Client Co-Manager. Together the Project Co-Managers are responsible for project quality planning to include:

- Quality Planning Process
- Quality Assurance Process
- Quality Control Process
- Quality records to be kept

Quality is one of the P2 Themes and is entirely consistent with the P2 LEAN Framework. In the P2 LEAN Framework, the acceptance criteria, which are documented in the Project Brief, form the standard against which the quality of the process and the quality of the delivered products is assessed.

Risk Management Plan

A solid Risk Management Strategy is essential because a P2 LEAN project is a high-risk project—basically because it is a complex project. This is simply a reality of the complex project landscape and for that reason, a continual effort at managing risk is critical to P2 LEAN project success. To assure that risk management happens, a member of the Core Team will have management responsibility for risk across the entire project life span. A complete Risk Plan is documented in the PID. This plan is equivalent to the P2 Risk Theme with adjustments due to the complexity and uncertainty associated with agile projects. See the P2 2009 Edition (AXELOS, 2009) for details on developing a Risk Management Plan. The only change from the P2 Risk Theme brought on by P2 LEAN is assigning risk management to a Core Team member for the project life span.

The Risk Management Plan includes a plan that embraces:

➤ **Risk Identification**

There are four risk categories: technical risks, project management risk, organizational risk, and external risks. Each of these categories can impact the five parameters that define the scope triangle, and they should be identified. A matrix, such as the one shown in Figure 10.2, is a good template to use as a checklist for that identification exercise.

➤ **Risk Assessment**

The ECPM Framework utilizes a worksheet that is highly recommended for use in the P2 LEAN Framework. Figure 10.3 is an example of the

RISK CATEGORIES	SCOPE TRIANGLE PARAMETERS				
	Scope	Time	Cost	Quality	Resources
Technical					
Project Management					
Organizational					
External					

Figure 10.2 Risk Identification Template

RISK TYPE	SCOPE TRIANGLE	EVENT NO.	EVENT	Y/N	Prob.	Impact	Priority	Mitigate Y/M/N
External	Scope	ES01	Changing competition	Y	M	M	L	M
		ES02	Unexpected regulations	N				
	Time	ET01	Vendor priorities	Y	H	H	H	Y
	Cost	EC01	Expecting higher prices	N				
	Quality	EQ01	Poor production yield	Y	L	L	L	N
	Resources	ER01	Misunderstood contract	N				
		ER02	No vendor resources	Y	H	M	H	Y
		ER03	Program budget cuts	Y	M	M	M	M
		ER04	Support staff layoffs	Y	M	H	H	M

MITIGATION LEGEND

Y	Yes
M	Monitor
N	No

LEGEND:

VH	Very High
H	High
M	Medium
L	Low
VL	Very Low

Figure 10.3   Candidate Risk Driver Template and Assessment Worksheet

External Risk rows of that worksheet. See Wysocki (2014) for a complete worksheet. The candidate risks will have been collected from previous similar projects and the worksheet can be tailored to those risks as well as others that may apply.

Team resources will have to be allocated to deal with these risks and their likely impact. There are any number of models that might be employed. The P2 LEAN Framework prefers simplicity whenever possible. To that end, the P2 LEAN Framework uses a risk/benefit matrix. Figure 10.4 is a 5x5 matrix and is our recommendation, but there have been occasions where 3x3 and even 10x10 matrices have been used.

The matrix is populated with the assessed risks and the shading tells the story. Risks that fall in the darkest cells are ignored. Risks that fall in the lighter shaded cells will be considered if resources are available. Risks that fall in the lightest shaded cells require action to be taken.

> ### Risk Mitigation

There are five mitigation strategies that can be employed for each risk. They are:

- **Accept**—There is nothing that can be done to mitigate the risk. The co-managers just have to accept it and hope the event does not occur.

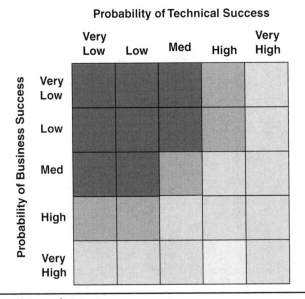

Figure 10.4   Risk/Benefit Matrix

- **Avoid**—The project plan can be modified so as to avoid the situation that creates the environment for the risk occurring.
- **Contingency Planning**—If the risk event occurs, what will you do?
- **Mitigate**—What can you do to minimize the impact should the risk event occur?
- **Transfer**—Pass the impact should the risk event occur (i.e., buy an insurance policy to cover the loss caused by the impact).

➢ **Risk Monitoring**

For those risks that will be monitored, it is a good strategy to establish tripwires. These are conditions that, if they happen, a response is put in place to mitigate the impact. For these risks another tripwire is established for further mitigation responses. A Risk Register should be kept and posted in a place where the team will see it.

Project Controls

This process establishes control points and reporting arrangements for the project, based on the project's size, criticality, risk situation, the customer's and supplier's control standards, and the diversity of interested parties.

In order to keep the project under control it is important to ensure that:

- The right decisions are made by the right people at the right time
- The right information is given to the right people at the right frequency and timing.

The Project Co-Managers are responsible for establishing the monitoring and reporting necessary for day-to-day control, and confirming the correct level of reporting and decision points for the Project Executive to ensure that the proper oversight is maintained. This is achieved by taking the following actions:

- Read the Project Brief to understand if there are corporate or program standards of controls to be used by the project
- Review the project's quality and risk plans to identify their control requirements
- Check the Lessons Log for any lessons relating to project control
- Confirm project tolerances have been set by the Project Executive
- Ensure that escalation procedures across all project management levels are in place
- Agree on the format and frequency of reports to the Project Executive

In the ECPM Framework, project control is center stage. Daily 15-minute team meetings are a required and effective control mechanism. The managers of the Work Packages that are open for work attend these meetings. They report the status of their Work Packages using the following statements:

- I am on plan.
- I am x hours behind schedule, but have a plan to be caught up by (give the date).
- I am x hours behind plan and need help.
- I am x hours ahead of plan and available to help other Work Package managers.

An update of risk status can be included. Any attendant problems are not discussed but are taken off-line with the appropriate parties. There is no taking of pizza orders for lunch or other irrelevant discussions.

Any variances from the Stage Plan or the Work Packages are immediately identified and corrective actions applied before the variance becomes a significant problem. This approach minimizes the need for a formal reporting structure and supports the lean principles upon which the P2 LEAN Framework is based.

High-level Project Plan

The Project Brief has been approved and the P2 LEAN Project can enter the SET-UP Phase, where the initial plans are developed. There are two plans to be developed. The first is a high-level plan for the entire project. Recognizing that the goal and solution may not be well-defined, the High-level Project Plan will be an outline of how the project will be approached from a management perspective rather than a detailed plan. That outline becomes reality as a result of a sequence of stages whose products contribute to the goal and solution. The actual management approach will have been designed in Chapter 9. With that in hand, a High-level Project Plan will include the following activities:

- Write the Project Product Description
- Create the product breakdown structure (PBS) for the known products
- Decompose the PBS for the known products
- Write the Product Descriptions
- Identify resource requirements
- Document the plan

At the completion of each stage, the Project Plan will be updated (see Chapter 11).

Executing the above list of tasks produces the High-level Project Plan and is the primary input to creating the Next Stage Plan. As part of its decision on whether to proceed with the project, the Project Executive needs to know how much it will cost and how long it will take. Details of the Project Plan also feed into the Business Case to indicate the viability of the project.

If the Project Executive makes a general decision to proceed with the project, it needs to have more detailed information about the costs and time of the next stage before committing the required resources.

A PBS should be created at this time, containing all the high-level requirements. This is a hierarchical description of all the requirements that must be present in the solution in order to deliver the business value expected. The PBS should be decomposed, where necessary, to provide more information on what needs to be part of an acceptable solution. At this point, we do not descend to low-level detail or move farther into the technique to look at *how* we will provide the products.

The Project Co-Managers are responsible for delivering the products from this activity. This is achieved by taking the following actions:

- Review the Project Brief to understand what the project has to deliver, along with any prerequisites, constraints, external dependencies, and assumptions
- Understand the selected project approach
- Check the Lessons Log for any appropriate lessons
- Check the risk and scope banks for anything that might affect the Project Plan
- Identify any planning and control tools to be used
- Decide on the method of estimating to be used
- Review the four strategy documents to assess what allowances in planning should be made to meet the time and resources needed for their work
- Use product-based planning to create the Project Plan
- Confirm the availability of the required resources
- Create or update configuration item records for the products in the plan
- Analyze project risks
- Modify the plan accordingly
- Decide on a tentative breakdown of the project into stages
- Decide on the average stage length

- Review the conditions of satisfaction to see if it needs updating
- Initiate the Next Stage Plan activity
- Check that both plans meet the requirements of the quality management strategy

Create the First Draft of the Benefits Realization Plan

The BRP is a term that appeared in P2 2009 but was never defined. P2 2009 defines the Benefits *Review* Plan and states that it will be part of the program's BRP. No discussion of a BRP was included in TSO 2008. The term fits very well with our treatment of benefits strategy and planning, so we have adopted it and provided details appropriate to the P2 LEAN Framework. It will also add two activities to the P2 LEAN Framework Planning Process. We will have occasion to develop a Benefits Realization Strategy (BRS) and a BRP. The BRS and BRP are defined in Chapter 4 and discussed in detail in this chapter. The BRP is updated in Chapter 11 and finalized in Chapter 14.

The project is approved based on the business value that it will return to the organization. That doesn't happen by accident—it must be designed into the project, i.e., it requires planning. That will happen first through establishing a BRS, which we discussed in Chapter 4. That will become the guide to a continuous product improvement program. Second, this occurs through the support of a plan at the stage level to encourage that improvement.

> **Definition: Benefit**
>
> A measurable positive impact on the business from having implemented one or more of the project products that have been accepted by the client.

Project products have to meet the acceptance criteria for the solution to be acceptable to the client. Once the client accepts and deploys the project products, the products should result in benefits accruing to the business. These benefits will be observable over a period of time, often long after the project has been closed and all but its Project Executive moving on to other assignments. Some benefits will be measured by existing business processes, but if measuring accrued benefits will be required, that must be spelled out with a plan.

Rather than simply walking away when the end product has been handed over, there is a requirement to create a BRP, describing when and how measurement should be made of the achievement of the expected benefits. This plan is outlined during initiation, refined at each stage end, and finalized as part of closing the project. The co-managers are responsible for its creation, but since the project team will be disbanded at the close of the project, responsibility for implementing the BRP belongs to the Project Executive.

Figure 10.5 is a graphical depiction of the BRS that we have designed into the P2 LEAN Framework. Implied in the BRS is a cause-and-effect relationship. The cause is meeting the acceptance criteria and implementing the project products. The effect is to change the business in some way. Now, some of these benefits will have been identified in the Business Case and may be the basis for approving the project for further planning. There will also be benefits that accrue from effects that were not visualized. Let's take a deeper dive into the consequences of deploying the project products.

The deployment of the approved project products will have consequences with respect to the benefits accrued. Most of those consequences will have been expected, others not. The intended consequences are those that will have been described in the Business Case and will generate business value, i.e., benefits. There will also be consequences that were not expected, i.e., unintended consequences. These could be positive or negative with respect

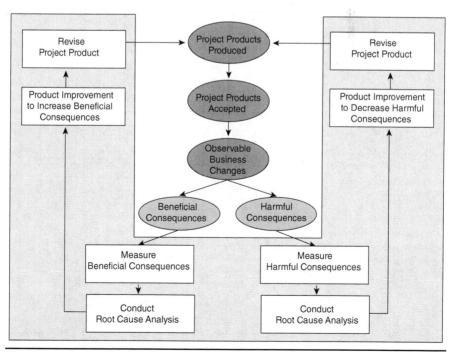

Figure 10.5 Benefits Realization Strategy

to the business value generated. A continuous product improvement program is designed into the P2 LEAN Framework, so the BRP will include programs to increase the beneficial consequences and decrease the harmful consequences. These will all involve adjustments to the project products. Some programs will be significant enough to initiate new project mandates.

For those in the P2 community who are new to the complex project world and agile projects, the P2 LEAN Framework will require an adjustment. An agile project can be a major cultural shock to many senior managers because it can take them outside of their comfort zone. They wanted to know exactly what they were going to get, when they would get it, and how much it would cost. That is old school; in an agile project that specificity is not possible. All the developer could do is say something like, "If you give me $50,000 and six months, your representative and I (ah—the co-managers) will do our best to deliver an acceptable solution." There is no guarantee and there can't be one.

If the project involves an unsolved problem or an untapped business opportunity, how could anyone ever state the actual benefits that will be achieved? You can't. No one can. All a sponsor can do is make a statement like, "If you agree to deliver $1,000,000 in net profits or increase sales revenues by 10 percent within three years, I will approve your project." So now you know what the acceptance criteria are, and you set out to achieve them. However, there are unknown unknowns!

So you put a plan together that you and your co-manager hope will deliver that expected business value. You both have done the best you can with the plan. (You have fully implemented the P2 LEAN Framework by the way!) But you don't really know what you will achieve. No one does. All you and your co-manager can do is your best effort. Hopefully it will be good enough, but it might not. So what do you do? Shoot the co-managers if they fail to deliver?

Nobody can really tell you that, or even if the project will find a solution, let alone one that achieves the expected business value. Maybe there is no solution. That could be one reason why it is an unsolved problem or an untapped business opportunity. So how do you approach a P2 client given this reality?

Template for the PBS Plan

The PBS Plan includes:

- A description of the acceptance criteria and the metrics that will be used to measure them.

- A list of the expected benefits that will occur from each of the acceptance criterion.
- When and how will the metrics be reviewed?
- Who from the Client Team will perform the review?
- Time and cost to perform the review.
- For each observed change:

Beneficial Consequence:

- ✦ A description of the observed consequence
- ✦ A link to the expected benefit
- ✦ Measurement used
- ✦ Calculation of the achieved benefit
- ✦ Description of the root cause analysis carried out

Harmful Consequence:

- ✦ A description of the observed consequence
- ✦ Measurement used
- ✦ Calculation of the impact of the consequence
- ✦ Description of the root cause analysis carried out

It may be that a benefit will accrue gradually, so there needs to be a number of reviews of certain benefits at different times. For example, if a benefit was increased performance by staff, there could well be a learning curve to get used to the new process/procedure/software. How much has performance improved after a week, a month, three months?

Measurement of the achieved benefits of the project's end products may not be possible until sometime after the client has begun to use the end products. Part of the project's work is to plan for those measurements, even though the project team will have been disbanded before that plan is required.

Work begins by taking measurements of the situation as it was at the start of the project. This is needed to ascertain what business changes have taken place after use of the project's end products.

Based on these, a strategy is now needed to guide those who do the post-project review on what needs to be done, when it should be done, what skills are needed, and what the likely cost will be. As this is a complex project, the full benefits may not be known at the outset. There also may be harmful consequences that are as yet unknown.

This plan should be updated at the end of each stage as more about the deliverables becomes known and finalized near the end of the project.

Next Stage Plan

The first stage is the Project Initiation Stage, and at this point, that has been completed. Its purpose was to establish the project management approach and prepare the PID, which is used to gain authorization to begin the Project EXECUTION Phase. The input to the Next Stage Plan is the updated PBS and PFD (product flow diagram) from the just completed stage. That plan included the following:

- Probative Swim Lanes products
- Integrative Swim Lane products
- Next Stage duration

See Chapter 11 for more details.

Next Stage Team Plan

The Next Stage Plan is input to the preparation of the Work Packages that will be needed to deliver the stage products. The Next Stage Team Plan will include the following:

- Work Packages to develop the products for each swim lane

See Chapter 11 for more details.

Assemble Project Initiation Documentation

The PID encapsulates all the information discussed previously. The PID is necessary for the Project Executive to make the decision on whether to go ahead to the next stage of the project or not. It also forms a formal record of the information on which this decision was based, and can be used after the project finishes, when judging how successful the project was.

PUTTING IT ALL TOGETHER

The PID is the minimum detail needed by the Project Executive to make an up or down decision for Project EXECUTION. It is used for the Initiation Stage, which is the first stage, and for all subsequent stages which are the product delivery stages. The documentation is comprehensive but satisfies the minimal information requirements for continued project approval. Thus, it is consistent with the lean principles upon which the P2 LEAN Framework is grounded.

PART 4: PRINCE2 LEAN AND THE EXECUTION PHASE

The project has been validated from a business perspective and a project management approach was designed and approved by the Project Executive. All that is left to do is the project and the delivery of the expected business value. Part 4 consists of four chapters that cross the project life span.

Chapter 11: *Preparing for the Next Stage* discusses the transition from a just completed stage to the next stage. To begin that transition, the Scope Bank must be updated to reflect the deliverables from the swim lanes and the product breakdown structure. The Next Stage Plan can then be created and the Project Initiation Document updated.

Chapter 12: *Executing the Stage Plan* discusses the process of Managing a PRINCE2 (P2) LEAN Stage Boundary and dealing with issues, risks, and exception events.

Chapter 13: *Closing the Stage* discusses the events that take place as the stage approaches the time box. P2 LEAN takes variance from P2 in that a Stage Plan is not changed during execution of P2 LEAN. It might be terminated early for a number of reasons but it is not changed. If the time box expires, any unfinished products are returned to the Scope Bank for later prioritization and scheduling. The Bundled Change Management Process is executed between stages, not within stages. This is a departure from P2 practices. It preserves the integrity of the Stage Plan and the lean principles and allows for better decision making and control of the change process.

Chapter 14: *Closing the Project* discusses the activities that take place once the project has been approved for closure. Product implementation, training, product installation, project post-audits, project documentation, and administrative contract closure are the primary activities that take place.

11

PREPARING FOR
THE NEXT STAGE

You can never plan the future by the past.
—Edmund Burke, English statesman, orator, and writer

Any plan is bad which is not susceptible to change.
—Bartolommeo de San Concordio, Florentine painter and writer

CHAPTER LEARNING OBJECTIVES

This chapter will provide readers the knowledge or ability to:

- Understand the power of the Bundled Change Management Process as a lean tool
- Appreciate the guiding influence of the Benefits Realization Strategy and Plan
- Update the Project Initiation Documentation (PID) as the proposal to the Project Executive for the authorization to continue to the next stage of the EXECUTION Phase of the project

At this point, the Project Mandate has been further analyzed and a Business Case developed that produced a feasible project that has since been approved by the Project Executive. The project is now in the SET-UP Phase. The deliverable from this phase is the PID. The PID contains all of the information that is needed to authorize putting the project into the

EXECUTION Phase. The purpose of this chapter is to prepare for the next stage. There are nine activities that conclude with authorizing the Next Stage:

- Update the Scope Bank
- Complete the Bundled Change Management Process
- Create the Next Stage Plan
- Create the Team Plan
- Update the PID
    + Update the High-level Project Plan
    + Update the Benefits Realization Plan
    + Update the Business Case
- Authorize the Next Stage

OVERVIEW

This is a key chapter, as it is the guide to the EXECUTION Phase. The key inputs to this chapter are the deliverables from the just completed stage and the output is the Next Stage Plan. The clearinghouse for these activities is the updated Scope Bank and it is reflected in the updated PID. Figure 11.1 captures these activities.

UPDATE THE SCOPE BANK

The Scope Bank is the cumulative history of the project. In that regard it is not unlike the Daily Log. It goes well beyond the issues, risks, lessons, and any quality management issues. The Scope Bank also tracks the history of the planned versus actual deliverables from all previous Probative and Integrative Swim Lanes, the history of change requests that have been acted on and those that are in the queue waiting for a decision and prioritization, an updated product breakdown structure (PBS) and product flow diagram (PFD), and finally the updated High-level Project Plan. All of this data is used to update the PID and create the Next Stage and Team Plans. In this section, let's take a deeper dive into the details of the Scope Bank.

Analyze Actual versus Planned Product Deliverables

At the end of a cycle, unfinished deliverables are returned to the Scope Bank for reprioritization. As a result of learning and discovery of the just completed cycle, unfinished deliverables may never get a high enough priority

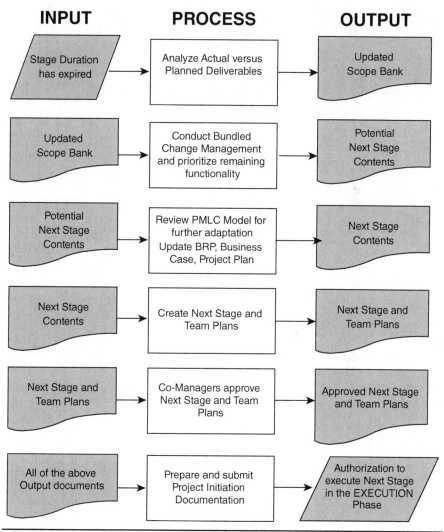

INPUT   **PROCESS**   **OUTPUT**

Stage Duration has expired	Analyze Actual versus Planned Deliverables	Updated Scope Bank
Updated Scope Bank	Conduct Bundled Change Management and prioritize remaining functionality	Potential Next Stage Contents
Potential Next Stage Contents	Review PMLC Model for further adaptation Update BRP, Business Case, Project Plan	Next Stage Contents
Next Stage Contents	Create Next Stage and Team Plans	Next Stage and Team Plans
Next Stage and Team Plans	Co-Managers approve Next Stage and Team Plans	Approved Next Stage and Team Plans
All of the above Output documents	Prepare and submit Project Initiation Documentation	Authorization to execute Next Stage in the EXECUTION Phase

Figure 11.1   Prepare and assemble the Project Initiation Documentation

to be completed in a later cycle. This is quite common, especially when you consider the fact that the work of the stage build plan should be completed according to its priority. The question, then, is what is its priority with respect to other prioritized functions and features waiting in the Integrative Swim Lane list in the Scope Bank?

Any Functionality and Features Planned and Integrated in the Previous Cycle

These are the deliverables from all previous Integrative Swim Lanes, in other words, the current solution. What was delivered will be used to update the solution through the PBS. So, the PBS is a hierarchical map of the current solution. It should be posted in the Team War Room. Through experience, we have found that the updated PBS is one of the most visual artifacts produced in an Effective Complex Project Management (ECPM) project and will carry over into PRINCE2 (P2) LEAN projects. It is also used as an idea generator for planning Probative Swim Lane contents.

Any Functionality and Features Planned but Not Integrated in the Previous Cycle

A stage ends when its time box expires or if all planned deliverables are complete. What was planned in the Integrative Swim Lanes for the just completed stage may not have happened for a variety of reasons. This is not the result of change. It is the result of running out of time or experiencing some other event that prevented the orderly completion of the Stage Plan. Since the stage time box is fixed, any schedule delays that cannot be recovered will result in some Integrative Swim Lane deliverables not being integrated into the solution in the just completed stage. These incomplete deliverables will be returned to the Scope Bank for reprioritization and consideration in some later stage.

Learning and Discovery

The client will need some time to evaluate the most recent contributions to the solution. That evaluation has two aspects to it. The first aspect will be the experimentation with the newly expanded solution, paying particular attention to the functions and features added in the just completed Integrative Swim Lanes. Are other changes suggested from what was just produced? The second aspect is the results from the Probative Swim Lanes. Did you learn about any new functions or features? Are there any clues about other parts of the solution yet to be built? Will additional Probative Swim Lanes be needed to further define these discoveries, or can they be planned for inclusion in the solution through future Integrative Swim Lanes?

Learning and discovery will involve an unedited cumulative list, including ideas generated in the just completed stage and all other ideas not acted upon. Once acted upon, an idea might end up in a future Probative Swim

Lane or Integrative Swim Lane. Until then, the idea remains in the Scope Bank.

Any Changes that Took Place in the Business Environment During the Previous Cycles

These changes will happen outside the control of the project team. A competitor introduces a new or upgraded product that competes directly with the deliverables you expect to produce in your project. This brings a traditional project to a screeching halt in almost every case, but that is not what happens on an ECPM project. Like a good athlete, the co-managers anticipate such changes and can adjust accordingly. Whatever solution existed at the completion of the previous stage may have sufficient business value to be competitive now. If not, all is not lost because the ECPM project can adjust deliverables going forward, and come into the market at a later time with expanded functionality and features.

Probative Swim Lane Results

The Integrative Swim Lanes are well defined, and the development and the stage build plan established. The Probative Swim Lanes are very different. They can be highly speculative, and can change depth of investigation and directions at any time. A good Probative Swim Lane investigation needs to be as adaptable as the situation dictates. The best return will be from a hands-off management style. Let the creative process unfold without any constraints except the stage time box. The Probative Swim Lanes are designed to expand the depth and breadth of the solution. The major question is: Has anything been learned about further enhancements to the solution? A Probative Swim Lane may have three results: to integrate; modify and repeat; or abandon.

Integrate: An Enhancement to the Solution Has Been Identified

Another piece to the solution puzzle has been discovered! It may have taken several Probative Swim Lanes spread over several cycles to reach that conclusion. The discovery may be so significant that a celebration is in order, but don't order the pizza just yet. The solution piece needs to be documented and placed in the Integrative Swim Lane queue for prioritization and consideration in a future Integrative Swim Lane.

Modify and Repeat: This Direction May Produce Results and Should Be Continued

The idea shows promise. Continuing in the same direction or some other discovered direction will be appropriate. It needs to be documented and placed in the priority list for consideration in a future Probative Swim Lane.

Abandon: Nothing New Has Been Identified and this Direction Should Be Abandoned for the Time Being

No idea is ever removed from the Scope Bank. What does not seem like a fruitful direction now may turn out to be valuable later in the project. As work proceeds on a Probative Swim Lane, results may suggest that the basis for the swim lane does not seem like a fruitful direction to pursue. The less that is known about the solution, the more likely that result will be. From experience, the best advice is not to *throw the baby out with the bath water* too soon. I have experienced situations where a past Probative Swim Lane did not produce any immediate insight, but later provided an idea that did. Just remember to put all Probative Swim Lane results (both good and bad) in the Scope Bank for future reference.

Search for New Functions and Features

The less you know about the solution, the more challenging the identification of Probative Swim Lanes and the higher the risk that you will not find that solution at all. Because the project team is journeying into the unknown, do not be discouraged by short-term results. Sometimes it will take several false starts before a promising direction is discovered. Even then, it may take several additional Probative Swim Lanes to fully explore a discovery and then implement it through one or more Integrative Swim Lanes.

Updated Scope Bank

The Scope Bank is the depository for all information on past performance and the potential contents of future cycles. From a graphic perspective, the analysis of project performance follows from longitudinal reports. A simple graphical report is a primitive earned value analysis (EVA), such as the one shown in Figure 11.2. The trend in the gap between *planned* versus *completed* is the important message contained in this report. But it is the effect and a deeper analysis that is needed to discover and correct the cause(s).

The important questions to be answered here are: Did the stage meet its objectives? Did the stage meet its planned functional specifications? If not,

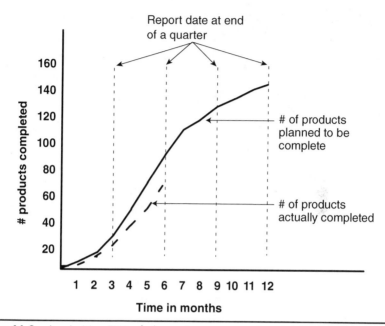

Figure 11.2 A primitive EVA of planned versus completed deliverables by stage

where are the variances? The answers will provide input into planning for the objectives of the next stage and the functionality to be built in the next stage. Remember, you may have already specified objectives and functionality at a high level for the next stage in the Version Scope Phase. So, we have the original scope and potential revised scope to review as we consider what the next stage will contain.

A cumulative history of project performance metrics should be maintained. These metrics should inform the project team about the rate at which convergence to an acceptable solution is occurring. Frequency of changes, severity of change, and similar metrics can help. One metric that has been found useful is to track the size of the Scope Bank over each stage. Figure 11.3 shows three trends in Scope Bank size that have occurred in client engagements.

- **Increasing at an increasing rate**

  An increasing rate of client involvement is the trend displayed in Figure 11.3(a). It indicates a client whose involvement has increased over time, and it probably indicates that the solution is diverging instead

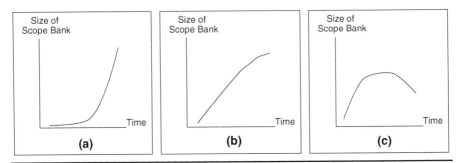

Figure 11.3   Tracking Scope Bank size

of converging. Changes beget changes, and those changes beget even more changes. Sometimes, a change reverses an earlier change! Although it is good to have increased client involvement, it may have come too late for this example. If you see a pattern like this, it may be too late for any corrective action to be taken. Your intervention should have come much earlier so that you would have a chance to work with the client to increase their involvement earlier in the project. The solution would have been to put some tripwires in place as early warning signs that client involvement is below expectations. If this increasing at an increasing rate pattern is what you are experiencing, you may have a run-away project. Whatever the case, you have a problem that needs immediate attention. Further analysis of the underlying causes is needed.

- **Increasing at a decreasing rate**

  Figure 11.3(b) shows that the size of the Scope Bank is increasing at a decreasing rate. That may be a good sign in that the size of the Scope Bank may eventually turn to an actual decrease. That fact that it is still increasing is not good. Like panel (a), it might be indicative that the solution is diverging. Such a trend suggests that it may be too late.

- **Decreasing at an increasing rate**

  Figure 11.3(c) is the desired trend. It shows an exemplary level of client involvement early in the project and good solution convergence. The Scope Bank size should increase for a while. Sooner or later, as the work converges to the final solution, the size of the Scope Bank should start to decrease and continue decreasing until the project has ended.

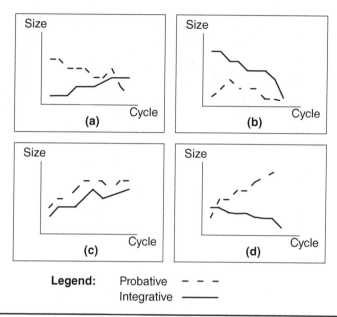

Figure 11.4   Size of Probative versus Integrative Swim Lanes

Tracking the Size of Probative Swim Lanes and Integrative Swim Lanes

The overall size of the Scope Bank is a good indicator of project performance, but it does not tell the whole story. For that, we need to look at the relative sizes of the two swim lanes over time. At the next level of detail, track the relationship between the Probative versus Integrative Swim Lanes over the history of the project. Keep in mind that Probative Swim Lanes supply Integrative Swim Lanes, and that supply needs to be consistent for good stage planning purposes. Figure 11.4 is an example of this type of report. It shows all four possible relationships between the two swim lanes: one is increasing and one is decreasing (a) and (d), both are increasing (c), or both are decreasing (b). Each pattern carries at least one interpretation.

Scope Bank Status Reports

Scope Bank Status reports are longitudinal reports showing the changes and trends in the different contents of the Scope Bank. Changes and trends are simple concepts, but there is a lot of information here and a lot of guidance for future stage planning. As the project progresses, the relationship between the size of the two swim lanes change. Depending on those relative changes, the project can be in trouble or converging as expected toward an acceptable solution.

Figure 11.4(a) generally denotes a successful project. The number of Probative Swim Lanes is decreasing while the number of the Integrative Swim Lanes is increasing. In other words, ideas are being translated into actual solution components. This is the ideal situation. The size of the Probative Swim Lane will continue to decrease as the solution is nearing as complete a solution as is possible for this version. It remains to be seen whether or not the success criteria have been met and business value achieved. There are still a number of Integrative Swim Lanes that are prioritized for inclusion in future cycles. At some point in time, these lanes should begin to decrease, and decrease continuously until the project ends. The project has all of the earmarks of being a success.

Figure 11.4(b) paints a different picture and can be interpreted as follows: both swim lane sizes are decreasing; the numbers of Probative Swim Lanes are decreasing and are not producing usable solution parts, as reflected by a decreasing number of Integrative Swim Lanes; and nearly all Integrative Swim Lanes are complete. If the project is early in its history, the situation is not good. This may be the best that can be done. Either the solution will be acceptable for now, or more work needs to be done. This project is essentially complete, and the current solution may or may not be acceptable. If not, then terminate the project and transfer the resources to a more encouraging solution approach. On the positive side, the solution is nearly complete and that is the reason for the decrease in the size of the Probative Swim Lane. The remaining question is the business value delivered by this solution.

Thus, early in the project, the focus should be on Integrative Swim Lanes. As most of these parts are integrated, the focus will shift to Probative Swim Lanes. Try to keep a good supply of Probative Swim Lanes in each stage so that there will be a steady supply of function and feature additions being discovered and available for integration into the solution. This strategy protects the project from having an incomplete solution and no new ideas for functions and features to be added. The closer the project product is to convergence on the final complete solution, or expending the time and money allocated to the project, the number of Probative Swim Lanes compared to Integrative Swim Lanes should diminish. Late in the project, the goal is to get as much of the solution defined and operational as is possible.

An example should help to illustrate these concepts. This example is an ECPM project where most of the solution is known at the start of the project. For this example, the early cycles will consist mostly of Integrative Swim Lanes. As they are moved out of the Scope Bank and integrated into the solution, their numbers in the Scope Bank will decrease. As learning and discovery takes place, the number of potential Probative Swim Lane ideas waiting in the Scope Bank to be acted upon will increase. That increase is due mostly to learning and discovery about the solution from actually building the solution through the Integrative Swim Lanes. By spreading the Integrative Swim Lanes across the early cycles, you might also discover that the lower priority functions and features that were once thought to be part of the solution may no longer be relevant. You would not know that if you simply used the first stage to build the entire then-known solution. Give considerable thought to that situation. It may save you from wasting the precious time of the developers.

The Project Co-Managers will want to keep a healthy balance between the two types of swim lanes so that there will always be functions and features to be added or discovered. Probative Swim Lanes grow the solution by feeding ideas with business value to the list of functions and features waiting for a priority in the Integrative Swim Lanes.

As the project commences, keep the relative number of ideas for each type of swim lane in balance. What is considered balanced is a subjective decision, something the co-managers get a feeling for as the project progresses. At some point in time, the numbers of each type in the Scope Bank will decrease. This means that the solution is stabilizing and no new ideas are coming forth. Hopefully, the solution is stabilizing into a solution that has acceptable business value. That will always be the final question in an ECPM project. As the project completion deadline approaches, or as the budget is nearly exhausted, the effort should shift entirely toward planning Integrative Swim Lanes and away from Probative Swim Lanes. Your goal is to get as much of the defined solution implemented as possible. Leave untested ideas for the next version.

This is the same interpretation as in the case of Figure 11.4(a). The only difference is that this pattern reflects a project that is much closer to completion than the one described in Figure 11.4(a). It is unlikely that the few remaining Probative Swim Lanes will introduce new solution features. This project is essentially complete.

Figure 11.4(c) shows both swim lanes increasing in size. This is the pattern you would expect to see for a healthy project. The list of functions and features to be integrated is growing, as is the list of ideas for future function and feature exploration. The Probative Swim Lanes are producing good results. If it is early in the project, the project appears to be healthy and should continue. As the project moves into the later stages, both swim lanes should begin to decrease in numbers.

Figure 11.4(c) can also be describing a runaway project. Even though the size of both prioritized lists is increasing, the appropriate question may be related to solution convergence. Is the solution converging to something that will achieve the expected business value? If this pattern continues, that is a strong signal of solution divergence. If not, and the numbers in each swim lane begin to decrease, the project is healthy.

Figure 11.4(d) shows an increasing Probative Swim Lane size and a decreasing Integrative Swim Lane size, and has the following interpretation: the solution is about as complete as it is going to be for the approach taken. Missing parts of the solution continue to be elusive. The increasing number of ideas is not producing any meaningful additions to the solution. This project may be spinning out of control and another approach might have been more productive. You also have to admit that the solution has not been discovered. Either the problem is unsolvable or you may be looking for a solution in the wrong places. In either case, the project should be terminated.

COMPLETE BUNDLED CHANGE MANAGEMENT PROCESS

The lifeblood of a successful complex project is change. Without change, an incomplete solution will never evolve to an acceptable complete solution. The first principle to learn is that every change is a significant change. What that means is that the change process must be open, simple, lean, and as painless as possible to the client, for that is where the bulk of the changes will originate. The P2 LEAN Framework includes a unique Bundled Change Management Process (Figure 11.5) that meets these criteria. Adopt and adapt that process to P2 LEAN projects and you will seldom go wrong.

Note that when the Change Request is received, it is reviewed, and if accepted without change, is added to the Scope Bank. Only when the stage is complete will the change request be analyzed and further action taken. If the change is approved it will be available as early as the next stage.

What that means is that every change requested by the client must be documented in a Project Change Request. Figure 11.6 is an example. That document might be as simple as a memo, but might also follow a format provided by the project team. Only when the request is clearly understood can the project team evaluate the impact of the change and determine whether, how, and when the change can be accommodated.

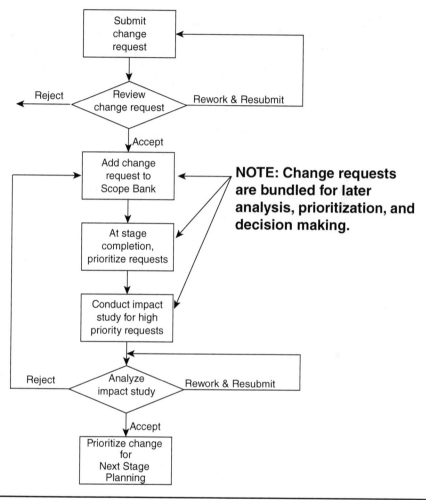

Figure 11.5   Bundled Change Management Process

Change requests can arise at any time and can come from any one of several sources. Furthermore, the request can be well thought out or just a statement like: What would it be like if we could...? Both extremes must be accommodated by the request form that formally enters the idea into the project. The request process begins with a statement from the individual making the request. It is designed to allow the requestor to provide as much detail as is available. The last thing you want is to have a requirement that

Project Name
Change Requested By
Date Change Requested
Description of Change
Business Justification
Action
Approved by   Date

Figure 11.6   Change Request Form

creates an obstacle to suggesting a change. Rather, you would rather have a request form that encourages ideas.

The Action section is critical to the process. It allows the project team to clarify any part of the request. It must be understood in the context of the current solution and future stage planning.

Review Change Requests

One of the strengths of bundling change requests is that every request is reviewed, critiqued, and considered in relation to all of the other open change requests. During Next Stage Planning those change requests are reviewed along with any learning and discovery that occurred during the just completed cycle. There may be some hidden synergies waiting to be exploited in the coming cycles. That is far more effective and efficient than any one-at-a-time approach. It gives the project team the opportunity to group similar open change requests for better decision making and use of resources. There will be situations where the grouping of similar change requests may generate other changes that otherwise would not have seen the light of day.

Add Change Requests to Scope Bank

Until Next Stage Planning starts, the Scope Bank is the holding pen for all change requests. Other than clarifications (the action section), no analysis is done at this early stage. The change request might be categorized according to how it relates to requirements and/or the current solution. That gives better visibility into how change requests might be leveraged as a group rather than individually.

At Stage Completion, Prioritize Change Requests

This prioritization is usually related to how the open change requests align with the possible content of the next cycle. This prioritization is usually nothing more than a classification (like Must Do, Should Do, Could Do, Won't Do [MoSCoW], ABC Analysis, etc.) so that a group of change requests can be further analyzed for inclusion in the next cycle.

Conduct Impact Study for High Priority Change Requests

This is the first detailed analysis of only those change requests that are relevant to the next cycle. The impacts can be to requirements satisfaction, solution development, generation of incremental business value, and risk/complexity/cost/duration estimates.

The response to a change request is a document called a Project Impact Statement. It is a response that identifies the alternative courses of action that the co-managers are willing to consider. The requestor is then charged with choosing the best alternative. The Project Impact Statement describes the feasible alternatives that the co-managers were able to identify, the positive and negative aspects of each, and perhaps a recommendation as to which alternative might be best. The final decision regarding the choice of alternatives rests with the requestor.

The Project Impact Statement involves looking at the project plan, assessing how the change request impacts the plan, and reporting the results to the project team. The project team may return it to the co-managers for further analysis and recommendations. The change request may be accommodated or even rejected with reasons given to the requestor.

Analyze Project Impact Studies

This analysis is designed to build content that will be input to the Next Stage Plan. It is an excellent tool for complex project management. Among the factors to consider are:

- **Schedule**: Any changes to the schedule will almost always have negative effects on completion dates.
- **Resources**: Their availability has already been accommodated in the current stage and project schedules. Schedule changes will almost always upset those commitments and add time to stage and project completion.
- **Risk**: If the changes only impact future cycles, those can be managed. But if the changes impact previous cycles, they can be very disruptive. The point here is that the disruption may result in rework of components of the current solution. The cost of these disruptions needs to be compared with the incremental business value as part of the decision to accept the change.

Prioritize Changes for Next Stage Planning

While you might think that the selected changes start at the top of the priority list and work down until available resources and stage duration limits are reached, that is not necessarily the case. For example, some Change Requests may hold promise of generating excellent business value but the associated risk is high, development time is excessive, and resource requirements are scarce. All of this may give way to Change Requests that deliver business value faster even though it may not be to the level of some other Change Request.

Change Requests can generate Probative or Integrative Swim Lane Work Packages for the next stage. Change Requests focus on *what* is needed in the solution, but not *how* those Change Requests can actually be implemented. The *how* may have several alternatives, and it is not obvious which, if any, are the best choice. That calls for some number of Swim Lanes to investigate the alternative *hows*. In the more obvious situations, the *how* will be obvious, so an Integrative Swim Lane will be planned.

CREATE THE NEXT STAGE PLAN

The Updated Scope Bank and the decisions from the Change Request Process are the major inputs needed to create the Next Stage Plan. That process is shown in Figure 11.7.

The co-managers are responsible, but creating the Next Stage Plan is a team event. This event includes the following actions:

- Check for any changes to the client's quality expectations and acceptance criteria
- Check the Scope Bank for any issues which will affect the Next Stage Plan

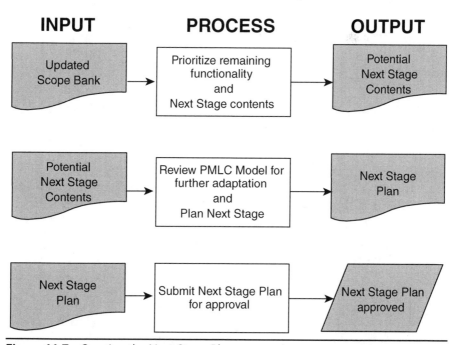

Figure 11.7   Creating the Next Stage Plan

- Review the Project Plan for the products to be produced in the next stage
- Review the Risk Register and Scope Bank for entries that may affect the next stage
- Use the product-based planning technique to create the draft Next Stage Plan
- Document any changes to the personnel of the project team
- Review the Quality Management Plan for the quality standards and procedures to be used
- Add any formal quality reviews and any other quality checks required
- Enter details of quality checks and involved personnel
- Ensure that the plan includes all required management products
- Check the plan for any new or changed risks and update the Risk Register
- Modify the plan, if necessary, in light of the risk analysis

CREATE THE TEAM PLAN

The PBS for the products to be developed in the Next Stage Plan may require further decomposition to allow for accurate estimation of their development time and cost. The completion criteria described in Chapter 4 will be applied to the stage PBS. With the stage PBS in hand, the Work Packages for the stage PBS products can be created. These will be approved by the co-managers.

UPDATE THE PROJECT INITIATION DOCUMENTATION

The P2 LEAN Project Brief has been approved by the Project Executive. That approval is not approval to do the project. It is approval to propose how that project will be executed. Resource requirements and schedules are needed so that costs and benefits can be measured and a decision made as to the real business value that will result. All of this detail will be reported in the PID along with a request to approve entry into the P2 LEAN EXECUTION Phase. The Input-Process-Output diagram shown in Figure 11.7 offers the details of how that PID will be created.

This updated version of the PID followed from just having completed a stage. The completed stage might have been the first stage—the Initiation Stage—or it might have been a development stage. A PID update requires an updated Scope Bank, which includes integrating the results from the just completed stage. The updated PID includes an updated High-level Project

Plan, an updated Benefits Realization Plan (BRP), and an updated Business Case.

Update the High-level Project Plan

The High-level Project Plan can now incorporate the products delivered from the just completed stage. Those results will have been captured in the updated PBS and PFD. All of this is reflected in the enhancements to the solution.

Update the Benefits Realization Plan

As each stage is executed and updates taken, the benefits expected and benefits delivered will change. Then there are the benefits that follow from both the intended consequences and the unintended consequences. The unintended consequences can be either beneficial or harmful. Obviously the co-managers will want to take actions that will improve the beneficial consequences and minimize or remove the harmful consequences. A root cause analysis for these consequences need to be conducted immediately so that adjustments to the BRP can be made and included in the Next Stage and Team Plans. There will also be results from the BRP that was executed during the just completed stage.

Unintended and especially harmful consequences can be problematic. The results of a root cause analysis might suggest revisions, and even that improvement initiatives be conducted to reduce or remove harmful consequences. These will probably result in changes to the BRP.

Update the Business Case

The Business Case is the client and organizational view of what the solution will mean to the business. As the solution evolves, the Project Product Description will often change. More details will have become available to further populate the PBS and PFD. The objectives and acceptance criteria as documented in the Project Brief will also be affected. All of these changes will impact the Business Case.

AUTHORIZE THE NEXT STAGE

The updated PID contains all of the information that the Project Executive will need in order to authorize execution of the next stage. The decision to authorize is based on the fact that:

- The products delivered to date have met or will meet the acceptance criteria
- The variance between planned deliverables and actual deliverables has been well-managed
- The Probative Swim Lane and the Integrative Swim Lane backlogs have been well-managed
- The resources assigned to the project team are sufficient to meet the Next Stage Plan
- The current solution has every indication of converging upon an acceptable solution

If the project is aligned to a program or portfolio, the above criteria must be in line with the acceptance criteria of the program or portfolio.

PUTTING IT ALL TOGETHER

The updated PID is the minimum detail needed by the Project Executive to make an up or down decision for the launch or continuation of the EXECUTION Phase. The authorization that is requested will put the project into a prioritized list for execution or specify an actual start date for the Next Stage.

12

EXECUTING THE
STAGE PLAN

To improve is to change; to be perfect is to change often.
—Winston Churchill, English Prime Minister

To tend, unfailingly, unflinchingly, to-
wards a goal, is the secret of success.
—Anna Pavlova, Russian ballerina

CHAPTER LEARNING OBJECTIVES

This chapter will provide readers the knowledge or ability to:

- Appreciate the significance of Probative Swim Lanes and Integrative Swim Lanes and their interaction with one another
- Interpret the size and trends between the two types of swim lanes
- Conduct a daily 15-minute team meeting
- Execute the Stage Plan as approved

The successful execution of the Work Packages is the essence and strength of a stage. The Probative and Integrative Swim Lanes are very different and their plans are very different as well. Probative Swim Lanes are journeys into the unknown. Some will be successful in their journey of discovery, others will reach dead ends. But in all cases, Probative Swim Lanes contribute to learning about the solution. The products of a Probative Swim

Lane are generally answers to questions and assumptions that lead toward the learning and discovery of product components. Integrative Swim Lanes are production related, in the sense that they update the solution with the products from previous Probative Swim Lanes.

Executing the Next Stage Plan involves these seven activities:

- Authorize Work Packages
- Execute Work Packages
- Review Stage status
- Capture, examine, and escalate issues and risks
- Take corrective action
- Accept Work Package products
- Deliver the Work Package products

AUTHORIZE WORK PACKAGES

The Stage Plan and Team Plan have been approved. These plans include the Work Packages and thus this authorization is a mere formality in the PRINCE2 (P2) LEAN Framework.

EXECUTE WORK PACKAGES

The Work Packages are under the management control of a Task Leader. In some cases they will have a small team to support their efforts. Work Packages are of short duration (usually two to six weeks). They may have a precedence diagram to assist with scheduling and other management control tasks.

> If it isn't in the approved Stage Plan, it is out of scope for the stage. Managing a stage means executing the Stage Plan *without change*!

REVIEW STAGE STATUS

Stage status is reported at 15-minute daily team meetings. These meetings are status briefings only and should be attended by all of the Task Leaders who have Work Packages open for work but not yet completed. Problem resolution is handled offline and with the participation of the involved individuals only, not the team. These 15-minute meetings allow communications to be verbal, not written, and replace many of the P2 report requirements. No problems or issues regarding the stage status or performance of any Work Package against its plan go unnoticed for more than 24 hours. This is the real strength of the project controls features of the P2 LEAN Framework. It is low in non-value-added work and also demonstrates how real-time communication replaces documented reports and preserves the lean characteristics of the P2 LEAN Framework.

CAPTURE, EXAMINE, AND ESCALATE ISSUES AND RISKS

Issues and risks are captured at the daily team meetings. Issues are assigned to the most appropriate team member and risks forwarded to the Risk Manager for processing. Those issues that affect the current stage will be assigned the highest priority for resolution. To the extent possible, the Stage Plan is preserved as originally approved. In a complex project, completing all products planned for a stage is done if possible. That may sound strange because it flies in the face of common practice, but keep in mind that we are executing a project that comes with unknown unknowns. All that can ever be promised is to do the best the team can do in the face of this uncertainty. That is the reason the Stage Plan should be held inviolate. The alternative is to not do any stage planning, but that borders on chaos—especially among the resource managers!

Where an issue threatens to go beyond tolerances, and the Project Co-Managers believe that corrective action cannot be taken within the authority limits imposed by the Project Executive, then the issue must be brought to the attention of the Project Executive for advice. Escalating issues and risks that threaten tolerances should not be seen as a failure. The Project Executive should be made aware of potential problems far more than the actions to be taken when the event has already occurred. Escalation is achieved by taking the following actions:

- If a recommended response has been shared, check for its impact on the Stage and Project Plans, Business Case, and Benefits Realization
- Revise the recommendation if any problems are found with it
- Direct the Project Executive recommendation to the Project Co-Managers

TAKE CORRECTIVE ACTION

Corrective actions of issues discovered during the stage that affects stage performance must be escalated and solved immediately. To the extent possible, the actions taken should not compromise the Stage Plan, especially actions that will change the schedule. The end date of the stage is not altered for any reason other than stage termination or early completion of all Work Packages.

The Project Co-Managers take any necessary actions to remedy the issues that have arisen and that will affect the Stage Plan if not addressed. If the corrective action is to issue a new Work Package or revise an existing one, then the relevant Task Leader will be involved. This is achieved by the co-managers by taking the following actions:

- Ensure that all necessary information about the issue has been gathered and is available
- Identify alternative corrective actions
- Evaluate the effort and cost of the options and the impact of the options on the Stage and Project Plans, Business Case, and risks
- Where necessary, seek advice from the Project Executive
- Select the most appropriate option
- Implement the corrective actions via a new or revised Work Package

ACCEPT WORK PACKAGE PRODUCTS

Upon the stage time box expiring, the completed products are accepted if they meet the acceptance criteria for that stage. This is a client decision based on previously established acceptance criteria that have been verified by the Acceptance Test Procedure for the stage.

There must be an understanding and agreement between a Task Leader (or an individual) and the relevant Project Co-Manager on any delegated work, constraints, interfaces, reporting requirements, and tolerances. The team manager has to be satisfied that the Work Package requirements are reasonable and achievable. This will be reflected in the Team Plan.

DELIVER THE WORK PACKAGE PRODUCTS

This is the formal act of integrating the Work Package products into the solution. That does not imply deployment however. Deployment is subject to the organization's release strategy and schedule. That release schedule will, at most, be quarterly, but usually semi-annual or even annual.

There has to be a process to deliver the requested product(s) and to document the agreement that the work has been done satisfactorily. This is achieved by taking the following actions:

- Update the Team Plan to show completion of the Work Package
- Deliver the completed products for integration into the solution
- Advise the Project Co-Managers that the solution has been updated

PUTTING IT ALL TOGETHER

The stage of a P2 LEAN Project is a unique component. It is unlike the stage of a P2 Project. That uniqueness derives from the fact that a P2 LEAN Stage is executed with a management approach that is largely self-contained. That is the supporting rationale of the Co-Manager Model. All of the authority and expertise needed to successfully execute the project is assigned to the team. The only decision that is reserved to the Project Executive is the approval (or not) of any of the six types of P2 LEAN plans (see Chapter 4 for a refresher on these plans). That does not preclude the co-managers from reaching out to the Project Executive for any other advice or needs as might arise.

13

CLOSING THE STAGE

You've got to think about "big things" while you are doing small things, so that all the small things go in the right direction.
—Alvin Toffler, American writer and futurist

If thou well hast begun, go for the right;
It is the End that crowns us, not the Fight.
—Robert Herrick, English poet

CHAPTER LEARNING OBJECTIVES

This chapter will provide readers the knowledge or ability to:

- Understand that the Stage Plan duration is fixed and does not change
- Protect the Stage Plan without change
- Apply the business rules for closing a stage
- Utilize the Scope Bank as the depository for Work Packages that were not completed in the current stage

With few exceptions, a PRINCE2 (P2) LEAN Stage closes when the time box for that stage has expired. The desired outcome is that all products planned for that stage have been completed. Some major change in the internal situation or external markets may render continuation of the stage and in some cases even the project. This is a decision to be considered by the co-managers and the Project Executive. Stage time boxes are never increased, although a stage may be terminated early.

CLOSING A P2 LEAN STAGE

In the P2 LEAN Framework, a Stage Plan is sacrosanct. It does not change for any reason. It may terminate early either because all of the Work Packages planned for that stage have been completed and the time box has not yet expired, or some risk event has occurred and made continuing the stage a waste of time and resources. In most cases, a stage closes because its time box has expired. Figure 13.1 is the Input-Process-Output diagram for closing the stage.

Normal End of Stage

The normal end of a stage occurs when the time box expires, and has nothing to do with the swim lanes being completed. Any planned work that is

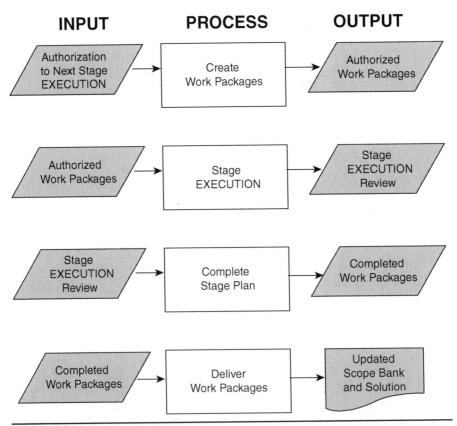

Figure 13.1   Closing the stage

not finished is returned to the Scope Bank for reprioritization and consideration in a later stage. If the Stage Plan has scheduled the development of the stage deliverables based on their position in the prioritized list, then nothing is lost. The work that is not completed will have a lower priority and can be rescheduled perhaps for the next stage, unless its new position on the prioritized list has placed it out of reach of that next stage.

Advice for Scheduling Tasks

To the extent possible, schedule Work Packages and tasks in priority order. That order should be based on business value. That practice gets the most business value into the solution earlier, rather than later. Technical dependencies may affect the priority order. Tasks that cannot be completed within the stage time box will be of lower priority. Incomplete Work Packages are returned to the Scope Bank to be reprioritized to be considered in a later stage.

Abnormal End of Stage

There are two situations to discuss with regard to an abnormal end of a stage: when all Work Packages in the Stage Plan are completed ahead of schedule or not completed within the stage time box.

All Work Packages Completed Ahead of Schedule

First, all deliverables could be completed ahead of schedule. If so, end the stage and proceed to the End Stage Assessment. For each of the swim lane teams, this means finishing their work as soon as possible. Just because the Work Package Manager finishes early does not mean they should stretch out the work to fill the available time. Parkinson's Law has no place in a P2 LEAN Project!

Work Packages or Tasks Not Completed Within the Stage Time Box

It is the end of the workday on Wednesday and the current stage is scheduled to finish at the end of the first shift on Friday. Harry is managing a Work Package in an Integrative Swim Lane and he comes to a co-manager asking for a two-day extension so he can finish his scheduled integration testing at the end of the first shift on Tuesday. It would be nice to get the functionality integrated into the solution. Should you grant the extension? The answer is a qualified *no*.

The Stage Plan and its time box are *sacred* for several reasons. If you said yes, what should the rest of the project team do—just make work to fill the two days? That is a waste of time and the P2 LEAN practitioners are lean practitioners and do not waste time. While Harry is working on his assignment, what does the rest of the project team do? If they work on another project, you might lose them, and then what would you do?

In a P2 LEAN Project, the unfinished work from a stage is returned to the Scope Bank for reprioritization for a later stage—for example, the next stage. There are no exceptions to this rule.

Review Stage Status

It is better to check the status of a stage on a regular basis and take action to avoid potential problems, rather than have problems occur as a surprise, and then have to react to them. The objective is, therefore, to maintain an accurate, up-to-date picture of the work and resource utilization within the stage. The daily 15-minute team meeting is designed just for this purpose. Within the context of these 15-minute meetings, the following should be considered, if appropriate:

- Review progress and forecasts against the Stage Plan
- Review resource consumption against plan
- Decide on and implement any actions in response to problems that have arisen
- Report any changes in the status of any risks
- Check for any changes external to the project which may impact it
- If the end of the stage is approaching, trigger creation of the Next Stage Plan
- If the end of the project is approaching, trigger the Closing a Project Process

PUTTING IT ALL TOGETHER

A Stage Plan is prepared under the guidance of the co-managers and authorized by the Project Executive with every intention of completing it as planned. But that is not the world of the complex project. It is a world filled with the uncertainties and complexities that arise from unknown unknowns and flexibility is the key. "If you don't succeed today, you can come back tomorrow and try again." That could be the mantra of the co-managers. Despite any optimism, planning for that eventuality is smart. The process of learning and discovery is fraught with dead ends and misguided attempts. As long as the cumulative learning and discovery is included in the planning for the Next Stage, the effort will have been rewarded.

Holding the Stage Plan as inviolate and not open to change is a different strategy than is practiced in P2. In the P2 LEAN Framework, every change request is received and held in the Scope Bank for analysis and consideration in the Next Stage Plan. That preserves the lean practice and creates a situation for better decisions during the change management process.

14

CLOSING THE PROJECT

We cannot afford to forget any experiences, even the most painful.
—Dag Hammerskjold, Former Secretary General of the United Nations

We judge ourselves by what we feel capable of doing, while others judge us by what we have already done.
—Henry Wadsworth Longfellow, American poet

CHAPTER LEARNING OBJECTIVES

This chapter will provide readers the knowledge or ability to:

- Understand that the EXECUTION Phase is a dynamic event in the PRINCE2 (P2) LEAN Project. It is repeated for every stage and may have occasion to change the project management model on a stage-by-stage basis.
- Recognize that closing the project is a milestone event in the life span of a product—in that it accepts the current version as the best that could be deployed given current knowledge and capacity of the organization.
- Use the Scope Bank as the bridge between the current version and the next version.

Closing the P2 LEAN Project is fairly routine. The practices are somewhat different than the P2 Framework, however. The client's acceptance of the delivered products occurs when the Acceptance Test Procedure (ATP) has

213

been met. That procedure triggers the co-managers to perform this sequence of events:

- Recommend project closure
- Authorize project closure
- Create the End of Project Plan
- Deploy products to production status
- Evaluate the project
- Prepare End of Project Report

The end of a complex project is a signal to the client that the team has done its best to deliver an acceptable solution and meet the planned benefits and expected business value. The end includes two major activities: install the project product and conduct the Post-Project Audit. Those two activities are the focus of this chapter (see Figure 14.1).

EFFECTIVE COMPLEX PROJECT MANAGEMENT PROCESS FLOW DIAGRAM

Closing a P2 LEAN Project is but one step in the life of a project product. It may be the beginning of the product's life span or the continuation of it with a new and improved *next version*. In the complex project world, each version is related to any preceding versions through the Scope Bank. In that sense it is the history of the product. With that as the reality, the close of this version must establish the transition to the next version.

CO-MANAGERS RECOMMEND PROJECT CLOSURE

A recommendation for closure of the project originates with the co-managers and is sent to the Project Executive. This event is triggered when the co-managers agree that all acceptance criteria have been met. Checking off all of the items on the ATP is that triggering event.

AUTHORIZE PROJECT CLOSURE

This authorization follows from the Project Executive upon verification by the client that the project product meets the ATP checklist of requirements. That is the ultimate *doneness criteria*. Benefits realization will usually follow sometime later in the project product's useful lifetime.

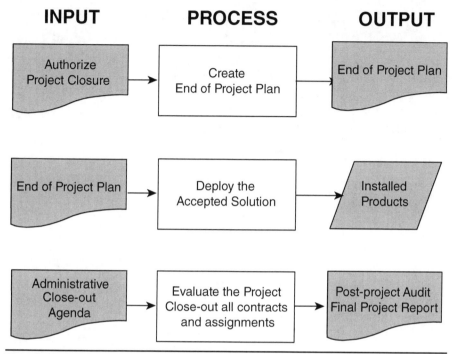

Figure 14.1   Closing the project

Project closure includes completing the following tasks:

- All required products have been integrated into the solution and met all acceptance criteria
- The solution has been deployed to production status and placed under warranty
- The support and maintenance teams have been put in place to service the warranty
- All outstanding issues have been resolved
- Recommendations for consideration in the next version of the product are in the Scope Bank
- Lessons learned during the project have been archived and are accessible to other project teams
- Project performance has been reviewed against the Project Initiation Documentation
- Plans are in place to measure the Business Case objectives and Benefits Realization Plan (BRP)

CREATE THE END OF PROJECT PLAN

Project closure can be normal or premature. Normal closure will follow when all requirements have been met. A premature closure will follow when the project is terminated before all requirements have been met. This type of closure will ensue after some catastrophic event that renders continuing the project a poor business decision.

The End of Project Plan is created through the following actions:

- Update the Project Plan with the actual products delivered from the final stage
- Review the final project product description
- Ensure that, where applicable, those who will be responsible for maintenance and support of the products are ready to accept the product
- Prepare a request to the Project Executive to release project staff and set a date for the formal closure of all documents, invoices, and reports

Just as a Stage Plan may not be completed, so might a Project Plan be incomplete. While many of the reasons may be the same as early stage termination there are some stark differences too. Some of those reasons include:

- A change in the project's priority in the program or portfolio, or a change in its relevance to the Corporate Strategic Plan
- Actions of competitors that might compromise the project product's viability and competitive position rendering continuation a bad business decision
- A technological advancement that replaces the current technological approach to the project product design and requires a significant change in the Project Plan

In addition to the closing actions listed above, the following would be causes for an early termination of the project:

- Identifying any finished or unfinished products that have some salvage value and might be used elsewhere
- Raising any problems caused by the premature termination of the project via the Project Executive and onto corporate/program management

One of the protections offered by the P2 LEAN Framework is that at any point in time there will be a validated solution that can be deployed and begin to generate business value and benefits. Whether or not that solution will be deployed is a separate business decision of the Project Executive and corporate management. The project and its products are not simply abandoned. Every effort will be made to salvage anything useful from the terminated project. This is achieved by taking the following actions:

- Update the Scope Bank, noting the premature close of the project
- Update the Project Plan with final details of costs and times from the terminated Stage Plan
- Check that all issues have been closed and any incomplete ones transferred as follow-on action recommendations
- Check that any open risks that might affect the operational environment have been transferred as follow-on action recommendations
- Ensure that, where applicable, those who will be responsible for maintenance and support of the products are ready to accept those products that were completed or are in a state where use can be made of them
- Ensure that the reason for premature closure is recorded in the Lessons Log
- Prepare a request to the Project Executive to release project staff and set a date for closing all contracts and invoices

DEPLOY THE ACCEPTED SOLUTION

There are three release strategies that are in common use:

- **Single release:**

  This is an old practice that occurs only on simple projects. Multiple releases have been shown to have good return on investment and are in common practice in the learning and discovery stages of a complex project. Current release strategies are designed to generate business value early. One of the weaknesses of a single release strategy is that business value is still an expectation, but all of the time is exhausted and resources spent before any deliverables are released.

- **Releases occur according to an established organizational release plan:**

  P2 LEAN Projects will learn from releases that occur according to an enterprise release plan. That may not be in the best interest of the P2 LEAN Project, but is least disruptive and in the best interest of the enterprise as it attempts to absorb change in the most effective and efficient way.

- **Intermediate releases decided by the co-managers:**

  These are, of course, in the best interest of the project as it works to find and integrate learning and discovery. The feedback gained from the intermediate release of deliverables is valuable. The issue is how effectively the enterprise can absorb change and the ability of the project team to support those intermediate releases. Organizations that use this release strategy will often deploy solutions into a test environment rather than across the entire organization.

The first step of closing a version is to go live with the accepted solution. This commonly occurs in computer systems work. The installation can involve phases, cutovers, or some other rollout strategy. In other cases, it involves nothing more than flipping a switch. Either way, some event or activity turns things over to the client. This installation triggers the beginning of a number of close-out activities that mostly relate to documentation and report preparation. After installation is complete, the deliverables move to support and maintenance status, and the project is officially closed.

There are four popular methods to install deliverables: the phased, cutover, parallel, and by-business-unit approaches.

Phased Approach

The phased approach decomposes the deliverable into meaningful chunks and implements the chunks in the appropriate sequence. This approach would be appropriate in cases where resource limitations prevent any other approach from being used.

Cut-over Approach

The cut-over approach replaces the old deliverable with the new deliverable in one action. To use this approach, the testing of the new system must have been successfully completed in a test environment that is exactly the same as the production environment.

Parallel Approach

In the parallel approach, the new deliverables are installed while the old deliverables are still operational. Both the old and the new deliverables are simultaneously in production mode. In cases where the new system might not have been completely tested in an environment exactly like the production environment, this approach will make sense. It allows the new system to be compared with the old system on real live data.

By-business-unit Approach

In the by-business-unit approach, the new deliverables are installed in one business unit at a time, usually in the chronological order that the system is used. Like the phased approach, this approach is appropriate when resource constraints prohibit a full implementation at one time. Similar to the by-business-unit approach would be a geographic approach where the system is installed at one geographical location at a time. This facilitates geographic differences, too.

EVALUATE THE PROJECT

A Post-Project Audit is conducted to review both the project management process that was used and the product that was delivered from that process. The main focus of the Post-Project Audit is to check how you did with respect to the success criteria, to document what you learned that will be useful in the next version, and to begin thinking about the functionality for the next version.

As part of the Project Brief the co-managers established measurable business outcomes and a BRP. These became the rationale for why the project was undertaken in the first place. The project will have been considered a success if, and only if, these outcomes and benefits were achieved. In many cases, these outcomes cannot be measured for some time after the project has been completed.

Take the case of a project impacting market share—it won't happen next Tuesday; it may happen several quarters later. However, the time frame is part of the success criteria statement as well.

What the client team and the development team believe to be the best mix of functionality has been built into the solution. The project is done. The deliverables are installed, and the solution is in production status.

The Post-Project Audit is an evaluation of the project's goals and activity achievement as measured against the project plan, budget, time deadlines, quality of deliverables, specifications, and client satisfaction. The log of the project activities serves as baseline data for this audit. The following questions should be answered:

1. Was the Project Goal Achieved?

- Does it do what the project team said it would do?
- Does it do what the client said it would do?

The project was justified based on a goal to be achieved. Either that goal was or was not achieved—and the reasons for this must be provided in the audit. This achievement can be addressed from two different perspectives. The provider may have suggested a solution for which certain results were promised. Did that happen? Conversely, the requestor may have promised that if the provider would only provide, say, a new or improved system, then certain results would occur. Did that happen?

2. Was the Project Work Done on Time, Within Budget, and According to Specification?

Recall from the scope triangle discussed in Chapter 2 that the constraints on a project are time, cost, and the client's specification, as well as resource availability and quality. Here, you are concerned with whether the specification was met within the budgeted time and cost constraints.

3. Was the Client Satisfied with the Project Results?

It is possible that the answers to the first two questions are yes, but the answer to this question is no. How can that happen? It's simple: the conditions of satisfaction changed, but no one was aware that they had. The project manager did not check with the client to see whether the needs had changed, or the client did not inform the project manager that such changes had occurred.

4. Was Business Value Realized?

Check the success criteria to see if business value was realized. The success criteria were the basis on which the business case for the project was built and were the primary reason why the project was approved. Did you realize that promised value? When the success criteria are used to measure the improvement in profit, market share, or other bottom-line parameters, you may not be able to answer this question until sometime after the project is closed.

5. What Lessons Were Learned About Your Project Management Methodology?

Companies that have or are developing a project management methodology will want to use completed projects to assess how well the methodology is working. Different parts of the methodology may work well for certain types of projects or in certain situations, and these should be noted in the audit. These lessons will be valuable in tweaking the methodology or simply noting how to apply the methodology when a given situation arises. This part of the audit might also consider how well the team used the methodology, which is related to, yet different from, how well the methodology worked.

6. What Worked? What Did Not Work?

The answers to these questions are helpful hints and suggestions for future project managers and teams. The experiences of past project teams are real *diamonds in the rough*—you will want to pass them on to future teams.

7. What Was Learned About the P2 LEAN Framework?

The refinement of the P2 LEAN Framework for this project was a cooperative effort between the co-managers. This will be a continual process that will be done for every new project. If you think of the P2 LEAN Framework as a thought process rather than a fixed procedure, you will understand why it will continually change and improve in the process. In every project, look for ways to improve the P2 LEAN Framework. Discover and learn about the solution to an improved adaptive complex project framework.

The Post-Project Audit is seldom done, which is unfortunate because it has great value for all stakeholders. Some of the excuses for skipping the audit include:

- **Managers don't want to know**—They reason that the project is done, and what difference does it make whether things happened the way you said they would? It is time to move on.
- **Managers don't want to pay the cost**—The pressures on the budget (both time and money) are such that managers would rather spend resources on the next project than on those already completed.
- **It is not a high priority**—Other projects are waiting to have work done on them, and completed projects do not rate very high on a priority list.

- **There is too much other billable work to do**—Post-Project Audits are not billable work, and people have billable work on other projects to do.

The Post-Project Audit is critically important, especially in a learning organization. It contains valuable information that can be extracted and used in the next version of this project and other complex projects. Organizations have such a difficult time deploying and improving their project management process and practice that it would be a shame to pass up the greatest source of information to help that effort. Don't be misled, however, actually doing the Post-Project Audit takes a commitment because it competes with other tasks waiting for attention, not the least of which is probably a project that is already behind schedule. Implementing the P2 LEAN Framework requires a continuous process and practice improvement program. Completed projects are your most valuable source of ideas for that improvement program.

The business outcome was the factor used to validate the reason for doing the project in the first place. If it was achieved, chalk that one up on the success side of the ledger. If it wasn't, determine why. Can something further be done to achieve the outcome? If so, that will be input to the functional specifications for the next version.

There is also a lesson here for everyone. If projects are limited in scope and they fail, and there is no way to rescue them, you have reduced the dollars lost to failed projects. The alternative of undertaking larger projects is that you risk losing more money. If there is a way of finding out early on that a project is not going to deliver as promised, cut your losses. The same logic works from stage to stage. If you can learn early on that a version will not work, kill the version and save the time and cost of the later stages.

In a traditional project the client would find out a project was not working only after all the money was spent, and then a great deal of trouble might be involved in killing the project. The traditional thought went, "After all, there is so much money tied up in this project, we can't just kill it. Let's try to save it." That is costly and unnecessary.

PREPARE END OF PROJECT REPORT

The contents of a final report are unique to each organization. Ideally, the co-managers would write a report on the final version, but assistance by the Enterprise Project Support Office (PSO) or the appropriate Division PSO can be used.

OBSERVATIONS ON THE NEXT VERSION

Project deliverables (whether products or services) have a finite productive life. The challenge to management is to know when that life will expire and when to begin the project for Version 2. The Version 2 project should begin sufficiently in advance of the estimated expiration date for Version 1 so that its deliverables are ready for prime time.

The contents of the Scope Bank from Version 1 should be preserved and will make good input for the Version 2 project.

CELEBRATING SUCCESS

Public recognition of those who were responsible for the success of the project is good for the soul and a great morale booster, too. The most effective reward we have ever seen was a project sponsor arranging a videotaping of each team member at work and giving each member a copy. Tee shirts, coffee mugs, and even banners displayed on the team members' work stations will be appreciated, too. Be creative! You don't have to spend a lot of money, either—*it's the thought that counts.*

PUTTING IT ALL TOGETHER

The Project Mandate has been acted upon and a final product was delivered to the client. The P2 LEAN Project Team's response may not have delivered the expected business value, but a best effort was made. The actual deliverables will have satisfied the Project Mandate to the fullest extent possible. A version of the solution has been deployed and the actual benefits are being tracked. The deployed solution will have a useful lifetime, after which it will be retired. The Scope Bank will have been updated with the final solution, but will probably still contain prioritized Probative and Integrative Swim Lanes that could not be executed within the previous version constraints. That, as well as the deployment experiences, will provide the input for the next version. The plan for the next version will eventually be requested in a new Project Mandate and will be submitted for approval.

PART 5: PUTTING IT ALL TOGETHER

To wrap up our presentation of the PRINCE2 (P2) LEAN Framework, we have two short chapters to offer. Chapter 15 is a high-level look at the organizational infrastructure that is recommended to support the P2 LEAN Framework. The emphasis is on the Project Support Office (PSO). It is a version of the Project Management Office that focuses on support, not compliance. If your desire is for a lean and agile P2 environment, P2 LEAN should be your process of choice; and the PSO the delivery vehicle. And finally, Chapter 16 is a summary of the reasons why a P2 LEAN Framework will be beneficial to your organization. Both P2 and the Effective Complex Project Management Frameworks contribute to these benefits.

15

ORGANIZATIONAL INFRASTRUCTURE

There is nothing more difficult to take in hand, more peril-
ous to conduct, or more uncertain in its success, than to take
the lead in the introduction of a new order of things.
—Machiavelli, *The Prince*

If we view organizations as adaptive problem-solving struc-
tures, then interferences about effectiveness have to be made,
not from static measures of output, but on the basis of the pro-
cesses through which the organization approaches problems.
—Warren G. Bennis, President, University of Cincinnati

CHAPTER LEARNING OBJECTIVES

This chapter will provide readers the knowledge or ability to:

- Revise an existing Project Management Office (PMO) to support the PRINCE2 (P2) LEAN Framework
- Design a P2 LEAN Project Support Office (PSO)
- Know the mission, objectives, and structures of the P2 LEAN PSO
- Know the services and functions performed by the P2 LEAN PSO
- Leverage a hub and spoke PSO structure for the P2 LEAN Framework benefit

- Define and support the project management position family and professional development
- Provide services to align human resources with project staffing needs

Your organization put a project management methodology in place and established a PMO to insure standards specification and compliance, administrative support to executive management, and consulting support to project managers and their teams. A P2 LEAN Framework has been developed and the PMO needs to expand its support to this new framework. The traditional PMO will not be configured with the services to support the P2 LEAN Framework and the broader Complex Project Landscape. In this chapter, we discuss supplementing an existing PMO to support the P2 LEAN Framework. Notice it is not a replacement—it is a supplement.

If a PMO has not yet been established in your organization, this will have to change. A P2 LEAN Framework has been designed in a manner that will not succeed without a strong infrastructure to support it. This chapter is devoted to defining or redefining the PMO. We call that infrastructure a PSO and discuss its organization and the services it will need to provide for the P2 LEAN Framework to thrive and mature.

WHAT IS A P2 LEAN PSO?

Several varieties of PMOs are in use in contemporary organizations. Each serves a different purpose. Before you can consider establishing a P2 LEAN PSO in your organization, you have to understand these differences. The purpose of this section is to describe those variations and ascertain what form is best suited for your organization. A good working definition of a PSO is:

Definition: P2 LEAN PSO

A P2 LEAN PSO is a permanent organizational unit that provides a portfolio of services, resources, and information specific to the support needs of P2 LEAN Project Teams and the Project Executive.

So, the PSO is a traditional PMO whose support services have been adapted to a P2 LEAN project environment.

ESTABLISHING THE PSO MISSION

If you have decided that a PSO will be established, the first order of business is to determine the mission of your PSO. The following list gives some examples of possible mission statements:

- Provide overall management and administrative support to the Alpha Program
- Establish and monitor compliance with the chosen project management methodology
- Provide a comprehensive portfolio of support services to all project managers on an as-requested basis

All three of these mission statements reflect the types of PSO that might be in place in the enterprise. They are also cited in the *Project Management Body of Knowledge (PMBOK® Guide)*. The first statement is the typical mission statement of a Program Office. It provides administrative support for a program, which comprises a group of projects related to something called the *Alpha Program*. This type of mission statement will be very common in organizations that operate large programs consisting of many projects.

The second statement is a very limited mission statement. Often such a statement doesn't find much favor with project managers. Even though this mission statement is not popular, it is necessary in any PSO that is worth the price. A standard must be established, and there must be compliance with that standard, but it doesn't have to be expressed in terms that suggest a military-like enforcement. Including strong support services in the mission statement will go a long way toward satisfying the project manager who is desperate for support and can live with the compliance monitoring and with the standard.

The third statement is more to my liking. It seems to be more supportive of the things a project manager is looking for in a PSO. This is my choice, and its purpose fits comfortably with a name like Project Support Office. A PSO will still have some of those military-like functions to perform, but the mission statement suggests that they are surrounded by and dominated by a comprehensive list of support services. It seems to define a package that can be sold to project managers as well as to senior managers.

PSO OBJECTIVES

Assume that you have adopted the third statement in the preceding list as the mission statement of your PSO. Because the PSO is a business unit, its objectives should be framed in business terms. The following list illustrates some examples:

- Help project teams deliver business value
- Increase the success rates of projects by 5% per year until it reaches 75%
- Reach Capability Maturity Model Integration Level 4 Maturity

The first statement is a bit vague, in that it passes the business reason for the PSO to the project teams. However, this places the responsibility for achieving business value on the shoulders of the client. That is as it should be. The project manager and project team are the facilitators. The client has to define value and make it happen. The PSO is not responsible for business value. If you want to hold the toes of the PSO to the fire, then either the second or third statement will do the job. They are very specific and can be easily measured.

HUB AND SPOKE PSO ORGANIZATIONAL STRUCTURE

The hub and spoke structure is an example of a PSO that is both enterprise-wide and functionally based. In very large organizations, the PSO may be organized in a hierarchical form. The hub is where the enterprise-level unit (also known as the central office) is housed. It is a high-level PSO that sets project management policy and standards for the enterprise. If only the hub form is in place, then all of the functions of the PSO will reside there. In time, as the organization grows in its maturity and dependence on the PSO, these functions may be carried out at the business unit or division level by regional PSOs (the spokes), who take their process and policy direction from the central PSO. The hub is typically staffed by high-level project executives whose focus is strategic. At the end of a spoke is a regional or functional PSO, which has operational responsibilities for the unit it represents. Obviously, the hub and spoke configuration works best in those organizations that have a more mature approach to project management. It is not a structure for organizations new to project management. Those organizations should focus on a hub structure first and then expand to the spokes as their practice matures.

Figure 15.1 illustrates the final form of the demand-driven evolution of the PSO hub and spoke structure. In preparation for the PSO, the hub and spoke organizational structure is probably the only organizational structure that makes good long-term business sense.

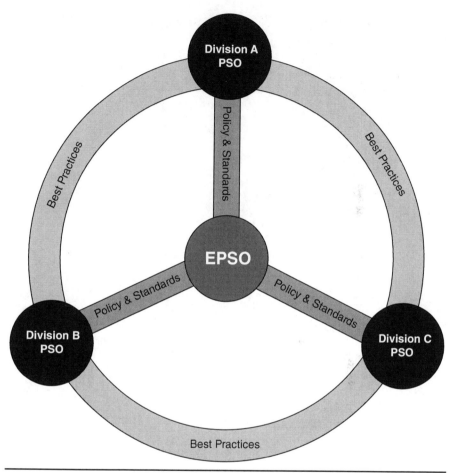

Figure 15.1   PSO hub and spoke structure

As demand in a division increases, the spoke that feeds that division is established. The initial discipline of the EPSO (Enterprise Project Support Office) will probably be project management (PM) because of the strong historical roots of the PMO. There is already a growing trend in establishing a Community of Practice (COP) and Center of Excellence (COE) in business analysis (BA), so that will most likely be the second discipline that is integrated into the EPSO. That will give the EPSO a strong generalist orientation in PM and BA. From that point the Information Technology (IT) and business process disciplines can be added as demand grows for specialists in the division PSOs.

At some point in time, usually when two or more division PSOs are in place, COPs and COEs for all four disciplines will emerge. They may support all four disciplines in an integrated model or support single disciplines as the BA COP now does. These will be the only direct communications link between division-level PSOs. A sharing of best practices will develop, as will training, consulting, and other support services that can be shared. Some of these can continue to be offered by the EPSO.

P2 LEAN PSO SUPPORT SERVICES

If you have a PMO, you already provide a portfolio of services. It may not be sufficient to support the P2 LEAN Framework, however. We provide the following list for your consideration. There are a number of functions specific to supporting the P2 LEAN environment. They are grouped into seven support service areas.

Project Support

This function encompasses all of the administrative support services that a PSO might offer to a P2 LEAN Project and its project teams. The project support services provided to the Project Executive and the senior managers includes:

- Provide advice to the Project Executive
- Participate in the strategic alignment of a P2 LEAN Project and its stages
- Manage archives of project documentation
- Implement and manage database of lessons learned
- Implement and manage risk database

The services provided to the co-managers and the project teams include:

- Responding to requests from the co-managers on preparing the Next Stage Plan
- Assist co-managers with resource allocation between swim lanes
- Schedule updating and reporting
- Time sheet recording and maintenance
- Report production and distribution
- Report archiving
- Report consolidation and distribution
- Project notebook maintenance

The PSO project support services remove as much non-value-added work from the project team as it can. In the spirit of lean, the project team should be focused on the work of the project and not be burdened by so-called *administrivia*. More important, the PSO staff will be much more knowledgeable about how to provide these services because they will be very familiar with the tools and systems that support them. A goal of the PSO is to provide this non-value-added work at a lower real cost than would be incurred if done by the project team.

Consulting and Mentoring

Professional project consultants and trainers are available in the PSO to support the consulting and mentoring needs of the project teams. In this capacity, they are a safe harbor for both the co-managers and team members. The PSO professional staff members are available on an as-requested basis. They stand ready to help with any specialized assistance. The following is a list of the consulting and mentoring services they are prepared to offer:

- Business Case development support
- Facilitate requirements elicitation sessions
- Facilitate project and stage planning sessions
- Risk assessment and mitigation planning
- Project interventions
- Mentor and coach co-managers
- Mentor Project Executives
- Participate in Project Review Boards

The PSO professional consultants are the most experienced project managers in the company. Their experiences are broad and deep. Because they have heard and seen most situations, nothing will surprise them. They are qualified to help the co-managers even in the most complex of circumstances.

Methods and Standards

Methods and standards represent a service that every PSO must provide. A good return on investment from a PSO will not happen without a standard methodology and a means of monitoring and compliance. That is the role of the P2 LEAN Framework. But it is not a methodology. In simple terms, it is a pantry out of which the chefs (co-managers) create a recipe (a specific Project Management Life Cycle (PMLC) Model for managing their project).

The establishment, monitoring, and support of the P2 LEAN Framework are major undertakings for a newly formed PSO. Perhaps more than any other task that the PSO will perform, this one affects the culture and operation of the organization. Its definition must involve as many stakeholders as possible. It is a cultural change in every business unit that is involved with projects and project management. The affected parties must have an opportunity to be involved in establishing the project management processes and the standards to which they will later be held accountable or the whole effort will be for naught.

The following list contains the services included in this function:

- Develop and implement the generic P2 LEAN Framework
- Participate in Project Review Sessions
- Conduct post-project reviews
- Monitor and control performance of the PSO
- Establish and monitor standards
- Product breakdown structure (PBS) construction
- Project network diagram development
- Bid preparation and contract administration
- Risk assessment
- Status reporting
- Bundled Change Management Process
- Documentation

Vetted Portfolio

- Maintenance and support of the vetted portfolio of tools, templates, and processes
- Evaluate and accept additions and revisions to the vetted portfolio
- Provide a business process to receive, evaluate, and add to the vetted portfolio

Software Tools

Every P2 LEAN PSO should be looking for productivity improvements. As teams become dispersed, it is essential that they remain productive. In this technology-crazed business environment, one can't let time and distance erect barriers to performance. The P2 LEAN PSO is the only organizational unit that can provide the support needed for the ever-changing set of software tools available on the market. It is responsible for soliciting, evaluating, selecting, and contracting with vendors of these tools. The following list describes the software services that the organization depends on the P2 LEAN PSO to provide:

- Software evaluation
- Software selection
- Software acquisition and licensing
- Vendor negotiations
- Software training
- Software management and maintenance

The ultimate test of viability is the perceived value added by the co-managers. The PSO needs to take the co-managers' positions in conducting its evaluations. Their activity should be needs driven and the P2 LEAN Project Teams can provide those needs.

Training

Training curriculum development and training delivery may be assigned to the PSO, depending on whether the organization has a centralized training department and whether it has the expertise needed to develop and deliver the needed programs.

Training in project management has probably been around longer than any other methodology an organization is likely to have. Unfortunately, senior managers incorrectly assume that the solution to their high rate of project failure can be found by giving everyone some training in project management. They are looking for that silver bullet, and there simply isn't one to be found. What has happened in many organizations is that several different project management training courses have been taken by the professional staff. Accordingly, there is no central approach that they follow as a result of their training. In a sense, everyone is still doing his or her own thing (Maturity Level 1). Some follow the approach they were taught, others do what they have always done, and yet others teach themselves. Under the PSO, all of that needs to change.

One school of thought says that if you teach concepts and principles effectively, project managers will be able to adapt them to whatever situation they encounter. That sounds good in theory, but it usually doesn't work. I have found that most project managers don't want to think, and typically convey this type of message: "Just tell me what I am supposed to do. I'm not interested in the concepts and theory." That's a truly unfortunate attitude, but it's reality; you can't change it very easily. If you happen to attend one of my workshops, you will hear me say, "I'm going to teach you how to think like a project manager, so don't look for any recipes or task lists from me. I'll teach you how to build those for yourself."

The trends are clear. To be an effective project manager means that you must be a chef (able to build recipes) and not just a cook (routinely follow recipes). You have to be firmly grounded in the principles and concepts of project management. Every project is different—as is the best approach to managing those unique projects. The effective project manager takes the project characteristics and the environment (both internal and external) into account, and chooses and continuously adapts a best-fit PMLC Model for the entire life of the project.

With all of this in mind, the PSO and the organization's training department must jointly assume the responsibility of designing and implementing a curriculum that is aligned with the organization's project management methodology. Furthermore, the PSO must assume whatever responsibility the training department is unwilling or unable to assume. Whatever the case, the job must be done. The following list describes the training services that the PSO should be prepared to assist with:

- P2 LEAN Framework basics
- Advanced and specialized topics
- Curriculum design and development support of the training department
- Course delivery

When it comes to project management training, the relationship between the training department and the PSO must be collaborative. The development of the project management curriculum should involve both the curriculum development experts from the training department and the subject matter experts (SMEs) from the PSO. The curriculum can be delivered either by the PSO or by the training department. If it is to be done by the training department, then the curriculum design must have followed a facilitative design. That relieves the training department from having to find trainers who have practical project management expertise, which is difficult at best. In most cases the trainers should be project management SMEs. There is no good substitute for frontline experience by the trainer—no amount of book knowledge can replace experience.

Project Co-Manager Resources

Here the PSO provides a resource to project managers for advice, suggestions, and career guidance. Regardless of the organizational structure in which the PSO exists, the project manager does not have any other safe place to seek advice and counsel. The PSO is ideally suited to that role. A variety of human resource functions are provided. Some PSOs have project managers assigned to them. In these situations, the project managers are usually assigned to complex, large, or mission-critical projects to:

- Assist the Project Executive with staffing decisions
- Provide mentoring for the co-managers
- Promote the P2 LEAN Framework within the organization
- Execute specialized tasks for co-managers
- Recruit, select, develop, and evaluate co-managers

In the absence of a Human Resources Management System (HRMS) administered out of a Human Resources department, both project staffing and professional development of project managers is often the responsibility of the PSO. This might be done in collaboration with an HR department that administers an HRMS, but it must be done. Staffing projects with qualified project managers and team members is critical and complex, and the HRMS must have the capability of providing that support.

The final function in this service area includes a number of human resource services revolving around the co-managers. The following list is quite comprehensive—it encompasses assessment, development, and deployment services:

- Human resource development
- Identification and assessment of skills
- Assist the co-managers with the selection of team members
- Selection of co-managers
- Assessment of project teams
- Professional development
- Career guidance and development

Even when the PSO is responsible for assigning co-managers, it is unlikely that they will have that responsibility for team members. That rests with their functional managers in collaboration with the co-managers. The PSO is available to assist. This establishes a collaborative environment between a functional manager, the PSO, and the co-managers to act in the best interests of the organization, the project, and the individual.

Projects provide a lucrative source of development opportunities, but are often overlooked as such. They offer on-the-job as well as off-the-job opportunities. For example, suppose that Larry is the best planner among the current development co-managers. Curly is a new development co-manager whose planning skills are less than nominal. Moe wants to become a development co-manager, but knows very little about project planning. If Curly could attend one of Larry's planning sessions, it would be an on-the-job training experience, because Curly is improving a skill needed for his current job assignment. If Moe could attend one of Larry's planning sessions, it would be an off-the-job training experience, because Moe is acquiring a skill needed for a future position. The development part of a great HRMS would have the capacity to bring the Larrys, Curlys, and Moes together. I am not aware of any commercial HRMS that has that capacity.

Projects also provide another interesting on-the-job development opportunity that has been used with great success. A person who aspires to be a professional will always rise to a challenge. If you are given an assignment that aligns with your professional development plan and that you are qualified to complete except for one skill that you do not have, and you are given the opportunity to learn that skill and apply it to complete your assignment, you will rise to the challenge. You learn the skill and master it with succeeding assignments. Then you repeat the process with a new assignment that you can do except for a missing skill. You get the picture.

STAFFING THE EPSO AND THE DIVISION LEVEL PSO

The only staffing strategy that makes sense for the P2 LEAN Framework is a model that rotates experienced members of the P2 LEAN Project Teams between the EPSO, division-level PSOs, and their home business unit. That accomplishes three very important things:

- They maintain a professional relationship and credibility with their peers in their home business unit
- They seed their home business unit with practices and techniques used elsewhere in the EPSO and division-level PSOs
- When they return to a PSO, they bring best practices back from their home business unit and pick up some clues about improving existing tools, templates, and processes

Most attempts at spreading best practices across the organization have been a disappointment. "My project is different," and "Not invented here," are the major obstacles.

Rotations are a great way to reward a professional and give them a chance to recharge themselves. This is especially important after a really tough assignment. The rotation can happen in two ways:

- Between projects, when they are *on the beach*, they can be assigned special projects within the PSO. These would be short-term projects.
- They can periodically take a sabbatical from their business unit to be assigned a major project within the PSO or simply provide consulting support across the organization. These could be competitive assignments awarded based on a proposal. The proposal could be unsolicited or a response to a request for proposal from the PSO. These are great ways for the PSO to do process improvement projects.

Other Considerations

There are three support areas that are becoming more central to the role of the PSO of the future. They are briefly discussed in the following sections.

Portfolio Support

Many PSOs already provide this support to portfolio managers. That will increase and strengthen. The PSO of the future will provide project proposal intake services, evaluation, alignment, and prioritization services to the portfolio managers.

Assigning Project Managers

The PSO of the future will maintain the skills and competencies inventory of existing and *wanna-be* project managers. This, coupled with their current and future assignments, will be the input that guides assigning project managers to new projects.

Career and Professional Development of Project Managers

This support service must be centralized, and the PSO is the logical home for such a service. The project management subject matter expertise resides in the PSO and not in the HR department. The PSO will have its eye on the trends in projects and is in the best position to give advice on areas of need for skilled project professionals.

PUTTING IT ALL TOGETHER

The EPSO and division-level PSOs are key to the implementation and maturation of a P2 LEAN Framework environment. That is the operational level component. At least as important is the behavioral level component. The complex project landscape is a challenging landscape that depends on creativity, flexibility, and courage of conviction to be successful. That landscape is not supported by a controlled environment. Flexibility implies that the P2 LEAN Project Team must be vested with the authority to make its own decisions on how to manage their project. That means that the team must include all of the skills and competencies to make those decisions. The PSO hub and spoke structure can make that possible.

16

BENEFITS OF THE PRINCE2 LEAN FRAMEWORK

---

*It is probably not love that makes the world go around,
but rather those mutually supportive alliances through
which partners recognize their dependence on each other
for the achievement of shared and private goals.*
—Fred Allen, Chairman, Pitney-Bowes Co.

*Efficiency and economy imply employment of the right instrument
and material as well as their right use in the right manner.*
—Louis Dembitz Brandeis, U.S. Supreme Court Justice

*We have always found that people are most pro-
ductive in small teams with tight budgets, timelines,
and the freedom to solve their own problems.*
—John Rollwagen, CEO Cray Research

CHAPTER LEARNING OBJECTIVES

This chapter will provide readers the knowledge or ability to understand the
business value and benefits realization from implementing the PRINCE2
(P2) LEAN Framework for managing complex projects.

When you enter the world of complex project management, you are in
a world filled with risk and uncertainty. Your challenge as a project manager is to trade in your rule book and risk stepping outside of your comfort

zone—depending on your flexibility, creativity, and problem-solving skills to manage a complex project.

P2 LEAN is a framework that can be used to build a recipe for managing any type of project regardless of how uncertain, complex, or risky it may be. The project will revolve around finding a solution to an unsolved but critical problem or to creatively take advantage of an untapped business opportunity. The more complex and uncertain the project, the more value will accrue from having used the P2 LEAN Framework.

This chapter offers a look backward at what we have designed with a reflection on the value we will have added to future projects undertaken by the organization.

ORIGINS OF THE P2 LEAN FRAMEWORK

Both frameworks (see Figure 16.1) are adaptable to any type of project, and that allows us to keep the P2 LEAN Framework within the P2 practitioners' and professionals' comfort zones. We have designed the P2 LEAN Framework to stay as close to the P2 Framework as possible. But keep in

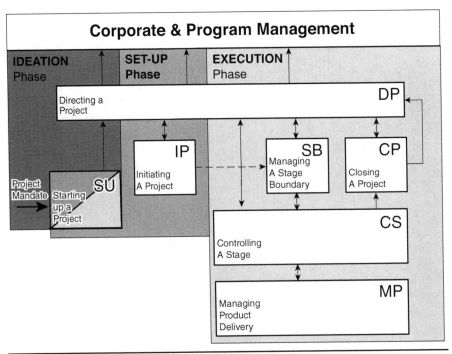

Figure 16.1 P2 and ECPM Framework alignments

mind that the P2 LEAN Framework is not the P2 Framework, and it is not the Effective Complex Project Management (ECPM) Framework, either. It is new and it is unique. Across the seven processes of P2, there are 44 activities. The P2 LEAN Framework utilizes 37 of those with little or no change and adds seven activities unique to the ECPM Framework. So the P2 community should find a home in the P2 LEAN Framework. We have done this intentionally to minimize the disruptive nature brought on by the change.

The P2 LEAN Framework is a lean and agile version of P2, and it is focused on applications. We found P2 to be an excellent presentation of *what* must be done and the P2 LEAN Framework an excellent presentation of not only *what* must be done, but *how* to do it. Even though there is a strong overlap between the P2 and ECPM Frameworks, there is a major difference, too. P2 is described in terms of how the seven processes relate to one another. That does not convey an intuitive understanding. From an applications perspective, an activity flow diagram is intuitive. To that end we offer the Product Flow Diagram (PFD) for the P2 LEAN Framework in Figure 16.2. It explicitly

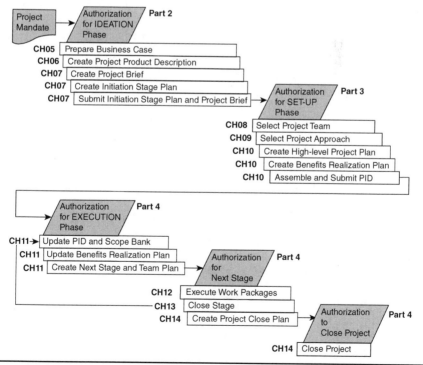

Figure 16.2 P2 LEAN Framework PFD

identifies 15 of the 44 activities. The remaining 29 activities are subordinate to these 15 activities.

The PFD is a linear flow with only one feedback loop from the Close Stage Activity to the Update Project Information Document (PID) and Scope Bank Activity. Our focus is on applications, so we developed PFD to aid the practitioner. There are several benefits to be gained from such an approach.

P2 LEAN BENEFITS GAINED FROM THE P2 FRAMEWORK

Having read the book, you will already be aware of some of the many benefits that use of the method can bring. Read the book again, and compare it to whichever method you have used to manage complex projects before. Your mind will explode with more and more of the benefits that P2 LEAN can bring. Let's just have a look at some of these benefits.

As was illustrated in Figure 16.1, P2 LEAN draws from two well-proven project management methods; PRINCE2 and ECPM. Both result from many years of development and refinement. And these are not years of theory, but of practical use—so everything in the method has been proven many times over in live (and successful) projects.

It is the most flexible project management method you will find with regular points at which you can review the project life cycle model that you chose and change it if the circumstances have changed. No other method offers this.

It is an ideal method for complex projects where you are uncertain of how to get to the end product, whether it is even possible to achieve it, or how to get there.

It puts control of the project into the hands of experienced and qualified Project Co-Managers. If you have been in project management for a long time, you will no doubt have come across situations where communication with the end users is either nonexistent or sporadic and strained. With P2 LEAN, the client and developer work hand-in-hand on a daily basis. This means that the developer never has to make assumptions on how the client performs a part of their business, and the client is never in the dark about what kind of a solution the developer is creating.

P2 brings a good method of risk analysis and management and a well-tested technique for planning—product-based planning. This forms an integral part of the work toward the quality that the client wants—quality *built in* is better than *quality bolted on at the end*. P2 LEAN carries that forward into its framework.

The P2 aspect of this method also brings a lot of help toward good communications, already on an even keel because of the day-to-day working together of the P2 LEAN Co-Managers.

The use of the P2 processes provides a secure platform to move through the project from beginning to end, and the addition of the ECPM Ideation and Set-up phases makes the method more comprehensive and self-contained. The P2 LEAN Framework integrates the best of the P2 and ECPM Frameworks.

The benefits claimed for adopting P2 are still there for users of P2 LEAN. Let's remind ourselves of some of them:

- P2 LEAN uses established and proven best practice and governance for project management. The benefits are even greater because we now merge two methods, both of which include different but complementary best practices.
- P2 is flexible, but using its flexibility takes a lot of experience. The chapter on tailoring the method just doesn't get you there on its own. P2 LEAN actually explains *how* to tailor the method.
- P2 LEAN uses much of the P2 vocabulary, so understanding and communication are made easy for those who know P2.
- P2 LEAN has adjusted the P2 project responsibilities, but we believe it has made the organization structure more effective, certainly for complex projects, which is where we are at. The structure defined in P2 LEAN also provides accountability and authority, and we believe that it improves on P2 in terms of delegation and communication.
- P2 LEAN has a similar structure of plans to P2 and actually gives a lot more information on what should go into each type of plan. For example, P2 LEAN describes an end-of-project plan, whereas P2 gives you little information. The Initiation Stage Plan and Benefits Review Plan are also covered in much more detail in P2 LEAN.
- P2 has a good *management by exception* philosophy, but P2 LEAN with its agile concept of rigid time and cost parameters for a stage removes a huge percentage of the exception situations. Problems and unfinished work are put in the Scope Bank for evaluation when planning the Next Stage.
- P2 uses the Project Board and Project Assurance roles to ensure the correct representation of sponsors and resource providers. P2 LEAN delegates most of this to the Project Co-Managers. Not only are the client and developer *involved*, they actually do the planning between them.

P2 LEAN BENEFITS GAINED FROM THE ECPM FRAMEWORK

The P2 LEAN Framework is new. It is unique in that it has integrated seven artifacts from the ECPM Framework that accomplishes two goals:

- The P2 LEAN Framework is a framework that describes not only *what* must be done, but *how* it can be done. Its architecture is structured around a PFD and is intuitive as a result. In so doing, it possesses a strong applications format.
- P2 has been evolved into an agile and lean framework. That framework is guaranteed to deliver better solutions, higher quality solutions, and increased business value over every alternate approach.

The P2 LEAN Framework is a significant addition to the arsenal used by the P2 community of practitioners and professionals. In that arsenal we have integrated 7 ECPM Framework artifacts. These are all unique to the ECPM Framework and have a long and successful history of applications.

Complex Project Co-Manager Model

In the complex project landscape, the projects are high risk. The search for a solution to satisfy an end state goal is not a certain event. Every skill and competency must be fully engaged. The Co-Manager Model has been used for over 25 years in the U.S. and has been fully vetted. Its benefits have been established:

- Promotes ownership
- Improves implementation success
- Delivers better quality solutions
- Increases project success

Requirements Elicitation

In the complex project landscape, goals and/or solutions are not clearly defined. In fact, there is no assurance that an acceptable solution can even be found and if found, might only satisfy a less lofty goal. Requirements elicitation has been a continuing problem and few thought leaders would claim that complete requirements can be determined at the start of a project. A new definition circumvents these obstacles. In the ECPM Framework requirements, elicitation is a two-step process. The first step defines a necessary and sufficient set of high-level requirements. These are quite similar to the Epics that P2 defines. In the second step, the stages help us to learn and discover the more detailed requirements.

Scope Triangle

The iron triangle is static and is obsolete! It has been replaced with the scope triangle. It represents the project as a system in balance and is a dynamic tool for decision making, problem solving, and change management. Figure 16.3 illustrates the scope triangle that has been taken from the ECPM Framework and planted into the P2 LEAN Framework.

Bundled Change Management Process

P2 processes change requests as they arise. P2 LEAN holds change requests in the Scope Bank and processes them during the planning process for the Next Stage. Bundling them in this way is more efficient and leads to better decisions, prioritization, and improved implementation. The lean principles are clearly preserved.

Scope Bank

The P2 LEAN Scope Bank has a number of similarities with the registers used in the P2 Framework, but it has the advantage of consolidating those registers into a planning resource. The Probative and Integrative Swim

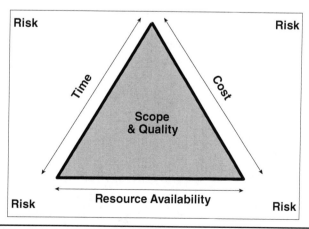

Figure 16.3 The P2 LEAN Scope Triangle

Lanes are the foundation of every P2 LEAN Stage. The complete history of the planned and actual stage products is preserved. Those histories are summarized and displayed in a variety of trend diagrams that assist the creation of the Next Stage Plan. Many of the PID elements are also archived in the Scope Bank for further planning support.

Probative and Integrative Swim Lanes

Probative Swim Lanes are unique to the ECPM Framework. They are journeys into the unknown where other unknown unknowns lurk. The search for unknown solution components is a high-risk search, thus, resource utilization must be done on a just-enough-resources basis. These are perfect examples of the lean principles in practice. Resources are committed to Probative Swim Lanes if and only if there is a demonstrated value for those investments. That investment is earned through successful delivery from the just completed stage.

Integrative Swim Lanes are virtually the same as the product development that is planned and delivered in the P2 Stages.

Probative Swim Lanes discover solution components. Integrative Swim Lanes add these components into the current solution. Other than that dependency relationship, the only connection is that both use the same finite human resources. Next Stage planning is a challenge, but is supported with the comprehensive Scope Bank.

Vetted Portfolio of Tools, Templates, and Processes

One of the greatest benefits of the P2 LEAN Framework is that it assigns maximum flexibility to the co-managers and their supporting project team members. There are no fixed *recipes* that the project team must use or follow. Rather they have free use of a vetted portfolio of tools, templates, and processes that have been customized for the enterprise. With minimal restrictions, the project team can use the portfolio as they see fit. In practice, that has been very motivating for the co-managers and their project team. They have the sense that they are really in charge of what they are doing.

PUTTING IT ALL TOGETHER

This is a solid list of proven benefits. As P2 LEAN gains from its use in the field, we expect there will be learning and discovery that will further strengthen the framework. After all, the P2 LEAN Framework is an agile project in process!

EPILOGUE

We have been privileged to be able to work together to bring complex project management to the next level of effectiveness and maturity. The PRINCE2 (P2) community and the Project Management Institute community will be the judge of how well we have met our objectives.

Our combined experiences uniquely qualify us to make this contribution. We are both retired, but remain active. We can both look back over several decades of involvement in the project management discipline. We have seen modern project management mature from its very beginning in the IT industry to its emergence as a strategic tool. Many problems persist and although the technology has become pervasive, the problems have not found acceptable solutions. They remain elusive and only materialize through creative and courageous efforts. The environment to do that is dependent on a risk-taking executive team. We believe the P2 LEAN Framework will change that, and we will continue our journey of learning and discovery. We see our contribution as a work in process, and we look for others to join our efforts and take up the challenges.

We both wish that our wisdom would have been granted to us much earlier in our careers. We both have so much more to contribute and so little time to do it.

Robert K. Wysocki
Colin Bentley

APPENDIX A: GLOSSARY

Accept (risk mitigation strategy): There is nothing that can be done that makes business sense to mitigate the risk. In other words, the solution costs more than the cost of the impact. Accept the risk and hope the event does not occur.

Acceptance criteria: A prioritized list of criteria that the final product(s) must meet before the customer will accept them; a measurable definition of what must be done for the final product to be acceptable to the customer. They should be defined as part of the Project Brief and agreed on between customer and supplier no later than the Project Initiation Stage. They should be documented in the Project Initiation Document (PID).

Acceptance Test Procedure (ATP): A checklist that specifies the performance characteristics or metrics that a product must possess in order to be acceptable to the client. The ATP is usually written by the co-managers and is included in the High-level Project Plan and might have limited application at the stage level. The ATP is written in such a fashion that no interpretation is needed to determine compliance. The metrics are collected. They are objective and not subject to debate. The acceptance criteria are either met or are not met.

Activity network: A flow diagram showing the activities of a plan and their interdependencies. The network shows each activity's duration, earliest start and finish times, latest start and finish times, and float. Also known as *planning network. See also critical path.*

Adaptive Model: This is one of the five Project Management Life Cycle (PMLC) Model types. The Adaptive Models are well suited to projects where very little of the solution is known at the outset of the project. Adaptive Models are those that can be modified during the EXECUTION Phase as a result of changes in project characteristics (often from solution discovery), changes to the internal organization, and changes to market conditions. P2 and the Effective Complex Project Management (ECPM) Framework are the only two models of this type. The P2 LEAN framework will become the third.

Avoid (risk mitigation strategy): Develop plans that avoid creating situations that might encourage the risk event. Instead, develop plans that tend to reduce the likelihood of those events occurring. For example, modify the High-level Project Plan and Next Stage Plan so as to avoid the situation that can result in the risk event occurring.

BA: Business Analysis or Business Analyst

Baseline: A snapshot; a position or situation that is recorded. Although the position may be updated later, the baseline remains unchanged and available as a reminder of the original state and as a comparison against the current position. Products that have passed their quality checks and are approved are baselined products. Anything *baselined* should be under version control in configuration management and *frozen*, i.e., no changes to that version are allowed.

Benefits: A measurable positive impact on the business from having implemented one or more of the project products that have met the acceptance criteria by the client.

Benefits realization: The practice of ensuring that the outcome of a project produces the projected benefits claimed in the Business Case.

Bundled Change Request Process: Adding all change requests received during a stage to the Scope Bank and processing them as a group as part of the planning activities for the Next Stage Plan.

Business Case: Information that describes the justification for setting up and continuing a PRINCE2 project. It provides the reasons (and answers the question *Why?*) for the project. An outline Business Case should be in the Project Mandate. Its existence is checked as part of the Project Brief, and a revised, fuller version appears in the Project Initiation Document. It is updated at key points, such as end stage assessments, throughout the project.

Change Request: A request from the Project Executive, development team members, client team member, user, or resource manager for a change to any requirements or product in the product breakdown structure (PBS). The referenced product may already be in the solution or prioritized for inclusion.

Chef: In the cook/chef metaphor, these are the project managers who can design management approaches to fit the project situation. They have access to the vetted portfolio of tools, templates, and processes for the design of their management approach.

Client Checkpoint: At the end of every stage, the product deliverables are incorporated into the solution and updates to the PBS and Product Flow Diagram (PFD) are made. The updated Scope Bank and additions to the change requests file are used to decide how the project should continue and then the Next Stage Plan and Team plan are developed.

Client Co-Manager: The person given the authority and responsibility to co-manage the project on a day-to-day basis to deliver the required products within the constraints approved by the Project Executive.

CMMI: Capability Maturity Model Integration. A grading of how mature a business's processes and procedures are.

COE: Center of Excellence

Co-Manager: P2 LEAN projects are co-managed projects. One co-manager manages the development team and the other co-manager manages the client team.

Complex Project Landscape: A 2x2 matrix defined by the goal and the solution. Each is either clearly defined or not clearly defined. At any point in time, the project aligns with one and only one of the 4 quadrants in the matrix.

Configuration control: Configuration control is concerned with physically controlling receipt and issue of products, keeping track of product status, protecting finished products, and controlling any changes to them.

Configuration management: A discipline, normally supported by software tools, that gives management precise control over its assets (for example, the products of a project), covering planning, identification, control, status accounting, and verification of the products.

Contingency planning (risk mitigation strategy): If the risk event occurs, this details your plan for responding.

Cook: These are project managers who are qualified to manage projects using established project management models or customized models designed by the chefs.

COP: Community of Practice. A group of people working to improve a specific set of tools.

Core Team: The main roles of the project management team, including Project Executive, Project Co-Managers, and Team and Task Managers.

Client: The person or group who commissioned the work and will benefit from the end results.

Critical path: This longest duration path through the Product Flow Diagram (PFD) for the current stage. Any delay in the tasks on this path will delay the stage and/or project completion. There may be more than one such path. The sum of the task durations on that path will determine the end date of the stage or plan.

Customer (or client): The person or group who will benefit from the delivered products. They will often be the User of the delivered products.

Deliverable: An item that the project has to create as part of the requirements. It may be part of the project product or an intermediate product on which one or more subsequent deliverables are dependent.

Development Co-Manager: The co-manager who is responsible for managing the teams that will develop the product.

DSDM (Dynamic Systems Development Method): An Iterative PMLC Model popular in the EU. It is defined by five major phases: Feasibility Study, Business Study, Functional Model Iteration, Design and Build Iteration, and Implement. Any of these can be repeated from the Implementation Phase until an acceptable solution has been delivered.

Earned Value Analysis (EVA): A graphic that shows the number of tasks that have been planned for a stage versus the number of tasks delivered from the stage. The trend over some number of stages carries a number of implications regarding how the project has been progressing from planned performance to actual performance. It is also the basis for further investigation as to the root causes. The trend is suggestive of systemic causes whereas a single stage display may suggest a cause inherent in the stage itself.

ECPM Framework: A robust portfolio of vetted tools, templates, and processes that can be customized to the exact management needs of a project to efficiently and effectively answer the following questions:

Project IDEATION Phase:
1. What business situation is being addressed?
2. What do you need to do?
3. What will you do?

Project SET-UP Phase:

    4. How will you do it?

Project EXECUTION Phase:

    5. How will you know you did it?
    6. How well did you do it?

ECPM Framework Scope Triangle: A representation of the project as a triangle whose sides are time, cost, and resource availability; whose inside are scope and quality; and which is embedded in risk. These six variables define a project as a system in balance. It is used to assist with decision making, problem solving, and change management.

End of Project Report: A report given by the co-managers to the Executive that confirms the hand-over of all products and provides an updated Business Case and an assessment of how well the project has done against its Project Initiation Document.

End Stage Assessment: The review by the Project Board and Project Manager of the End Stage Report to decide whether to approve the Next Stage Plan (unless the last stage has now been completed). According to the size and criticality of the project, the review may be formal or informal. The approval to proceed should be documented as an important management product.

End Stage Report: A report given by the Project Co-Managers to the Project Executive at the end of each stage. This provides information about the project performance during the stage and the project status at the end of the stage.

EPSO: Enterprise Project Support Office

EVA: Earned Value Analysis

EXECUTION Phase: A phase of the ECPM Framework in which an approved project or stage of an approved project is executed.

Extreme Model: A quadrant in the complex project landscape populated by projects whose goal and solution cannot be clearly known at the outset.

Feasibility study: A feasibility study is an early study of a problem to assess if a solution is feasible. The study will normally scope the problem, identify and explore a number of solutions, and make a recommendation on what action to take. Part of the work in developing options is to calculate an outline Business Case for each as one aspect of comparison.

Feature Driven Development (FDD) Model: A Feature Driven Development Model is an Incremental Model that partitions the deliverables into feature sets that are technically related and then builds the solution incrementally by feature sets. This model is not a client-facing model and does not easily lend itself to multiple releases. The FDD Model requires a complete definition of the solution as a precondition to using it.

Follow-on Action Recommendations: A report that can be used as input to the process of creating a Business Case/Project Mandate for any follow-on PRINCE2 project and for recording any follow-on instructions covering incomplete products or outstanding project issues.

Gantt chart: This is a diagram of a plan's activities against a time background, showing start and end times and resources required.

High-level Requirements: High-level Requirements define an end-state condition whose successful integration into the solution delivers specific, measurable, and incremental business value to the organization. The set of requirements forms a necessary and sufficient set for the attainment of all project acceptance criteria including the delivery of the expected business value.

HRMS: Human Resource Management System

Hub and Spoke: An organizational arrangement, usually of Project Support Offices (PSO). The hub would be the main office with sub-branches or spokes to other areas of the business; for example, geographically remote offices or departments related to different functional areas.

IDEATION Phase: A phase of the ECPM Framework in which an unsolved problem or untapped business opportunity is put forward as an idea for a project and a business case prepared for it's justification.

Incremental Model: An Incremental Model is a Linear PMLC Model that develops and releases the clearly defined and known project product through several releases. Incremental models require a complete definition of the requirements and the solution as a precondition to using the model.

Integrative Swim Lane: One or more Work Packages whose purpose is to integrate a new function or feature into the current solution. These may be the result of a Probative Swim Lane having made that discovery. There is no assertion that the solution has been deployed into production.

Iterative Model: An Iterative Model is one type of agile project management model. It is used in projects where most of the solution is known and can be used to learn and discover the missing parts.

Issue Log: Contains all issues raised during the project, showing its number, date received, to whom assigned, and status.

Lessons Learned Report: A list of actions and decisions that were taken that should be done and should not be done in future projects along with the results that will be realized.

Linear Model: This is the simplest of all PMLC Models. It is used with projects whose goal and solution are clearly known and will be delivered in one release at the end of the project.

LOB: Line of business

Mitigate (risk mitigation strategy): What you are willing to do to minimize the probability of the risk occurring and/or the impact it will have on the project.

MoSCoW: An acronym for *Must do, Should do, Could do, Won't do.* A method of grading the importance of requirements.

Off-specification: Something that should be provided by the project, but currently is not (or is forecast not to be) provided. This might be a missing product or a product not meeting its specification.

Operational and maintenance acceptance: Acknowledgment by the person/group who will support the product during its useful life, that it is accepted into the operational environment. The detail in the report will depend on the product itself. It could be in the form of an acceptance letter signed by the appropriate authority, or a more complex report detailing the operation and maintenance arrangements that have been put in place.

P2 LEAN Framework: The framework that evolves from having integrated selected lean and agile artifacts from the ECPM Framework into the P2 Framework.

Peer review: Peer reviews are specific reviews of a project or any of its products where personnel from within the organization and/or from other organizations carry out an independent assessment of the project. Peer reviews can be done at any point within a project, but are often used at stage-end points.

Phase: A part, section, or segment of a project, similar in meaning to a PRINCE2 stage. The key meaning of *stage* in PRINCE2 terms is the use of management stages, i.e., sections of the project that the Project Executive only commits to one at a time. A phase might be more connected to a time slice, change of skills required, or change of emphasis.

PMBOK®: Project Management Body of Knowledge

PMO: Project Management Office. A central administrative office for projects.

Portfolio: A collection of projects that share some common link to one another. That link could take many forms:

- Same business unit
- New product development
- Research and development
- Process improvement
- Staffed from the same resource pool
- Funded from the same budget

The projects are selected, planned, and managed under the guidance and approval of a Portfolio Manager. The Portfolio Manager is part of the Project Executive for the projects in their portfolio.

Post-project review: One or more reviews held after project closure to determine if the expected benefits have been obtained. Also known as post-implementation review.

PRINCE2: A method that supports some selected aspects of project management. The acronym stands for **PR**ojects **IN** Controlled Environments.

Probative Swim Lane: One or more Work Packages whose purpose is to investigate whether an idea or variation of a function or feature of a product might define part of the solution.

Process: That which must be done to bring about a particular result, in terms of information to be gathered, decisions to be made, and results that must be achieved. The P2 LEAN Framework consists of seven Processes: Starting up a Project, Initiating a Project, Controlling a Project, Managing Product Delivery, Managing a Stage Boundary, Closing a Project, and Planning a Project.

Product: Any input to, or output from, a project. PRINCE2 distinguishes between management products (which are produced as part of the management or quality processes of the project) and specialist products (which are those products that make up the final deliverable). A product may itself be a collection of other products.

Product-based planning: A four-step technique leading to a comprehensive plan based on creation and delivery of required outputs. The technique considers prerequisite products, quality requirements, and the dependencies between products.

Product breakdown structure: A hierarchical decomposition of all the known products to be produced during the project.

Product Description: A description of a product's purpose, composition, derivation, and quality criteria. It is produced at planning time, as soon as possible after the need for the product is identified.

Product Flow Diagram: A diagram showing the sequence of production and interdependencies of the products listed in a product breakdown structure (PBS).

Product life span: This is the term used in this manual to define the total life of the product, from the idea for the product, until it is removed from service. It is likely that there will be many projects affecting the product during its life, such as the feasibility study, development and enhancement, or correction.

Program: A collection of related projects selected, planned, and managed by a Program Manager. The Program Manager is part of the Project Executive for every project in their program.

Project Approach: A Project Management Life Cycle (PMLC) Model that is either a tailored standard PMLC Model, an enterprise designed model, or a model created from the vetted portfolio of tools, templates, and processes.

Project Brief: A description of what the project is to do; a refined and extended version of the Project Mandate that the Project Board approves and that is input to project initiation.

Project closure recommendation: A recommendation prepared by the Project Manager for the Project Executive to send as a project closure notification when the Project Executive is satisfied that the project can be closed.

Project Executive: The senior manager(s) who are responsible for ensuring that a project meets its objectives and delivers the expected benefits. They could be the sponsor, the program manager or portfolio manager, or all of these senior managers. They may act individually, or as a group, to ensure that the project maintains its business focus; is aligned to the corporate strategic plan, and that they are active participants in up/down decisions for project and stage plans.

Project Impact Statement: An analysis of a change request that focuses on the time, cost, schedule, and resource impact that follows from having accepted and implemented a change request. The impact is measured against the business value expected from having honored the requested change.

Project Initiation Documentation (PID): A logical document that brings together the key information needed by the Project Executive to start the project or stage following a sound plan.

Project Issue: A term used to cover any concern or query raised during the project.

Project life span: This term is used in this manual to define the period from the start-up of a project to the hand-over of the finished product to those who will operate and maintain it.

Project management: The planning, monitoring, and control of all aspects of the project and the motivation of all those involved in it to achieve the project objectives on time and to the specified cost, quality, and performance metrics, and to assure that its products meet the acceptance criteria.

Project management team: Covers the entire management structure of Project Executive, Development Co-Manager, Product Co-Manager, and the support team.

Project Mandate: Information created externally to the project, which forms the terms of reference and is used to start up the P2 LEAN project.

Project Notebook: A collection of all approved management and specialist products and other material that is necessary to provide an auditable record of the project.

Project Plan: A high-level plan showing the major products of the project, when they will be delivered, and at what cost. An initial Project Plan is presented as part of the Project Initiation Document. This is revised as information on actual progress appears. It is a major control document for the Project Board to measure actual progress against expectations.

Project Quality Plan: A plan defining the key quality criteria, quality control, and audit processes to be applied to project management and specialist work in the PRINCE2 project. It will be part of the text in the Project Initiation Document.

Project Review Board: Project reviews are conducted quarterly, at project milestones or other events and are conducted by a Project Review Board that is chaired by the Project Executive and supported by project managers who do not have a vested interest in the project under review. The co-managers present the project performance, planned versus actual product deliverables, problems, issues and risks, and corrective actions taken. The Project Review Board offers comments and may require other corrective measures to be taken.

Project Support Office (PSO): A group set up to provide certain administrative services to the Project Manager. Often the group provides its services to many projects in parallel.

Proximity (of risk): Reflects the timing of the risk, i.e., is the threat (or opportunity) stronger at a particular time, or does it disappear sometime in the future? Or does the probability or impact change over time?

PSO: See Project Support Office.

Quality: The totality of features and characteristics of a product or service that bear on its ability to satisfy stated and implied needs. Also defined as *fitness for purpose* or *conforms to requirements*.

Quality Log: Contains all planned and completed quality activities. The Quality Log is used by the Project Manager and Project Assurance as part of the reviewing progress.

Quality review: A quality review is a quality checking technique with a specific structure, defined roles, and a procedure designed to ensure a product's completeness and adherence to standards. The participants are drawn from those with an interest in the product and those with the necessary skills to review its correctness. An example of the checks made by a quality review is, *does the document match the quality criteria in the Product Description?*

Rapid Development Waterfall: A version of the Waterfall Model where parallel swim lanes are executed at the same time in order to reduce the project duration. The compression of work into shorter time boxes increases project risk by reducing the time available for problem resolution.

Request for Change: A means of proposing a modification to the current specification of a product. It is one type of project issue.

Requirements: A description of the user's needs. A detailed statement of what the user wants in terms of products, what these should look like, what they should do, and with what they should interface.

Resource Availability: Information on available resources, giving names, skill set, line manager, and description of availability.

Requirements: A description of the user's needs. See Specification.

Request for Change: A means of proposing a modification to the current specification of a product. It is one type of project issue.

Resource Managers: Those who have management responsibility over a particular resource. They are responsible for assignments and performance reviews if appropriate.

Reviewer: A person asked to review a product that is the subject of a quality review.

Risk: An event that can occur during the project life span with an estimated probability and that can impact the project with a negative result. The risk events that impact the project with a positive impact are not considered.

Risk Management Plan: Contains all information about the risks, their analysis, countermeasures, and current status.

Risk Register: Contains all information about the risks, their analysis, countermeasures, and status.

RUP (Rational Unified Process) Model: An iterative software development process framework created by the Rational Software Corporation, a division of IBM since 2003. RUP is not a single concrete prescriptive process, but rather an adaptable process framework, intended to be tailored by the development organizations and software project teams that will select the elements of the process that are appropriate for their needs. RUP is a specific implementation of the unified process.

Scrum: Scrum is an agile framework for completing complex projects. Scrum originally was formalized for software development projects, but it works well for any complex, innovative scope of work.

Scope Bank: The depository of all project activity. It includes:

- Open change requests
- Lists of learning and discovery from the prior cycle
- Current prioritized requirements
- The known PBS decomposition
- Priorities Probative Swim Lanes not yet acted upon
- Priorities Integrative Swim Lanes not yet acted upon

Senior Supplier: The Project Board role that provides knowledge and experience of the main discipline(s) involved in the production of the project's deliverable(s). Represents the supplier(s) interests within the project and provides supplier resources.

Senior User: A Project Executive role that is accountable for ensuring that user needs are specified correctly and that the solution meets those needs. Replaced in P2 LEAN by the Client Co-Manager.

SET-UP Phase: The P2 LEAN Phase that is purposed to develop the PMLC Model that will be used for the management of the project.

Specification: A detailed statement of what the user wants in terms of products, what these should look like, what they should do, and with what they should interface.

Sponsor: In a P2 LEAN Project, this individual is an executive who has assumed responsibility for providing the financial resources to fund the project.

Stakeholders: Parties with an interest in the execution and outcome of a project. They would include business streams that can affect or be affected by the outcome of a project.

Stage: A stage is a section of the project that delivers a solution component. The length of a stage may be dictated by the amount of products that the co-managers estimate can be completed during the stage. Stages are typically two to six weeks duration. The stage duration is set at the time the stage is planned and is not changed during stage execution.

Success criteria: A prioritized list of criteria that the final product(s) must meet before the customer will accept them; a measurable definition of what must be done for the final product to be acceptable to the customer. They should be defined as part of the Project Brief and agreed on between customer and supplier no later than the Project Initiation Stage. They should be documented in the Project Initiation Document.

Supplier: The group or groups responsible for providing the project's specialist products.

Task: The lowest level of decomposition in the PBS that meets the completion criteria.

Task Manager: The leader of a small group of team members. Reports to a Team Manager or directly to a Project Co-Manager.

Task network: A flow diagram showing the tasks that define the work of a stage plan and their dependencies. The network shows each task's duration, earliest start and finish times, latest start and finish times, and float.

Team Manager: A role that is assigned by the co-managers to develop the products defined in a specific Work Package or define some function or feature of the product.

Team Plan: The Work Packages that enable the Probative and Integrative Swim Lanes in the Next Stage Plan.

Team War Room: A real or digital space accessible only to the project team where all of the plans and documents on the project are kept and updated daily.

Tolerance: The permissible deviation above and below a plan's estimate of time and cost without escalating the deviation to the next level of management. Separate tolerance figures should be given for time and cost. There may also be tolerance levels for quality, scope, benefit, and risk. Tolerance is applied at project, stage, and team levels.

Transfer (risk mitigation strategy): Passing on the impact should the risk event occur (for example, through an insurance policy).

User(s): The person or group who will use the final deliverable(s) of the project.

Version: A specific form or variation of a product or subproduct. If a version of a product has been shared with others or if any changes are to be made, a copy is made of the product, then given a new version number, and the changes are applied to the new version. The old version is retained but never amended.

Vetted portfolio: The collection of tools, templates, and processes that the co-managers use to create the tailored PMLC Model for the management of their project.

Waterfall: A Traditional Project Management Model characterized by a linear sequence of phases with no feedback loops.

Work Package: The set of information relevant to the creation of one or more products. It will contain a description of the work—the Product Description(s)—details of any constraints on production (such as time and cost), interfaces, and confirmation of the agreement between the Project Manager and the person or Team Manager who is to implement the Work Package that the work can be done within the constraints.

APPENDIX B: REFERENCE BIBLIOGRAPHY

The following books and articles include those that have been referenced in the chapters and are recommended readings to further explain and enhance the content of the book.

AXELOS, 2009. *PRINCE2: Managing Successful Projects with PRINCE2*, The Stationary Office.

AXELOS, 2015. *PRINCE2 Agile*, The Stationary Office.

Bentley, Colin, 2010. *PRINCE2: A Practical Handbook, Third Edition*. Oxford, UK: Elsevier Ltd.

Bentley, Colin, 2015. *The PRINCE2 Practitioner: From Practitioner to Professional, Third Edition*. Abingdon, Oxon: Routledge.

Denning, Steven, 2011. *The Leader's Guide to Radical Management: Reinventing the Workplace for the 21st Century*. San Francisco, CA: Jossey-Bass.

Gray, David, Sunni Brown, and James Macanuto, 2010. *Game Storming: A Playbook for Innovators, Rulebreakers, and Changemakers*, Sebastopol, CA: O'Rielly Media, Inc.

IBM, 2010. *Capitalizing on Complexity: Insights from the Global Chief Executive Officer Study*, GBE03297-USEN-00, Somers, NY.

Maul, June Paradise, 2011. *Developing a Business Case: Expert Solutions to Everyday Challenges*, Boston, MA: Harvard Business Review Press.

Office of Government Commerce, 2008. *Portfolio, Programme, and Project Office*, The Stationary Office.

Patton, Jeff, 2014. *User Stories Mapping: Discover the Whole Story, Build the Right Product*, Sebastopol, CA: O'Reilly Media, Inc.

Poppendieck, Mary and Tom Poppendieck, 2003. *Lean Software Development: An Agile Toolkit*. Boston, MA: Addison Wesley.

Robertson, Suzanne and James Robertson, 2012. *Mastering the Requirements Process, 3rd Edition*, Boston, MA: Addison-Wesley Professional.

Wysocki, Robert K., 2010. *Adaptive Project Framework: Managing Complexity in the Face of Uncertainty*, Boston, MA: Addison Wesley.

Wysocki, Robert K., 2014a. *Effective Project Management: Traditional, Agile, Extreme, 7th Edition*, Indianapolis, IN: John Wiley & Sons.

Wysocki, Robert K., 2014b. *Effective Complex Project Management: An Adaptive Agile Framework for Delivering Business Value*, Plantation, FL: J. Ross Publishing.

INDEX